The Angels' Portion
Volume IV

A Clergyman's Whisk(e)y Narrative

VOLUME IV

Reverend Christopher I. Thoma

Angels' Portion Books

Text © 2019 by Christopher I. Thoma

FIRST EDITION

Angels' Portion Books
AngelsPortion.com

Front cover image: Fr. Thomas Clark
Back cover and interior images: Christopher I. Thoma, Jennifer A. Thoma, and Pixabay
Cover design and layout: Christopher I. Thoma
For more information visit:
https://www.angelsportion.com

Cataloging-in-Publication Data
    Thoma, Christopher I., 1972—
    The Angels' Portion: A Clergyman's Whisk(e)y Narrative,
    Volume IV / Reverend Christopher I. Thoma – 1st Angels' Portion Books ed.
    ISBN-13: 978-1-7341861-5-4
    1. Whiskey/whisky 2. Review, criticism, analysis 3. Christian theology 3. Narrative
    4. Fiction/non-fiction 5. Fan-fiction. I. Title. II. Subtitle. III. Series/volume.
    APB 2019; Beverages & Wine > Wine & Spirits > Whiskey

Printed in the United States of America.

For
all those I've observed

You've assisted in this effort unawares.

ENDORSEMENTS

It's the various distilleries throughout the world that make the whiskies, but it's Reverend Thoma's eloquence that makes me want to try them. He's incredibly clever, being careful with his wit and sorting his words so that the reader can't resist the lure of his narrative style. But often in the midst of his humorism, one realizes he's not just having fun. He's teaching, too, and as he does, he reveals a friendly depth as a storyteller that's refreshing for our day. His observations in all things—literature, family, culture, theology, politics, you name it—cause one to stop and think more intently than before. By the end of each review (if that's at all what you can call each of the chapters in this delightful volume), you will have discovered something of yourself and the world in which you dwell, and you'll be better for it.

DINESH D'SOUZA
Author and Filmmaker

Likely the real mind behind the incandescent light bulb, I'm betting Thoma invented the skull that goes on top of the Hurst floor shifter, too. He's a remarkable man. Chris—a glass of whiskey in one hand, a Bible in the other, AC/DC blaring at ear bleed levels—is my kind of Reverend. And I know he's armed to the teeth. I like that. If he writes something, read it. The man is all the way live and genuine, and his writing is the proof. If you're shy and don't get out much—basically introverted—make sure to read this book. It'll add new dimensions to your life you didn't even know existed. Who knows? You may even run away from home and become the leader of a pack of super models. Dig in. And dig in DEEP. Get, read, and share *The Angels' Portion*! You'll be more than glad you did.

THAYRONE X
Host of "On the Edge with Thayrone"
WAAM Radio, Ann Arbor, Michigan

This is the fourth book in a must-read series of hilariously endearing stories. Some are sweet. Some are sour. All are completely relatable. Most of all, while they prove Reverend Thoma's mind is versatile, they also prove he's pretty twisted.

LAHNA TURNER
Comedian, Actress, & Songwriter

It seems the saying that the loneliest person in the world is a man on a rainy day with nothing to read may be only half true. Add whisky to the list of miserable omissions and only then is the saying complete. Chris Thoma—a Lutheran pastor, author, family man, and humorist—demonstrates this in the fourth volume of his *The Angels' Portion* series. He depicts both the wisdom and joys of an angelic palate, and he gives all glory to God, the generous giver of the divine elixir. Move over Mark Twain. Thoma is vying for your crown!

JIM WEST
Author of
Drinking With Calvin and Luther: A History of Alcohol in the Church

FAKE NEWS

"If you're reading this book, it's quite possible you're dead. Good thing for you the last I heard hell doesn't stock this volume."

DANTE ALIGHIERI
13th Century Author and Poet

"Thoma has captured the heart of whisky. Seriously. He literally cut it out of Whisky's chest and put it in a jar on a shelf near the bar in his basement. I'll bet Netflix is already making the documentary."

BILL HAGMAIER
FBI Special Agent and last man to visit with Ted Bundy

"This book should be required reading in all seminaries. In all my years, it's by far a budding preacher's best bet for sermon illustrations."

G.K. CHESTERTON
19th Century Author, Poet, and Theologian

"Thoma is the kind of son I always wanted, but never really had. Read his book. It's funny. And I'm in it."

DARTH VADER
Sith Lord and Alligator Farmer

No longer drink only water, but use a little wine for the sake of your stomach and your frequent ailments.

— I Timothy 5:23

"The Apostle Paul said this to the young pastor, Timothy."

"Yes, I know."

"Do you know what we can learn from his advice?"

"Alcohol is medicinal?"

"That, and had he ever visited Kentucky, he probably would've recommended something else."

CONTENTS

Contents

Contents

Canada and France

Contents

FOREWORD

I grew up in Kentucky.

In Kentucky, like bluegrass and horses, whiskey is sewn into the fabric of our identity. It's a part of our culture. It's a part of our economy.

In 1795, just three years after Kentucky achieved statehood, Jacob Beam, the patriarch of my family, began making and selling his corn whiskey. For seven generations since, there've always been descendants of the Beam's distilling somewhere in Kentucky.

Whiskey—bourbon in particular—has been a central figure for us. From celebrations to the need for first aid, bourbon has been there.

Here's an example.

It was in the fall of 1962, and not long after we'd just moved into our new home in Louisville, I'd been running around in the cool night air and took to a nasty cough. As the night progressed, so did the cough, and no one in the house got much rest—until after about

2 AM. It was then that my mother fetched me from my room, carried me to the kitchen, and sat me on the counter beside our brand new Coppertone stove. Just above my head was the cabinet that held the family's spirits. My mother pushed aside the medicines that just wouldn't do—the Crème de Menthe, the vodka, and a bottle of gin—and she took hold of the bourbon. Pouring a small portion into a milk glass, she added a teaspoon of sugar, and then much to my surprise, instructed me to drink it.

To a child whose palate is far more accustomed to milk and Kool Aid, it was the absolute worst medicine I'd ever choked down. Yes, it's true. For a moment, there was a genuine member of the Beam family wondering why anyone on earth would put such a thing into his or her body.

But it worked. The cough was gone—and I suppose it also cured me of desiring any pre-legal-drinking-age imbibing, too.

Apart from scenes like this, the memories from my childhood are bursting with vibrant recollections of great men and women hard at work making distilleries hum, enjoying life together, and celebrating with a glass from the fruits of their own labors. In the midst of it all, as I got older, I grew to learn that Kentucky's native spirit is best served with a story or two—sometimes true, sometimes not—each version more enthralling than the one before as the whiskey bottle got emptier and emptier.

In a way, this book reminds me of these things. It's an echo of the familiar moments involving whiskey and great storytelling at the Beam family reunions.

My guess is as you read it, you'll enjoy it all the same.
Along the way, you'll discover that Reverend Thoma has talent. Yes, when it comes to whiskey in general, his palate is definitely discerning. But it's what he does with language—how he brings the experience to you through words—that sells the whole experience.

This book is filled with reviews. But don't be confused. They're not what you'd expect. His style is unique, which I reckon is why this is the fourth book in a series that's growing in popularity. He doesn't give you the stale and typically inanimate review you can get from just about any whiskey review source out there. He brings you into something. He makes you a participant. And you're glad for it. I mean, when you find yourself among tortured and vomiting high schoolers at a cross country track meet and Thoma somehow connects it with Old Weller Antique, or you imagine scenes of Carrie Fisher as Princess Leia and it makes perfect sense in connection to a sampling of Ardbeg, you'll understand.

As a whiskey distiller, I have many whiskey review books on my shelves. Most are there solely for reference. Not so with Reverend Thoma's *The Angel's Portion* books. His books are there because they're fun, compelling, thought-provoking, and just all around enjoyable to read. No marzipan-generic-flavor-wheel-review stuff here. Everything between the two covers, like a great whiskey, has a beginning, middle, and end—an alluring scent, a tasty middle, and a captivating finish.

I just know you're going to enjoy this book as much as I did.

Now, before bringing this to a close, I must admit that when the good Reverend asked me to write this Foreword, I was both honored and humbled, but also more than a little intimidated. I certainly do not consider myself a writer. Growing up in Kentucky, I like to think that I took English as a second language in school. Please bear with me as I do what I can to wrap up with another and final accolade that Reverend Thoma deserves.

Distilleries are opening faster than, as we say in the south, green grass through a goose. More and more whiskies are making their way to your favorite liquor store shelves. This can make for a daunting shopping experience. Allow me to suggest that with the

Reverend's book in hand, you'll never be found unprepared while searching for the right bottle. If one bottle tempts you, check to see what the Reverend says about it. Rest assured that when you find his words on the edition, he'll have given you a "no holds barred" assessment. He doesn't mince words. He's sure to entertain you, but he's also just as sure to send you away with his exact thoughts on the whisky in question.

In short, buy this book, read this book, but most importantly, use this book. Use it to grow in your appreciation of whiskey. If anything, use it to relax. With your favorite dram in hand, just enjoy it for the really great read that it is!

Cheers,
Stephen Beam
President & Master Distiller, Limestone Branch Distillery

INTRODUCTION

It is a rare life that remains orderly even in private.
—Michel de Montaigne, *Essays*

"How do I introduce something I've already introduced three times before?" I asked.

Jennifer thought for a moment. "Well," she began, "when you only had three kids, how did you introduce the fourth?"

"Insightful," I replied. "But unfortunately, not very helpful."

"Why not?" she asked.

"Because when we got married, I was under the impression we were shooting for a maximum of two kids."

"So, what does that mean?"

"It means that I've never really formally introduced two of them. I've more or less been consigning their existence to the fact that you have trouble counting days and I can't say no."

"Whatever," she said, rolling her eyes and giving a half-smile. "We were meant to have four. And we love all of them."

True.

And yet I can't help but think that the woman uttering such words of motherly affection is the same one who, in the midst of fierce bedtime combat with her offspring, has been known to pierce the evening air with an earth-trembling, "Chris, I need a lime!"

I suspect the kids aren't fully aware of what she means by such words in those moments. I'm guessing they just think she's crazy.

But her words aren't lost on me. They form the clarion call that she's had enough of being a parent for the moment, and once the battle ends and the dust settles, tequila, salt, and limes will be required in the queen's tent—which, of course, I'm always more than happy to provide.

And why?

No, it's not what you're thinking. It has nothing to do with how we ended up with four children.

Rather, I keep tequila at the ready lest she one day find herself in need and yet ill-supplied. Having been pushed well beyond the borderlands of her coping skills, "Chris, I need a lime" could very well become "Chris, I need a whisky."

She doesn't like whisky, and yet people do what they need to do in the midst of war.

I used to wish that she liked whisky so that I'd have a compatriot with whom to share. But as I've described, here in the often overwhelming "two kids more than we expected" frame of our lives, I'm glad she doesn't. With the frequency of skirmishes that arise from among such a number, I dare say that there'd be very little whisky left in the kingdom for either of us to actually enjoy.

So, how does any of this lend itself toward introducing *The Angels' Portion, Volume IV*?

I don't know.

Perhaps it is merely to say that while I hope this particular volume will be as enjoyable for you as the three before it, you must know that beyond this point, whatever laughter you sound or tears you shed, all are born from an intersection with a grand beverage— an *interpreter* that I love—one that brings both enjoyment, and if employed rightly, is often a salve in the midst of the joyful wreckage resulting from a woman who can't count and a man who just can't say no.

Slàinte mhath!
The Reverend ✝

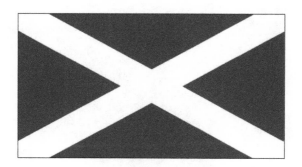

SCOTLAND

ARDBEG, AN OA, 46.6%

Did you lick my pizza?

Relatively speaking, we live in a small town. We have two traffic lights, one gas station, one small grocery store, a hardware store, a barber shop, and a "downtown" that includes a small restaurant, a Mason's lodge, and a dealer in antiques—although in my opinion, it's really just a shop full of the stuff left at the proprietor's door, except now, the items have price tags. We also have a Chinese restaurant right beside a pizza place—Little Caesar's—and both are housed in the same building that keeps the grocery store. Right across the street is a McDonald's, and as of last fall, a Taco Bell. Let it not be under-spoken that when Taco Bell came to town, for many of our citizens, the announcement alone was like winning the lottery.

So, where is this leading?

Well, the point is that anything we might need is only two or three minutes away, especially when it comes to an easy meal. For the Thoma family, as it is for many in our society hurrying toward exhaustion, pizza is quite often the mealtime solution. And with the latest trend of ready-to-go pizzas for five dollars each, you don't have to call in an order, nor are you to be concerned with the ideological turmoil that might unfold at your front door when faced with a fifty-five minute delivery snafu resulting in cold pizzas being handed to you by a driver who believes he should still receive a tip.

Here's a tip. Keep the pizzas, give me a refund, and make sure you use the GPS app on your phone to find your way back to the store. And while you're tapping on your phone, do us all a favor and delete your drug dealer's contact.

Anyway, many such establishments are adding to their services the ability for patrons to place an online order. This is true of the pizza place the next township over, which I am yet to mention serves the pizza we most prefer but rarely buy because it's more expensive and it takes longer to acquire, sometimes due to the delivery issues previously mentioned. Still, Jennifer took a chance and, for the first time, gave the online portal a try.

She tried it once. It didn't work. She tried it again. The same. A few more times and finally it took her order. But this minor obstruction was not the conundrum at the heart of this story.

Gladdened by her final success, and after about fifteen minutes of waiting, she called me over to take a look at the follow-up webpage she'd been provided for tracking the progress of her order. That's when I noticed something strange, something that concerned me—the guy who won't take a sip of water from a glass that's been touched by one of his own children for fear of catching some rare and incurable disease.

I was terror-stricken. Do you see why?

Flavor check?! What the heck is that?!

I don't want these guys flavor checking my pizzas. How do they do that, exactly? Do they take a bite? Do they lick it? I'll bet that one kid I see there from time to time—you know, the one who looks like he hasn't showered in about six weeks—I'll bet he licks the pizzas.

Time passes. Fifty-five minutes to be exact. The doorbell rings and I rush to the door. Jennifer hides out of sight because she knows what I'm about to do. My eight-year-old daughter, Evelyn, is standing beside me with her arms crossed, and as it so happens, she's wearing a fake mustache she received at school—because that's the way she rolls.

Although, I'll admit that with a fake mustache and a confident stance, she's pretty intimidating. More cop-like. *Good.*

"Hi," I say straight-forwardly.

"Hi," the delivery boy replies.

"How much do I owe you?"

"Here's your receipt. Just sign the bottom."

"Okay," I say, having first taken the pizzas and set them on the bench seat near the door. Mid-signature, I ask plainly, "Did anyone lick my pizzas?"

"What?"

"Did anyone lick these things?"

"I don't know what you're talking about?"

"We ordered online. The progress tracker on the website indicated that our pizzas passed the flavor check. How do you guys check the flavor of the pizzas, exactly?"

"Um. I dunno what that is. I don't go to the website very much."

"So, no one down there at the store is the official flavor tester— you know, charged with licking the pizzas before they go out?"

"I don't think so."

"You don't think so?"

"No one licks the pizzas, sir."

A prickly moment passes, and with an interrogative stare, Evelyn hands him an additional three dollars.

"Okay," I say. "Thanks."

"Um, have a good night," the kid replies and disappears into the evening.

The door still closing, Evelyn offers, "I don't trust him."

"Me either," I account. "These pizzas have been licked."

"So, what do we do?"

"I think you'll be okay to eat them," I say. "You're young, and your immune system is strong. Me, I'm older and more susceptible to illness. But I have it handled. I'll chase each bite with a sip of whisky. That's the only way to make sure whatever amoebas landed on these things get neutralized."

And so, to my whisky cabinet I go, having first called the family to assemble for dinner. Evelyn delivers the pizzas to the kitchen counter.

My preemptive dram, something with a reputation for laying waste to everything in its palatable path: Ardbeg. In particular, the An Oa edition.

I shouldn't say that this stuff lays waste to palates. An Islay distillery known and respected for bottling peat smoke "oomph," Ardbeg is not for the faint of heart, and for this reason, I selected it as an ally in the fight against licked pizzas. Nevertheless, the An Oa, for all of its smoky armament, is reasonably smooth and really rather light-hearted.

The nose is a sweet-butter wash of Ardbeg's moniker peat, mildly so, with undercurrents of lemon cake and maybe even a little bit of something nutty—roasted almonds, perhaps.

In the mouth, there's a certain serenity that arrives, ushered along on a similarly lapping tide of sweet-butter and burn. Just behind it comes a gentler wave of warmed citrus and a little bit of pepper.

The finish is ashy and dry, leaving a behind an oily lick of the peat smoke. And it's a good lick.

In all, the An Oa is just strong enough to bring a sense of security, making one feel as though, after a few swigs, any undesirable bacteria that has found its way into the stomach will be rendered impotent. In this light, even if the label offered that each bottle had passed a flavor check, I wouldn't be concerned. At 46.6%, Ardbeg has it handled. In the current circumstance, the dram pairs well with a slice or two of licked pizza, and that alone makes it worthy of your time and money.

AUCHENTOSHAN, 12 YEARS OLD, 40%

Tick-tock.

Maybe you're like me and you rarely feel as though you have enough time to get much of anything done.

As a child, perhaps sitting in a droning lesson with an inanimate teacher, I'd watch the clock and judge myself sentenced to purgatory. The barest creeping of the minute hand would fool me into thinking that time moves far too slowly, that perhaps endings were far less common than beginnings.

As an adult, there is a different awareness. I'll discover myself in conversation almost as exciting as the lesson from youth. A guarded glance at the clock affirms time's familiar pace, and yet there is an alternate sense that the most profitable hours have flitted away with a hummingbird's stride.

"Time speeds away irretrievably," we think, not realizing Virgil already penned the phrase. But no matter. The instincts of both are right. Time is the most expensive fruit in the basket, and it's also the one that ripens and spoils the quickest.

Mindful of this, I've learned to multitask in some pretty incredible ways. I have articles, blog posts, and sermons to write each week. I have a spouse and four children to whom time must be devoted. I have day and evening meetings to attend, classes to teach, and visitations to make. Among a great number of other things, I also have my health to consider. I need time on a treadmill to loosen up my decaying frame and keep my waistline in check. A day or two of no walking and this 40-something feels a little more like an 80-something.

But again, as time breezes by, I've learned some things about myself.

I've learned that even as I could never read in a moving car, I can read perfectly fine on a treadmill. I've discovered that rather than trying to find a laptop desk made for my treadmill, I was capable of designing and employing my own from the scrap lumber in my garage. I've become aware that I can type about two thousand words in an hour at that homemade miniature desk on the treadmill. I've learned that I can do these things with great confidence, never once relying on the safety tie that stops the treadmill if I suddenly trip and go flying through the closet door behind me.

In other words, as time and tasks have pressed against me, I've learned I'm a death-defying exerciser who gets an incredible amount of study and writing accomplished at four to five miles per hour.

Admittedly, it takes a certain measure of skill to get so much accomplished in such a short period of time. Auchentoshan knows I speak the truth. The distillery's 12-year-old edition is nothing less than the Doogie Howser among a good number of the whiskies I've enjoyed as of late.

This triple-distilled delight wafts scents of the better, darker fruits in time's basket, all of which have been carefully malted at peak ripeness. Another draw suggests a sprinkling of wood spice.

The palate is enchanting. It presents itself with a gentle youthfulness, but then begins reciting lofty lines of spicy vanilla and raspberry prose. A twelve-year-old, you think? It can't be.

The finish betrays time's truest nature. It's gone much faster than you'd expect. Nevertheless, the moment together was anything but dull, and the finish reminds of the fruits that spoke so clearly.

Overall, the Auchentoshan 12-year-old edition infers that while a little over a decade in the barrel was certainly sufficient for crafting a superb dram, one can only imagine what a few more years in the barrel would have delivered.

I'm guessing something in the superhero range—like Doogie Howser bitten by a radioactive armadillo.

BOWMORE, DARKEST, 15 YEARS OLD, 43%

Round One

Even as Autumn is upon us, my front yard looks great. Its grass is plush and full, rivaling any professionally cultivated yard in town. My backyard, not so much. There aren't any bare spots, but the grass grows thick and full in a limited number of island-like spots. Everything else remains thin.

I think it may have something to do with the deer that pass through fairly regularly. Over the years, as I've mowed, I've learned that there are certain locales where I should tread with care because that's where they do their business.

Speaking of mowing, I should set up a video camera and share the experience with you.

Seriously.

You know how most folks will mow in straight lines, gradually making their way across the yard until it's finished? Yeah, that's not what you'd see in my video, at least not in the backyard. I pretty much just wander around, going from patch to patch until I get them all. I figure it's a waste of time and gasoline to mow a yard that doesn't necessarily need it, and yet, if I don't regularly mow those portions that get fuller than the others, it starts to look pretty crazy.

That second or third time I decided to do it this way, I noticed my southern-most neighbor peeking through the blinds of his patio door, and I imagined the conversation he was having with his wife at that moment.

"Honey, come take a look at this."

"What is it?" she asks.

"I think Thoma only mows his yard when he's drunk," he replies.

"His poor wife," she says, gently nudging aside one of the blinds to observe.

I suppose the next time I see them spying, I'll just go ahead and wave. And the next time I have a chance to talk with them, I already know what I intend to say.

"Hey, John!" I'll say, waving excitedly.

"Hey, Chris," he'll reply uneasily from the mouth of his garage.

"So, did you see those bright lights in the sky last night?" I'll ask in all seriousness.

"Bright lights?"

"Yeah, the lights. I sure hope they didn't wake you and the dogs."

"I didn't see them," he'll continue puzzled. "What was going on?"

"Oh, nothing," I'll continue. "Just a couple of alien spacecraft hovering over my yard."

"Alien spacecra—?"

"—Yeah," I'll interrupt. "I've been doing the 'crop circle' thing in the back yard to help coordinate their eventual invasion.

They promised they wouldn't eat me or my family after the war. Not really sure what they have planned for you and everyone else. They did say that I could be governor of the east coast territories. Let's hope you're left in my jurisdiction, right? Anyway, I think with my latest attempt at the language, I may have misspelled something. They stopped in last night to help with the conjugation."

"Yeah, okay," he'll say and take a step back, the garage door closing between us.

I have to admit that when I'm done mowing this way, I get a kick out of going into my upstairs bedroom which overlooks the backyard in order to better view my handiwork. The results are always rather spectacular.

The best part is that what used to take me about an hour, only takes thirty minutes.

The second best part is that the neighbors think I'm crazy, which is okay by me. It makes the solitude of my home all that more enjoyable. After a typical, and very long day, when I get home, I don't need to be fearful that anyone from the neighborhood is going to stop in for a visit when they see the Millennium Falcon... I mean, the minivan... pull into the driveway. Although, I suppose if the "alien invasion" idea gets around and people start believing that I'm actually in line for a prominent position in the new world order, I may get more visitors than ever before, all putting their hopes in my benevolence.

I should probably rethink that strategy for explaining my strangely-mowed backyard.

I suppose I could go back to the intoxication idea, except I would qualify the booze part by saying that I'm not actually drunk, but rather performing a pre-mowing ritual that involves taking a sip of the 15-year-old Bowmore Darkest Sherry Cask Finished edition that results in a form of stunned ecstasy, ultimately causing me to wander around the yard.

I really like this whisky. The smoke, the sherry, the bite—it's all good.

The nose is masterful, almost otherworldly, at least in the sense that the sweeter sherry and the smoky character take equal turns steering the craft. What I mean is that both are so crisp that it's not difficult to concentrate on either. The smoke sets the scene beside a salty inlet from the ocean. The sherry is just beyond the mouth of the waterway, and as the smoke dissipates, the sherry takes over.

There is an oily nature to the palate. In it there is the suggestion of smoked berries, frosted pastry dough, and a wood spice bite. A second sip sees the smoke prevail.

The finish is absolutely delightful, rendering a semi-longer fade into something spicier, almost rum-like.

In all, this is a delightful dram, and it's certainly worth your dollars—coming in right around $70. Actually, it might even be worth ritualizing, as I posited even if only for the sake of excuse, in order to explain away whatever strange behaviors you perform before observing neighbors.

"So, Bill," your neighbor might say reservedly, "I couldn't help but notice yesterday when you were doing yard work that you dug up some of the flowers from my flowerbed and planted them in yours."

"I did?" you'll pretend.

"Um, yes Bill, you did."

"Oh, gosh, Tom. I'm truly sorry," you'll say in return. "Well, there's no reason to dig 'em up again. That could kill 'em. And I should probably tell you about my pre-yardwork ritual, just in case I ever do that again."

BOWMORE, DARKEST, 15 YEARS OLD, 43%

Round Two

B ecause there aren't too many things that scare me, if you ever actually see or hear me startled, it's most likely because I came face to face with a shark, or I was surprised by one of the four children in my home who walk and talk in their sleep.

For one, if I didn't know better, I'd swear my daughter Madeline is a Pentecostal vampire. I say this because it's not all that uncommon in the evening to travel past her bedroom and hear her speaking in a conversational voice, uttering the kinds of gibberish you might hear at a tent revival. But brace yourself as you stand there in her doorway listening to her speak in tongues. At any moment, she may sit straight up and slowly turn her head toward the doorway, reminiscent of Michael Myers from *Halloween*, or the undead master vampire, Kurt Barlow, in Stephen King's *'Salem's Lot*. Perhaps more terrifying is that even with her eyes closed, she somehow knows who it is that's standing in her doorway.

"Daddy!" she says with a forceful whisper. "Can I have another hug and kiss before bed?"

"Go back to sleep, Madeline," is my typical response, which is really just an evangelical way of saying to her, "No way I'm giving you hug and a kiss right now. You're creeping me out. And besides, I'm not interested in becoming your next meal."

Harrison is another story altogether, although a similarly creepy one. There have been times when I've walked by his bedroom and found him standing at its center point in the dark with his eyes wide open. A distant stare and barely blinking, he's eerily cognizant that I walked by, and so with that, he turns toward the door to ask a question, something like, "Where are the birds for the soccer game?"

"They're in Nevada by that rock that looks like a coffee maker," I might say, because it really doesn't matter what answer I give. "Now, go back to sleep, Harry." And then he does.

In moments like these, instances that occur after sundown, moments that involve ominously pale children stirring from motionless sleep to hover in tenebrous spaces, I'm a little on edge, and so the only darkness I'm willing to venture into is a deeply ambered whisky like the Bowmore 15-year-old Darkest edition.

Matured in an inspired combination of both bourbon and sherry casks, it's the final three years spent in Oloroso sherry casks that gives Bowmore 15-year-old, one of the most beautifully balanced Bowmores, the rich, deep color reflected in its name, and its warming finish.

A gift to me from a friend visiting Scotland, the nose of this sampler dram actually entices one into a peaty shadowland of smoked citrus fruits and vegetal meats. With a sip, the dusky end-of-day somnolence turns to a crisp and wide-eyed night of smoke, sweet and sour oak, and Werther's soft caramel chews.

The medium finish speaks in tongues—of men and of angels—with peppery washes of singed and salty fruit, it grabs hold tightly and pulls you back for another sip.

Considering these things, I'd say it's a worthy addition to any bar. It certainly seems to have the ability to make darkness less bothersome. Which reminds me...

I think that one of the creepiest, and perhaps most humorous, of the sleepwalking occurrences so far was when Jennifer and I were watching a movie and Harrison suddenly appeared out of nowhere—as if he'd emerged from the darkest corner of the room. He was wearing sleep pants but no shirt, and with a semi-literate mumble, he complained that he was cold. Wondering how in the world he made it down the stairs without us seeing him, I told him to go put a shirt on and get back into bed. He did. A few minutes later he emerged once again from the same dark space to say he was still cold—except this time he was wearing a shirt but had taken off his pants.

It was all very spooky. My wife, of course, asked me to shepherd him back to his room.

"No way, José," I said, rejecting her request. "This is all a trick. He's trying to get one of us alone in the darkness—like that creature from 'The Thing.' As soon as I'm distracted and pulling the covers up and over him, his face will split open and tentacles will fly out and pull my head clean off. I'm sure the little sleepwalking ghoul can find his way back to his room on his own."

"You're a horrible father."

"Seriously, just point him in the right direction and then give him a little nudge."

Getting the look, I attempted to negotiate further.

"Okay, I'll take him to his room, but just to put him in it and then close the door. How's that?"

"I'll do it," the loving, but foolhardy, mother sighed.

"Yeah, you will," I whispered, but well after she had already departed.

BRUICHLADDICH, OCTOMORE, MASTERCLASS 08.2, 8 YEARS OLD, 58.4%

To unicorns!

"We're in the ditch here at Kellogg's, folks," the portly honcho at the furthest end of the board room table roared. "Nobody's eating Frosted Flakes anymore. Tony the Tiger just isn't keeping us above water like he used to."

"We lost the millennials a long time ago to Frappuccinos and veggie bagels stuffed with kale," another at the table began. "And now they're all having kids and feeding them the same garbage."

"True," the boss replied, scratching his chin and easing backward into his chair with a deflated sigh. "So, what do we do?"

"I don't know," the same executive offered, "but unless we come up with a new product, something irresistible to both the kids and the parents, the days of cold cereal will be nothing more than a questionable Wikipedia page for junior high kids doing history reports."

"Do any of you have any ideas worth sharing?" the chief asked, rocking in his chair and waving an open palm in frustration around the table. "Does anyone here have anything?"

One hand went up.

"Of course, we need to be true to who we are as a company," a younger executive offered in a voice betraying her nervousness, "but we also need to be asking ourselves what millennials and children both have in common, and then we need to try to meet them there."

A moment of silence passed.

"Go on," the boss motioned.

Shifting slightly in her chair, the young woman continued, "I've been thinking about this, and I think that since we're pretty much about slapping cartoon characters onto boxes of sugary globs of addictive carbohydrates, I figure the only thing we need to do to recapture the millennial market is to figure out what's at the heart of their beliefs and then continue to do what we do best."

Another moment passed.

"Keep going," the boss nodded.

"If you really think about it, millennials and their children have a lot of the same characteristics."

"They do?" the person beside her asked.

"Sure they do," she replied.

"Pedagogically speaking, children are fairly straightforward and simple, right? You don't necessarily need to use flowery language to gain their interest. In fact, the simpler, the better. The same goes for millennials. They want a straight answer and that's that. Flowery stuff like, well, details, sort of bogs them down."

"Sure," the boss agreed, "but how do we turn that into breakfast cereal?"

"Well, this is where we can be who we are and make the connection."

The whole room appeared to rise from a common slouch into a fuller posture of attentiveness.

"Children believe in mythical, fairytale-like things. Millennials do, too. For kids, it's things like mermaids and dragons. For millennials, it's believing in things like free healthcare, socialism, or that they're going to be millionaires without ever actually having to get a job. You know, things like that."

The boss' stale concern was becoming an enlightened smile.

"So, you see," the young executive finished, "we only need to think of a fairytale character for our next cereal. No more talking tigers and toucans, but something truly mythical that both kids and millennials may actually believe is real."

"Do you have a creature in mind?" the boss asked, his voice now blooming with intrigue.

"Unicorns," the young woman said.

Silence won the immediate moment, but soon the room was filled with sighs of optimistic relief.

"Brilliant!" the boss exclaimed, matching the room's buoyant cheer. "I can see it now: Ulysses the Unicorn cereal! And we'll plaster him across a bright colored box with flowers and—"

"—No name for the unicorn, sir," she interrupted. "Remember, these folks just want us to shoot straight. I say we just call the cereal 'Unicorn Cereal' and that's it. I know it's weird, but that's all we need to do."

"That's it?"

"Yep, that's it," she said resolutely. "Of course we'll probably put some sparkly rainbows in the background, too. Rainbows only enhance the fairytale nature of the box's primary icon."

"Does it matter what kind of cereal we put inside?" another leaned in to ask.

"Probably not. In fact, we can probably just take a cereal we already have in stock and stick in it there. They're all fairly habit forming. Maybe just dye some Fruit Loops a different color."

Bruichladdich, Octomore, Masterclass 08.2

"Again, brilliant!" the boss called out. Looking to the executive at his left, "Bob," he said decisively, "get the ball rolling on this right away!"

"I'm on it," he said. "Meeting's over, folks. Let's get to work."

The meeting's muse stood up to leave with the crowd, but the boss called to her. "Not you, my young friend. I want you to take a walk with me."

Gathering her things, she made her way around the table and joined him through a different door. Bob followed by a few paces.

"I knew there was a reason we put you in charge of packaging," the boss said, opening the door to his corner suite. "And now it's time to celebrate that decision."

"Thank you, sir," she said, smiling and taking the corner seat of the leather sectional. "I'm glad to contribute." Only a few paces away, her boss counted three rock glasses from a cabinet followed by a bottle she couldn't quite see.

"And since we've been talking about beasts of the mythical variety," he chuckled and pulled the bottle's cork, "I've been saving this limited edition whisky for just such an exceptional moment."

"He's opening the Bruichladdich Octomore Masterclass 8.2," Bob whispered as he took a seat beside her on the sectional. "That's a big deal."

Even from a distance, with the first pour she could smell what reminded her of evening campfires near the beach with her family as a child, the ocean's salty breezes gathering the crackling cinders and cooled ash in its streams.

"Smells nice," she said, taking a dram from the boss' hand.

"This whisky isn't the oldest in my collection," he said, handing another dram to Bob and then taking one for himself. "But just like you, young lady, age isn't necessarily a qualifier." The compliment made her smile. "The whisky was aged for about eight years," he continued, "but its upbringing is one of incredible refinement. It was finished in three different types of wine barrels— Mourvèdre and Sauternes, both from France, and then another from Austria, but I don't remember the type."

"To unicorns!" Bob offered, lifting his glass to the others.

"Unicorns!" they announced together and then sipped.

"This is great," she said. "It tastes a little like orange marmalade on buttered toast."

"Burnt toast," Bob gurgled through a swallow. "It's incredibly peaty. And oily. You like this stuff, sir?"

The boss' eyes were closed as he savored the dram. "Yes, I do," he said through a grin. "It's hefty and thick in every way. But there's also a sweetness, like cupcake batter and cream frosting. And the finish has a medium, almost sparkly warmth to it." He opened his eyes. "It's so well balanced it's fantastical, just like our new product is going to be, thanks to you," he said, motioning his glass to the youthful executive.

"Do me a favor, will you?" he asked. "When you're getting the packaging together, put a cupcake on there somewhere to memorialize the moment we took back the millennial market."

"I can try," she started, "but remember we need to keep it simple. Cupcakes don't really have anything to do with unicorns, sir."

"Well, then, make it a magic cupcake," he said. "In fact, you'd better suggest that the cereal is actually made from these magic cupcakes and not unicorns. This whole idea could backfire if the millennials over at PETA get the wrong idea."

"Good point, sir," she said.

"To unicorns and magic cupcakes," Bob said, raising his glass again.

"To unicorns and magic cupcakes!"

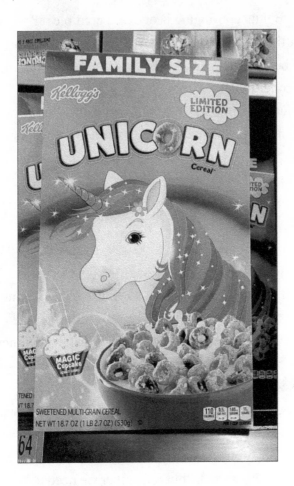

COMPASS BOX, GREAT KING STREET GLASGOW BLEND, 43%

Who would you force-choke if you could?

"So, what did you bring this year, Reverend?" Vader asked dryly, unwilling to reveal his joy at seeing one of his only, truest friends. "And what took you so long?"

"The usual traffic on I-4," I replied. Setting a bottle hidden within a paper bag onto the table, I patted his shoulder, "Good to see you, Darth. How's Edith?"

"Edith is fine," he said. "How are Jen and the kids?"

"Fine," I said, pulling a chair away from what was a round table pushed into a darker corner of the room. Vader kept on.

"And I-4 through Orlando is always like that," he growled. "It takes about hour to go four miles on that stupid road. And it doesn't matter what time of day it is." He took a sip from a near-empty water glass. "Every time I pass a speed limit sign at two miles an hour, I use the Force to throw a few cars in front of me into the ditch. It's a way to cope. I always feel a little better after doing it, and it helps me feel like I'm actually getting somewhere."

"Makes sense," I said and thought, *I wish I had your skills. Although, I probably wouldn't use them on traffic.*

"I heard that," he said. "Who would you force-choke?"

"Nobody," I said, swiftly changing the subject. "Before I tell you what I brought this year, tell me why we're meeting here at the Big Fin Seafood Kitchen instead of our usual place."

"It's more for you than for me," he replied. "Didn't you say that one professor friend—?"

"—Peter Scaer," I interjected.

"Didn't you say he hassles you for going to Florida every year and eating at Red Lobster instead of a more authentic seafood joint?"

"He also poked a little fun at me for going to see the ocean and never going in it," I added as dryly as Vader's initial greeting.

"You never told him what happened to you when you were younger?"

"Nah," I replied. "And I don't think he knows that I get a few Red Lobster gift cards here and there from folks in my congregation throughout the year. Those things help with the vacation bill."

"Whatever."

"Whaddya mean, 'whatever'?"

"Dude, I use the Force on the people around us every year. We never pay our bill at Red Lobster. And we won't pay tonight, either."

"You're gonna use it on someone in here?"

"Well, actually, no. At least I better not have to use it. I know the former owner—Bobby Moore—and he still has pull around here, so I get my food and drinks for free."

"That's really nice of him."

"Well, I sort of tossed him into a ditch on I-4 a few years back, and he promised to take care of me at his restaurant if I didn't do it again. Since then, we've been friends. Nice guy. Good food in this place."

"My visit with you isn't the only time we go to Red Lobster, Darth," I said, attempting to return to the original premise.

"Whatever," he replied, taking another sip. "So, what did you bring?"

"I stopped by the usual place in Davenport and picked up a bottle of the Great King Street Glasgow Blend from Compass Box." I reached for the menu. "I've never had it."

"You don't need that," Vader said, giving a nod. "I already ordered for you."

"What did you order?"

"It's a surprise—something authentic that you need to try."

"Is it spicy?"

"Maybe."

"I don't do spicy, Darth."

"I know."

"Then why—?"

"—Don't worry about it, Thoma," he interrupted. "Just pour the whisky."

I took the bottle from the bag just as two rock glasses lifted from the bar across the room. The bartender smiled, giving the impression that Vader had done this before. Weaving through a bustling crowd, the glasses hovered to our table, finally coming to rest at the center.

"Do you guys need some ice?!" the bartender called, but in that same instant, began gurgling and reaching for his throat.

"Greg should know better," Vader buzzed in a whisper. I could see his left hand at his side clinching at nothing.

"Let 'im go, Darth," I said. "He's the barkeep. He has to ask folks that question."

Vader released him. I poured. We both heard Greg's raspy swearing through his coughs.

"It's not a Lagavulin," I said, pushing a two-finger dram to Vader, "but it does have a little bit of smoke to it, which I thought you might like."

We both nosed our glasses.

"Compass Box never seems to let me down," I said. "This is nice."

"I smell wine," Vader offered. "The sherry is strong with this one."

"I get that," I volleyed. "And the smoke is just light enough to put the sherry in the front."

We sipped simultaneously. The Sith Lord's mouthful was bigger than mine. A few moments of savoring and we gulped.

"Hardly any smoke in the palate," he said, "but there is a good bit of caramel. And some of the wood from the barrel."

"The sherry is definitely a sweet wine and not dry," I said. "And you're right about the wood. You can taste the char."

We both sipped again.

"Are you getting almonds?" I asked.

"Barely," he replied. "The smoke is definitely more evident the second time around."

"It carries into the finish, too," I added, "along with a little bit of what seems like sour cherries."

"But it's not a bad end."

"No, it's not. Medium finish, I'd say. And the sour cherries work."

I reached to pour another set when the waiter arrived with our meal.

"One crispy alligator with remoulade sauce for you," he said, setting a well garnished dish before Vader. "And the same for you," he continued, setting its twin before me. "Can I get you anything else, Mr. Vader?"

"No, we're fine," Darth replied. "Is Bobby here tonight?"

"Not tonight," he answered shakily. "But he did say that if we saw you we should take good care of you."

"Whatever. Thanks."

The waiter turned to leave, but Vader locked him in place with a quick wave of his hand. "When you pass Greg over at the bar," he said, "tell him to stop asking me if I want ice in my whisky."

"I think he knows not to do it anymore, Mr. Vader," the waiter said. Vader released him and he hurried away.

"Alligator?" I said with a look of surprise. "Is that technically even seafood?"

"Sure is," he said. "And I eat 'em all the time down at the gator farm. When one of the older ones dies, I cook him on the grill. Gator is really pretty tasty, actually, and the crew in this place grills 'em right. Not to mention the homemade remoulade sauce here is the best—just the right amount of horseradish. I'm actually glad I destroyed Bobby's car that day, otherwise I might never have come into this place."

"Remoulade sauce is spicy, Darth," I said, waving my hand to catch the attention of a waiter who already appeared to be making his way to our table. "I said I don't do spicy."

"Which is why the waiter is bringing you ketchup, Reverend," Vader replied with a half-chuckle. "I wouldn't want your professor friend to miss out on an opportunity, here."

"Nice. Your dark side is showing."

I poured the ketchup.

"So," Vader said, taking a bite, "if you could, who would you force-choke back in Michigan?"

DEWAR'S, THE ANCESTOR, 12 YEARS OLD, 40%

Dryer for sale. Like new. Rarely used.

For the sake of the children, Jennifer had better not die anytime soon. She's their best, most caring advocate. I say this after engaging in a few mid-Christmas-break scuffles over simple things like brushing teeth, taking showers, cleaning up bedrooms, and basic back-to-reality chores.

If Jennifer dies, there will be certain things that die with her.

For one, we own a number of various digital devices—iPads, iPods, both the PlayStations 3 and 4, a Wii, and a few other gadgets—all of which will be going into the casket with her. The kids will no longer have to worry about experiencing the tortuous symptoms of withdrawal when I tell them to turn them off and get ready for bed.

The next thing that will go away is the use of devices for listening to music while taking a shower. We're going to start giving the water heater a break. You're already in there thirty-five minutes longer than necessary. The last thing you need is a soundtrack to your little naked dance party. When your mother passes on and is no longer in place to coax me in other directions, you'll have eight minutes to get in and get out. After that, I'm turning off the hot water and the power to the room and you're going to have to finish in the icy darkness.

Another thing, I'm putting a much tighter cap on Christmas gift expenses. You've got too much stuff already, half of which you don't ever even play with. From here on out, you get three gifts at Christmas. And if you don't provide me with a list, you get nothing. Your mom's dead and I don't have a mother's intuition, so no list equals no gifts. Also, you will no longer be receiving gifts at other holidays. I always thought that was stupid, anyway. So, no more gifts on Valentine's Day, or Easter, or your birthd… Well, okay, I'll get you a gift on your birthday, but remember, you need to make sure you give me a list. I don't know that much about you. I just know that I had a hand in making and naming you. Other than that, as far as I'm concerned, when your mother dies, you're a squatter in my house and I'm being benevolent. No list equals no gift.

A couple of other things to keep in mind.

On the day of your mother's death, Legos officially become contraband. If you're caught with Legos, you get a week in the sweat box in the back yard. If I step on a Lego, you get two weeks. If I step on a Lego and no one fesses up to the smuggled goods, all four of you forfeit your birthdays for the year. The same goes for dirty dishes left in the sink or on the kitchen counter. Any dirty dishes found in either of these locales will be dumped into the perpetrator's bed. And while I'm at it, if I go to use the bathroom and there's no toilet paper on the roll, any remaining rolls in the house will be locked in my bedroom closet, where they'll be available for my use only. But recall that I am a benevolent overlord. I will provide each of the other bathrooms in the house with a sufficiently stocked bottle of hand sanitizer. Do what you must, just don't touch the curtains or any of the towels.

Lastly, everyone is responsible for their own laundry. If you don't do your laundry, you're going to have to wear dirty clothes. Dirty clothes stink. And guess what, even with dirty clothes, you're still going to school, and you'll most likely be labeled as the stinky kid. And because ninety-five percent of the clothing your mother has bought for you has to be hung up to dry, I'm selling the dryer. Seriously, I don't know why we shelled out the cash to buy the stupid thing. It's practically new, and on a day when laundry is being done, while it sits there idly staring at us all, the place looks a little bit like a terrorist blew up a laundromat. Right now, we only have two drying racks, which for a family of our size means that clothes are hanging everywhere—chairs, doors, on the bannister—everything is prime real estate for princess t-shirts, khakis, Under Armor sweatshirts, and polyester pajamas.

So, again, the kids had better pray that their mother outlives me, because if she doesn't, they'll have a whole lot more to worry about than the five stages of grief.

And let me tell you one more thing, if they… What?

No, I don't.

What do you mean I sound like a grumpy old man? I'm just…

No, I'm not being too harsh. When have I ever shown myself to be too harsh?

Well, okay, maybe you're right about Dewar's. Maybe I have been a little harsh with them. But I only say that now that I've tried The Ancestor 12-year-old edition, which I'll admit is actually pretty good.

It has a politely malty nose, one with slight impetuses of nougat and red papaya. There's even a dig of smoke deep down at its base.

In the mouth, the whisky presents peaches and cream along with the tiniest pinch of ash stirred into some warmed caramel. All of this departs hurriedly through the malt from the nosing.

Okay, so, if Jen dies, I'll go a little easier on the kids. How about this? How about they can each have four presents at Christmas instead of three, and they get fifteen minutes in the shower instead of eight? That seems kinder, don't you think?

And their Legos. They can keep their Legos.

Sheesh. Okay. And they can keep the digital devices.

But I'm still selling the dryer. That's a few hundred dollars' worth of whisky money just sitting there in the laundry room. That's just poor stewardship with the finances of a family that would be struggling with grief, and if there's anything about this particular write-up that's harsh, that's it.

GLENFIDDICH, EXPERIMENTAL SERIES #01, INDIA PALE ALE, 43%

I ♥ WHISKY.

I don't claim to understand the deeper trails that connect one email database to the next. In other words, I don't know how my primary email address might end up on this or that list, except to say that because I watch over it like I watch over my own children, it stays pretty secure. I use three other email addresses for the more risky communications in my life, and so far, they've been the ones to take the brunt of the email spamming barrages that pretty much anyone who uses email experiences. So, if I get some sort of message sent to my primary email address trying to sell me something, while I may not have signed up to receive the communiqué, it is usually hocking something that is in some way relevant and might be of general interest.

Knowing this, I'm not sure what to make of the message I received today, one offering a six-month free membership in an online dating service and adorned with the subject line "Meet Other Seniors over 50."

"But, I'm not a senior, yet," I whimpered sheepishly, taking off the eyeglasses that hardly work for me anymore because I'm in desperate need of bifocals. Setting them aside, I dropped a multi-vitamin and some ibuprofen into a gulp of coffee and added, "I'm only forty-five years old, for crying out loud. I'm practically a spring chicken."

The multi-vitamin is something my doctor forcefully recommended. The ibuprofen is for my knee and my terrible back, which both start their daily routines of throbbing pretty much as soon as I get out of bed.

Sigh.

Well, okay, so maybe the only things shattering the relevancy of this particular email are the facts that, first, my wife is still alive, and second, even if she weren't, I'd have to dig really deeply to find any interest in ever engaging in the dating scene.

Nope. No interest whatsoever.

Leave me with my laptop, my books, and my whiskies. No need to go outside. I'd be just fine being the pasty old man in the neighborhood you rarely see—except, of course, when he's out mowing the yard in his black "I ♥ WHISKY" t-shirt and blue-gray plaid shorts, all trimmed out quite nicely by his favorite red "Texas Towing" hat and black dress socks. I'd be pleased enough to be the pale widower who walks on his treadmill in the dimly lit basement, and even as he does, types away at sermons, articles, and whisky reviews for all of you.

Speaking of pale, in that digital moment of dreadful revelation, the Glenfiddich Experimental Series #01 India Pale Ale Casks edition was waiting. Even as the sun of my body and emotions appeared to be setting, it beckoned.

With a fanning scent of a more lemon-like citrus, hardly a nudge of hops rises in the mix, carrying along in its stream a nip of unseasoned oak.

A sip reveals far more rivulets of the typical whisky flavors than beer, and for that, I'm glad. The whisky is doing what it's supposed to do—which is to be uniquely accentuated by the pale ale casks and not completely rerouted by them. There is the distant sense of carbonation, which I found intriguing, and I'm thinking it's brought on by the ale's specter combined with the citrus noted in the nosing. There's even a little bit of something sweeter at the end—warmed honey, perhaps, and maybe even some brown sugar.

The finish is short, but still quite delightful, handing over a rather precise dosage of the hops you were expecting in abundance on the front end. It reminded me of what follows a glass of Blue Moon accompanied by the trademark orange slice.

The lighter nature of this dram, while it isn't enough to put hair on your chest, is well and good for reinvigorating a humble gent for confronting the fact that while he is, indeed, getting older, he isn't going to do so without a fight—which includes hiding this email from his wife, because the truth is, he's probably going to die long before her and he doesn't want her getting any ideas about remarriage.

Okay, full transparency. The real reason I don't want my wife thinking about remarriage is because I have several cabinets full of whisky, and odds are, I won't get through all of it before I breathe my last. Like any self-respecting whisky sod, I certainly don't want her meeting some guy who might end up picking through all of it. With that, all of you must now serve as witnesses to my last will and testament.

I, REVEREND CHRISTOPHER IAN THOMA, do hereby require of the one preparing my mortal remains:

Rather than using the traditional mixture of formaldehyde, glutaraldehyde, methanol, and other solvents for post mortem preparation, instead I ask for you to use all—and I repeat ALL—of my remaining whiskies lest they fall into the hands of a less-than-appreciative deadbeat who claims devotion to my surviving wife and begins squatting in my house. And if for some reason my remains are incapable of receiving all of the said whiskies, I hereby authorize the opening of each and every reasonable cavity in my body for housing what cannot be included in the embalming process. And if still there isn't room, I request a Viking funeral. Douse me in the whisky that remains, put me on a kindling boat in the pond behind my house, and light me up.

Addendum: The one bottle of Scoresby hidden in the mixer cabinet is forbidden from being used in the process.

GLENFIDDICH, PROJECT XX, EXPERIMENTAL SERIES #2, 47%

You need some joy.

"Evelyn, honey, I'm tired and I just want to pour myself a whisky, sit by the fireplace, and rest in the quiet."

"But you look like you need some joy."

"No, I look like I need some restful quiet. And a whisky."

"And some joy. You need some joy."

"Honey, I love you, but you need to go play somewhere else right now."

"I'm just gonna go right over here."

"And do what?"

"I'm going to get some of my joy out on the piano."

"Hey, Evelyn?"

"Yeah?"

"Do you see the top of the piano?"

"Yes."

"It opens."

"It does?"

"Yes, it does."

"Why?"

"Two reasons. First, so that when the piano needs tuning, the guy who does it can access the wires and make it sound as nice as can be. Second, so that fathers in need of restful quiet beside fireplaces can put their joy-filled children inside where no one will find them—at least not until the piano guy comes to tune it."

"I'm going to go be joyful upstairs with Madeline and Harrison."

"Thanks, honey. I love you."

"I love you, too."

Off she goes to spread her noisy joy with the others in the brood. But that's just it, right now her joy is noisy. I love joy. And I want it, too. I just don't want it to be in the decibel range of an eight-year-old girl singing "Jingle Bells" at the top of her lungs. I certainly don't want joy delivered by way of that same little girl beating our piano to death with her fists. Maybe tomorrow, but not right now.

Right now I want quiet joy—timid and caressing—lazily undulating around me with sounds no louder than the crackling of a fire and the accidental clink of a rock glass against a bottle of something nice. And perhaps a book. Something from Dickens would be suitable. It's been a while since I've read either of the two parts to *Dombey and Son*. Or I could go for a hasty tour through *The Cricket on the Hearth*, an original edition hand signed in 1846 by a Miss Milly Edgar and gifted to a man named Robert. It's a cherished edition, as well as an easy read, one I could complete by a third of the bottle. But it would need to be a savory bottle. Alas, as with the book, the answer is before me.

The Glenfiddich Project XX edition is at hand and available for completing the scene.

Its cork on the table beside me and two fingers worth in the crystal, a generous scent of spiced fruitcake and sweet cream is free to roam among the warmed airstreams curling up from the fireplace's flame. A sip and a savor allows red berries, caramel, and ginger to meet me just after eyeing the dedication page.

TO

LORD JEFFREY
THIS LITTLE STORY IS INSCRIBED
WITH
THE AFFECTION AND ATTACHMENT OF HIS FRIEND,
THE AUTHOR.

December, 1845.

The finish heartily negates any thoughts of choosing a different book or whisky for the moment. The mid-lasting citrus and cinnamon affirms that all is well, and that little else would match the delight being fostered.

Ah, but by the time I gather to page nine, I can hear so conspicuously and so cheerily a song drifting down to me from the upper floor of my home. It is one that speaks of jingling bells, a super hero who smells, and a sidekick who lays eggs. It is a tragedy of sorts, in that the hero's transport has lost a wheel resulting in the villain's escape.

Still, such a tragedy cannot pall my quiet joy. By way of the Project XX, it has, for the most part, been assuredly accomplished.

GLENGOYNE, 18 YEARS OLD, 43%

Germipaedophobia

The dishwasher was empty. The countertop was uncluttered and clean. The stainless steel sink glistened in the sunlight. Even the dish soap bottle had been wiped spotless of its water pocks.

I like it clean.

An empty yogurt cup in hand, a well-licked spoon in the other, the little girl shuffled across the kitchen floor and set both on the counter at the edge of the sink and skipped away.

"For crying out loud," I growled, having just hung up the dish towel, "at least put your spoon in the dishwasher!"

"Sorry!" she chimed, changing course and making her way back to the scene of the crime.

"No, you're not," I said.

"Yes, I am," she whined, beginning to open the dishwasher door.

"No, you're not. You do this every time."

"No, I don't."

"Yes, you do," I insisted. "And do you know why?"

"Why?"

"Because you're too lazy to put in the extra bit of effort it takes to throw the yogurt cup into the garbage and put your spoon in the dishwasher."

"I'm not too lazy!"

"Yes, honey," I said adamantly, "you are, and it's not just with spoons and yogurt."

"No, I'm not."

"Yes, you are," I said resolutely. "And do you know how I know this?"

Assuming she already knew the answer, her words got softer and slower, "Because my room is always messy?"

"Nope," I returned. "Because of your mother's side of the bathroom upstairs." The little girl's face donned a look of confusion as she wondered how her indolent habits had anything to do with her mother. I think I heard a collective breath from others in nearby rooms as they, too, awaited the logic in my statement.

"Come with me," I said, taking her by the hand. Arriving at the bathroom door, I pointed to the difference between the two ends of the countertop. One is very messy and the other is pristinely neat.

"When your mother lets you guys come in here to get ready for school or before bed, apparently you only have enough energy to go as far as your mom's sink. You don't have the strength to go another three feet to mine, and so all of the things you feel you need in order to brush your teeth—a toothbrush, some toothpaste, a few toys, some cat stickers, a rubber ball, and whatever else is essential for success—all of it piles up on her side of the bathroom."

"It does?"

"See for yourself," I said "I feel bad for her. In fact, I'm surprised she hasn't asked me to set up a mirror near the pond in the back yard so you guys can start getting ready out there."

Dropping to one knee, I looked into the little girl's eyes. "I know it'll be exhausting, and with such exertion, you'll probably need a glass of water halfway through the effort just to stay hydrated, but go downstairs to the kitchen and put your spoon in the dishwasher and throw your yogurt cup in the garbage, please. "

"Okay," she said with a half-smile and turned to go back downstairs.

"Give it all you've got, honey," I called to her. "You can do it." She said something in return, but I couldn't quite hear it. I can almost guarantee it was something snarky. But even as I strained to hear her words, I could hear in my head what I surmised would have been my wife's words in the moment.

> *I let them use my side of the bathroom because the first time they would've left a half-dried glob of spit and toothpaste in your sink, you'd have spun out with a stroke. That's why they don't use your side of the bathroom. Because they're afraid of walking in on you sprawled out and foaming in the middle of the floor.*

I could hear my secret reply just as easily.

Well, my dear, while you do put up with a lot around here, that particular truth didn't fit the lesson at hand. The little ne'er-do-well needed to learn more about ditching her sloven tendencies and less about my germipaedophobia; that is, my fear of coming into contact with the general grossness of children, namely, my own.

As a pastor of a church with a school, I'm around kids a lot, so in one respect, you have to give me some room with this one. I shake hands with a lot of people and I get hugs and high fives from countless numbers of kids. Not even my office is safe. My side of the bathroom serves as an innocuous space of sorts, a place where there's no chance of coming into contact with a miniature human who just mined something from his or her nose.

Go ahead and use mom's side of the bathroom, I say. I'll be over here having a drink and fearlessly interacting with all of the available space.

When it comes to cleanliness, I try to keep things at a certain level, which is one reason why I think I like the Glengoyne whiskies so much, especially their 18-year-old edition. It is a crisply sparkling rendition of a fresh and flavorful dram.

With a nose of sherry-sopped apricots, milk chocolate, roasted almonds, and a mention of coffee, this whisky tempts the idea that highland whiskies are the best. Of course no true whisky drinker would say that. Nevertheless, the purity of the breeze arising from this edition is close to being as good as it gets.

The palate is just as fine, offering the same sherry and chocolate, a pinch of ginger stirred into vanilla, and a silky lather of overly buttered caramel.

The finish—a short to medium wash of spiced apple rings and vanilla—confirms that while there certainly are some whiskies only worthy of being used to clean bathroom countertops caked in desiccated toothpaste and drool, there are indeed others to be held in the highest regard and enjoyed in one's safe space a few feet away from the sordid scene.

GLENGOYNE, CASK STRENGTH, BATCH 004, 58.8%

I'm not much for camping.

I've discovered as of late that I'm no longer a person who enjoys camping. I say this as one whose childhood was filled with such things.

I have many fond memories of spring, summer, and fall days begun in the morning dew beside a smoldering campfire and ended beside that same rekindled fire pit. And in between those bookmarks of daily existence, the hours were spent getting dirty and getting hurt—hiking, climbing trees, fishing, canoeing, and so many other activities that almost always resulted in the need to bandage up at least one in the troupe.

I think one of my favorite things to do was to wade waist-deep in the swiftly moving river that formed the northern edge of the campground my family frequented most. Like bald, uncoordinated, albino bears, my older brother (may he rest in peace) and I would try to catch the fish with our hands as the water pulled them past. We were never all that successful, although, I do recall a time my brother managed to snatch one, but the barbs on its fanned dorsal fin convinced him to set it free.

Another of my favorites was to pretend to be a primal hunter. Again, teamed with my brother, we'd fashion long tree branches into spears and creep through the shadowy underbelly of the forest's darker parts attempting to harpoon the chipmunks darting from tree to tree. We never caught a single chipmunk, but it was fun.

I suppose another of the best moments involved riding our bikes through the trails at top speeds. This was, of course, long before there were ever such things as mountain bikes or laws regarding helmet usage. We wore baseball caps, and our bikes were rattling pieces of crap we pretty much built ourselves. They had sparkling banana seats that could've just as easily been hung from the ceiling of a disco, and plastic license plates that said things like "CRUISN1" or "ROKNROLLR" we got from boxes of cereal like Honeycomb. They had baseball cards in the spokes to make them sound like motorcycles, and their frames were adorned with "The Dukes of Hazard" stickers we got from a bubblegum dispenser at the K-Mart where our mom worked as a cashier.

These were our ATVs. These were our camping stories.

But things are different now, and for me, the psychology of the whole thing has advanced far beyond what a kid may or may not have been capable of recognizing.

What I mean is that as a kid, it was necessary to comb your hair, tuck in your shirt, clean your room, and take a bath. When you went camping, none of those things mattered anymore. You could be dirty, and being dirty was the way to be free from the normal regimen of life. As an adult, the radius of life's filth expands to meet you both inside and outside of a campground scene, and with that, the opportunities to get dirty are less inviting. Again, I guess what I mean to say is that even as life is much harder and much messier, why would I want to put myself into a situation where the simpler things are much harder and much messier, too? When I come home from a day of psychological dirt—from dealing in the wretchedness of life—I don't want to be attacked by mosquitoes while walking to an outhouse that hasn't been cleaned since 1979. I want things to be easier. I want to be clean. I want my crystal rock glass, not a red Solo cup. I want to wash the cares of the day away in a shower that isn't made of rotting planks and crawling with spiders. I want to depart from that shower and make it to my favorite chair without feeling the need to return to the shower to wash off the dirt I gathered along the way to the chair. I want a fire, but I want it in a fireplace that's beside my favorite chair and brought to life with the flick of a switch. If it's raining, I want to experience the cloud's tears from my front porch and not in a tent that's filling with water because we didn't know its canvas base had a hole. I want to choose a whisky from one of my various cabinets, not the choice between cans of Coca-Cola or Country Time lemonade floating in a cooler that used to be filled with ice, but is now nothing more than a swimming pool for soggy cheese slices, a gallon of warm milk, and a package of hotdogs that didn't seal properly.

I want easy.

Of course, I might be willing to change my mind on all of this if I could just find a campground that doesn't have a sign at the entrance which reads: No Alcoholic Beverages Permitted.

You know what, forget what I just said. That's a Utopian idea. Just ask anyone who's spent the night in a campground that allows booze. It's anything but clean, easy, and restful. I just want to be home. In a sense, I want everything you'll find in a bottle of whisky from one of my favorite distilleries—Glengoyne.

Even when it comes to an oomph-capable dram like the Cask Strength Batch 004 edition, which hovers at an ABV very near to

60%, all of my previously mentioned descriptors fit. This is an easy, clean, and restful Scotch that serves to distract from any of the harsher things life pitched during the day.

With the first pry of the cork and a nose to the bottle, there's a generous stream of sherry and sweet cream. In the glass, while these remain, mixed berry coffee cake is added.

The palate is a bowl of sun-ripened cherries thinly coated with cinnamon and mingled with the coffee cake from the nose. The finish is nearly the same, with the only difference being a tap of black pepper.

Pleasant. Clean. Easy. Restful. Unlike the campground that welcomes imbibing campers—which is the same one with fireworks being set off at all hours of the night by raucous crowds revving KX150s and guzzling Bud Light.

HIGHLAND PARK, MAGNUS, 40%

You guys have that little thing you do.

I drive a Jeep Wrangler now. It's black. I named it Vader. Well, actually the kids named it Vader. I wanted to name it Drax the Destroyer.

This isn't my first Jeep Wrangler. I've owned two prior to this one. I sold the first one when I lived in Levittown, Pennsylvania. I had to. I lived in a shadier part of town, and with the soft top, I just couldn't seem to keep a decent radio in it—or anything else for that matter. Eventually when Jen and I moved back to Michigan, we bought another one. Although, not too long after that, we found it necessary to sell it and buy a minivan, mainly because I was the chauffer to and from school for four children. The Wrangler only had room for three and I didn't think Jen would be happy with me strapping one of the little ones to the roof, although I did prepare and present to her a lottery system just in case.

Anyway, I figured the day would eventually come when one of those kids would start driving his own car and I'd only need space for three. Well, that time has come.

Not only have I missed having a Wrangler during the Michigan winters, but I've missed the comradery that goes with it—the two-fingered wave that Wrangler pilots flash to one another from the steering wheel when they pass on the road.

Jen forgot all about the little gesture, but I didn't. Just today we were driving and she asked me why I waved.

"We just passed a Wrangler," I said.

"Oh, yeah," she replied. "You guys have that little thing you do."

"Yes, we do."

As a side note, I should clarify that I don't necessarily wave to the four-door Wranglers. Waving to them feels weird—like saluting an American flag with twenty-six stripes and a hundred stars.

I suppose being a whisky drinker has its Wrangler-esque moments. When you see another fellow in an establishment sipping a straight dram, well, it's not too out of place to lift your glass slightly and give a nod. That's the wave, and you don't give it to folks holding a mixed drink or sipping a beer.

However, I would suggest not doing it if you notice that the whisky drinker is crying, or you notice the barkeep reaching to refill his dram with Scoresby. In either of those instances, you should probably just ignore him. He's a four-door Wrangler. Just keep driving.

On the other hand, if you're feeling generous, you might order him two fingers' worth of the Highland Park Magnus. Doing this, you'll show him that no matter what has happened, it is possible for life to get a little better, or at a minimum, it's possible to recover from poor choices.

Now, before you get your hopes up about this whisky, you need to know that at $40 a bottle in the liquor stores, there are two reasons why it's the perfect gesture for a crying Scoresby drinker. First, it's not top shelf, which means the markup price will be reasonable. The second is that after a sour glass of the sewage that is Scoresby, the incredibly mild character of the Magnus will serve well to wash it away—like fresh rainwater washing away a clod of muck in the gutter.

But again, don't get your hopes up with this one. A sniff will leave you wondering if perhaps someone watered down your Scotch. There's barely a drifting of the maltiness you might expect from Highland Park. It takes a deeper dive into the glass to find the sherry and a very distant wisp of smoke.

The palate, as I already mentioned, is exceptionally dainty. Like the nose, a sip leaves you wondering if at one time there were a few ice cubes in your glass that eventually melted away. The smoke is more noticeable, but still it remains afar off. Concentrating—and I mean really concentrating—you may discover warmed whipped cream atop cherries and dusted with chocolate.

The finish is short. In fact, it's almost too quick to notice anything. I'd say I sensed salted butter.

I'll admit that over the course of the years driving our minivan, I did try to start a wave between the Chrysler Town and Country owners. It didn't work out, but not because I didn't give it my all. It's just that I felt that for the sake of all the soccer moms I should do something that looked a little more like jazz hands. I think I scared a lot of people. And not to mention I found myself flashing the animated pose every nineteen seconds because there are about a billion Town and Country minivans around here. By the time I arrived at my destination, I was exhausted.

In the end, I suppose I'm glad that didn't catch on. I'm a pastor. I don't need to be blamed for anything else.

HIGHLAND PARK, VALKYRIE, 45.9%

Boo.

Sometimes as my wife Jennifer is departing from any particular occurrence, she'll turn back to me and intently say, "That's not an Angels' Portion post!"

"Ah, but it is, my dear," I'll whisper under my breath. "It most certainly is."

She knows me all too well.

She knows I'm always watching. I'm always paying attention. I'm always ready to take the simplest of happenings, examine it, and then set it before all of you in all of its pure or profane glory.

And why shouldn't I? What is to be gained by keeping these little life gems hidden away?

I mean, why wouldn't I tell you about the time my daughter Madeline, as a one-year-old, caught the Rotavirus? And what is this illness? Well, I can tell you that explosive diarrhea is pretty much its defining characteristic. I can also relay that it is never a good idea to let your infected child bounce happily in an ExerSaucer wearing only a diaper—that is, unless you want to see the watery contents of her tiny intestines jetting out the sides of her little Pampers with each bounce's impact, drenching everything within a two-feet radius of her bright smile. Oh, and by the way, she was only wearing a diaper because I had to cut her out of a similarly soaked onesie she was previously wearing. Yep, I grabbed the scissors, cut it off of her, and threw it away. There was no chance in this lifetime that I was going to try to work her out of it and then put it into the washer.

Nope. Not a chance.

Okay, so, maybe that's not the kind of story you want to hear. And perhaps Jennifer is right to a certain extent. Some of these gems are better left unmined. But in truth, I think in certain moments she stops to level her mandate because she doesn't want to reveal her darker side—which I must say, is one of the facets to this beautiful woman that makes me love her so much.

By darker, I mean the following.

Are you familiar with the horror film entitled "Annabelle"? Briefly, it's about a doll that is possessed by a demon. I know that Jennifer has never seen it. In fact, she won't even watch the movie trailers for it. They are terrifying enough. I know that my seventeen-year-old son, Joshua, has seen it. In fact, he saw it with his friends in the theater when it first came out. When it finally made it to video, I rented it and he watched it with me. I thought it was lame—as I think pretty much all horror movies these days are lame—but I can tell you that by about halfway through the film, Joshua had moved from the end of the couch to within inches of me.

Now, as I've learned, the movie claims to be based on true events, and it turns out that the real doll is not at all like the amped up prop in the film, but is instead a rather soft and inconspicuous "Raggedy Ann" doll.

Guess what. We have one. Jen's mother made it for her when she was a child.

So, now that both Jennifer and Joshua know the doll's origin and style, Jen's childhood cuddler has taken on an ominous presence, and with that, they've both been working overtime to frighten one another with it—setting it on top of partially open bedroom doors so that it will fall on mom when she enters, or sticking it in a child's chair in the shower so that when the young man pulls back the curtain, he is startled enough to be heard downstairs.

But last night, I think it could be said that Jen took the lead in this little dance.

In the midst of midnight's pitched darkness, Jennifer crept into Joshua's room. He would be returning from a friend's birthday celebration in moments, and so she'd need to be swift.

With the doll in hand, and one of our son Harrison's remote control cars in the other, she duct-taped the doll to the top of the car and set it under the edge of Joshua's bed.

And then she waited.

Joshua came home, and after visiting with us for a few minutes, he made his way into his bedroom. But before he could flip the switch to bring his room to a comforting glow, the dimly beaming light from the hall barely washing the right measure of his bed, Jennifer hit the gas on the remote and out came the doll with a mechanized screech.

Let me tell you, if Joshua had been wearing a onesie, I'd have needed to cut him out of it. The Rotavirus has nothing on Jennifer, even as the boy promised his mother that she would pay for her crimes.

"And this is not an Angels' Portion post!" he said, angrily.

"Oh, yes it is, my good man. Yes it is. In fact, I have just the whisky in mind."

Alas, the Highland Park Valkyrie edition.

In Nordic lore, Valkyries were vicious female spirits—emissaries of Odin sent into the battles of mortal men, angel-like beings arriving with a measure of judgment, choosing the loathsome and cowardly for the Underworld, while selecting others for Valhalla or for joining the spiritual regiment that would be required for the final battle of the ages known as Ragnarok.

Yep, sounds like something Jen would be a part of if she were a Nordic demigod in service to Odin. Too bad she despises whisky, because this namesake dram is fit for such otherworldly deviants as she.

The nose of this delightful dram is one of cranberries and white chocolate—almost feminine in its initial gentleness. There's barely a hint of smoke. And I mean barely. In fact, you might not even discover it unless you know to expect Highland Park's signature incensing—this time reminiscent of smoked citrus zest.

The first sip is incredibly sweet, offering an inviting and generous splash of the citrus noticed in the nosing. Alongside, this beauty unsheathes an additional armament of honeyed cinnamon. But then its alluring smile turns to a more serious and menacing grin, reminding you of its rightful station at Odin's side with a tarry stir of cinders reminiscent of the Nordic god's furnace. This stays through the medium finish, with barely a mention of the fruitier delights that were first to arrive.

If anything, it makes for a great dram while following around and watching an otherwise gentle and kindly wife, a mindful and loving mother of four doing all that she can to set the stage for terrifying her seventeen-year-old son. It's nothing short of being the perfectly consumable soundtrack to her twisted scheming at 12:30 in the morning.

JOHN BARR, RESERVE BLEND, BLENDED SCOTCH WHISKY, 40%

Do you need a spoon to help pry it out?

E ach of my four children is incredibly unique.

Joshua, my oldest, is built with a confidence that arises from an ever-increasing intellect. And while he may often be very right about whatever he's debating at any given moment, that same intellect and confidence has the potential for getting him into trouble.

Madeline, the next in line, is beautifully graceful in both body and soul, and is so pleasant to be around that one is actually a lesser human being when she's away. She cries at the littlest things, and not necessarily because she's fragile, but because she cares about so much. She wants things to be good for everyone, and with that, she's always a light in dark places.

Harrison, the third among the crew, has a brilliant mind that is, more often than not, unhindered by his own body. In other words, he will sometimes offer truthful commentary when he should be silent. But on the other hand, his empathy runs deep, and his love for his family is unbreachable. In addition to all of this, his abilities with language are so far beyond the average person. I have a feeling that when it comes time to pass along the mantle of *The Angels' Portion*, he'll be the one at the keyboard bearing it.

But I think he's going to need his little sister's help, and here's why.

Evelyn, the last of the squad, is the strangest of them all.

Of course she's the absolute stereotypical girl when it comes to girly things. She cares affectionately for her baby dolls. She loves doing her nails. She adores unicorns and Disney princesses. She bears the brightest smile when bathing in the pinks and purples and yellows of this world's design. But she has a side that few are privileged to behold, and it causes her to respond in a moment's notice with shockingly unforgettable words and actions, most of which revolve around using the word "butt" or talking about poop.

Take for example a most recent scene in which she received a box of Skittles. Being the tormenting father that I am, I told her that I was going to sneak a few when she wasn't looking.

"Oh no, you won't!" she said emphatically. "I'm going to hide them under my pillow where you won't find them."

"Honey," I said, "you just told me where they'll be."

"Evelyn," her mother chimed in, "something tells me that putting them under your pillow wouldn't work, anyway. Daddy will probably find them."

"You know it," I said, taunting her.

"Well," she offered resolutely, "I'll just put them up my butt. You won't want them after they've been hidden in there, will you?"

There was nothing left to argue in that little exchange. She was right. I wouldn't be in the mood for Skittles if that happened.

Another milder example...

Evelyn was in a moment of struggle in the bathroom when she called out to Jennifer, "Momma, I'm trying to poop, but I can't!"

"Well, keep at it, sweetie," Jen replied with a kindly voice. "It'll happen."

Again, stepping up to my role as an instigating father, I called back to the little girl, "Honey, do you need me to get you a spoon so you can pry it out?" A short moment of silence passed before I heard a giggle.

If you think it'll help," she said with a tone of faux innocence.

It wasn't Skittles, but this *is* representative of the stranger stuff from which *The Angels' Portion* is often squeegeed—the weirder dimensions of life's normal doings—and Evelyn is more than brimming with the abilities to see them and deliver. I'm more than confident that Harrison has the literary skill to bring them to you personally.

And who knows which whiskies they'll like or dislike, especially when it comes to some of the bottom shelf, fringe whiskies that you only buy while on vacation—whiskies like the John Barr Reserve Blend.

The nose of this particular dram is most certainly light, giving over hardly a wafting of chocolate malt and an even lesser measure of peat.

The palate is a little more complex. Milky in its texture, it offers a sugared grapefruit tang that's not necessarily unpleasant, but that's only because it's lying just below a rescuing layer of caramel and malt that seems a little out of place.

The finish is short. This is good, because there's trouble in the fruit mix it's trying to share.

My thoughts: Go ahead and hide this one wherever you want—under your pillow, in your butt, or wherever. It'll be a long shot before I go looking for it again anytime soon.

What I didn't tell you in the beginning is that getting Harrison and Evelyn together to keep *The Angels' Portion* alive is probably a long shot, too. Right now, I think they're both putting in extra hours to get the other arrested and thrown into jail. I'm serious. These two are not the best of friends. I've thought about paying to send them to a team building seminar—you know, one that has them playing paintball in the woods or climbing rock walls. But in the end, it felt more like I'd be paying to test Harry's ability to survive a point blank shot of the paintball gun to his throat and an assessment of Evelyn's dexterity when Harry cuts her safety rope on the rock wall.

I'd rather be hopeful that God will sort it out in time while I spend my money on whisky—even whisky that's kind of "meh," like the John Barr Reserve Blend.

JOHNNIE WALKER, BLUE LABEL, GHOST AND RARE, 46%

But that's not how the game is played.

"Hey, Daddy," the little girl sing-songed while thumping down the stairs. "Do you wanna play a game with me?"

"Sure," I replied, knowing full well that I'd denied her too many times already. "What game do you want to play?"

"Let's play that game where we slap each other's hands," she said with just as musical a voice.

"You mean the one where I put my hands under yours like this," I asked and demonstrated, "and then try to move as fast as I can to slap the tops of your hands before you pull them away?"

"Yep, that's the one. Let's play that."

"Okay," I said. "So, who goes first?"

"You can try to slap my hands first," she replied. "But before we start, let's see if Joshua wants to play with us."

"Okay. He can go next."

"Oh, no," she said resolutely. "I was thinking that instead of you actually slapping my hands, you could slap Joshua, instead."

"Um, but, that's not how the game is played, honey."

"I know. But I don't really want you to slap my hands, and I think his room is messy. He won't be ready for you, so you'll definitely win the first game, and then you can just tell him you did it because his room is so messy."

"How messy is it?"

"Very," she reported sternly. "I can't even see his floor."

"But you're a much bigger slob than he is," I volleyed.

"Yeah, but I'm only eight. He's seventeen. He should know better."

A contemplative moment passed.

"Josh!" I called out to my eldest son.

"Yeah," returned a somewhat muffled voice.

"Do you want to play a game with me and Evelyn?"

"Sure. What are you playing?"

Now, I know what you're thinking about the scene I just described. And you're right. Making up new rules is a great way to spice up any particular game. I mean, who of us really wants to play Monopoly when there's no chance of a financial windfall from landing on "Free Parking"? Not me, that's for sure. And who wants to play Scrabble without being able to use proper nouns, spell a word backwards, or use foreign languages? Oh, heck no. As a pastor, what's the use of learning a bunch of different languages if I'm forbidden from employing any of them to destroy you during full-on Scrabble combat? Let me tell you, if I discover that the letters in my stash can be rightly arranged to spell out in *Latin* "aquabubalus," you'd better believe I'll be slapping those tiles down and asking, "So, who else wants some of this?"

In short, rule breaking can, sometimes, lead to a fuller enjoyment of God's gifts in any particular moment. Take for example the Johnnie Walker Blue Label Ghost and Rare.

I've never been a big fan of Johnnie Walker, and I must admit that when I received this generous Christmas gift from some very dear friends—Ed and Harry—I thought there might be a chance I could end up offending them when it came time to write the review. I have to be honest in the expressing of my impressions of every whisky I drink, otherwise my credibility as a reviewer will be shot. And Johnnie Walker and I haven't had a very good relationship over the years.

But here I am with what I would say is one of the best blended whiskies I think I've ever tried—even better than the Ballantine's 21-year-old. In other words, the time has come to break my "never-buy-Johnnie-Walker-whisky" rule, knowing that if I do, in the case of this whisky, it will be to my benefit.

As an inhalant, the Ghost and Rare is relatively mild—not stodgy like most of the other Johnnie Walker editions. This one offers up caramel apples, and maybe even an after dinner dessert plate of warmed brownie and ice cream. A little longer with the dram and there's the certainty of a pinch of mint in the ice cream.

The palate is incredibly delightful, carrying through with a deliciously buttery cream of toffee, sweet doughnut glaze, and blood oranges.

The medium finish—bearing an almost unnoticeable kiss of smoke—singles out from the nose and palate the apples and the buttery toffee, ultimately jettisoning pretty much everything else.

This is a costly dram, one that would almost certainly cause you to break other rules in order to purchase it, like the ones communicating that society typically looks down upon people who withhold food and clothing from their children—or rob banks—in order to afford such whisky.

Don't break those rules. Feed and clothe your kids, and earn your own money. But let's say you find yourself at a friendly dinner party where you just so happen to stumble across a bottle of the Ghost and Rare in the host's liquor cabinet. In that case, I think it makes sense to set fire to a couch so that while everyone else is distracted and working to put it out, you could fill a flask or two to take home.

I won't judge you. Unless, of course, the dinner party is happening at my house, and that was my couch and my bottle of the Ghost and Rare. In that case, I'll call the cops and let the local magistrate do the judging.

JURA, 18 YEARS OLD, TRAVEL EXCLUSIVE EDITION, 42%

Don't put the shovel away. It's June. It could still snow.

From among the many threads that form the fabric of this universe, there are things that appear to pair very well. Take, for example, doughnuts and milk. What a joyful combination and generous gift of the Creator!

There are others, of course, such as hotdogs and baseball games, the morning sun and a cup of coffee, a toilet and bad Mexican food, shoes and socks, movies and popcorn, my wife and her camera, and me and ibuprofen.

But there are things that do not go together, things like my kids and a tidy house, pastors in black clericals and glitter, plumbers and pants that fit, me and ibuprofen, and snow and the month of April.

Ah, yes, snow and April. Here I sit this springtime morn in the aforementioned month with a cup of coffee in hand observing the sun rising effortlessly sun in a cloudless sky, casting its bright beams of love upon my snow covered yard. Oh yeah, and the morning newscaster just announced that we should expect one to three inches more sometime this afternoon.

The thing is, I just moved the lawnmower from the shed to the garage, and I put into its place a cleaned snow blower. I put the shovels in the shed, too, being sure to situate them all the way in the back where they'd be out of the way and most difficult to reach, figuring I wouldn't need them again until next winter.

You know, my mower has a side chute that blows out the grass clippings. I wonder if it would work similarly with snow. I suppose it might, as long as I get to the snow before it gets too deep. I wonder what folks in the neighborhood would think of such things. On second thought, who cares? When it comes to my yard, they already think I'm either a little crazy or that I'm conspiring with aliens.

Just know that if I decide to try to mow my snow today, it'll be in style—shorts, boots with tall black socks, and an AC/DC shirt pulled over my winter coat. And maybe even a motorcycle helmet so that when I'm asked about it later, I can say that it wasn't me, but one of my alien friends doing me a solid.

Anyway, rest assured that before venturing out into the tundra-like landscape, I shall be pouring myself a short dram of something that pairs well with an arctic Michigan springtime. The Jura 18-year-old Travel Exclusive edition is perfectly suited for the task.

With a nose of chocolate, warmed caramel, and a distant but not unpleasant hint of vinegar, a deep intake stirs the body's warming element and sets one ready for the frigid task at hand. A sip does the same, giving gingered coffee and a citrus side that suggests warmer climates, but at the same time, reminds you that you don't live in Florida.

The finish is long, like a Michigan winter. But unlike the coldest and darkest of seasons, it's an enjoyable savoring of sour citrus and the promise that, while it feels like it might last forever, it won't. Eventually it will get warmer.

With that, I'm off to gas up the mower, although I need to try to find my boots. I'm pretty sure Jen may already have packed them away in the basement storage—because last week's warmer weather suggested doing such things.

Knockando, Master Reserve (1994), 21 Years Old, 43%

There's no "s" at the end of the word "Revelation."

"Hello, this is Pastor Thoma."

"Hi, I was supposed to be put through to Pastor Chris. Is he available?"

"Well, if you mean Pastor Thoma, whose first name is Chris, then that's me."

"Oh, great, well, Pastor Chris, I'm Tom from—" *I don't care where you're from, pal, and you just lost any chance of selling me anything* "—and I was wondering if you might have a minute to let me tell you about our new ten-week video Bible study series on the Book of Revelations."

"Well, actually, I don't really have ti—"

"Pastor Chris, this is really a great series, and I can personally guarantee it'll help you be successful in guiding your flock through a very important book of the Bible that a lot of folks find confusing. Do you find it confusing?"

"No."

"Well, that's because you're a pastor. But, Pastor Chris, I'll bet some of your people can't make heads or tails of the darn thing."

"I hear you, but I don't think—"

"I think you'll appreciate the series. It deals with the rapture, how to see modern events in light of Biblical prophecies, and a whole bunch more things that you may not have even thought about."

"Listen, Tom, I appreciate your call and—"

"And I can send you the series for free. You keep it for thirty days, and if you decide you don't want it, just send it back. You only pay shipping and handling. If you decide to keep it, you'll be billed three easy payments of only $59.99."

"I'm sorry, Tom, but I do need to go. I don't think I'm interested in—"

"I gotcha, Pastor Chris. You're a busy man. How about I call back in a few weeks to check and see if you've changed your mind? Maybe I could share a little more about the series when you have more time."

"That's fine, but when you call back, if I don't answer, just ask for Pastor Thoma."

"Will do. Pastor Chris, I do so thank you for your time."

"Right. Blessings in your day."

Click.

First of all, there's no "s" at the end of the word "Revelation." Stop adding one. It makes you sound foolish.

And second...

No offense to the Reverends out there who go by their first names in their churches and communities, but honestly, whose idea was it to start this silly practice in the Church, anyway? Sure, I get the point that some pastors *believe* their people feel closer to them when they are permitted to use their first names. And I get the urge to scratch the point's itch, especially as it appears to so many in the clergy as an avenue for personal or institutional relevancy. But as I've said in so many other places, the Church and her pastors have never had a problem with being relevant. The message we bring and the service we render are about as relevant as they get. The world may not see it that way, and that's to be expected, but where the hell are we in the match if right out of the gate the pastors themselves consider their stations as intrinsically less-than-relevant, that is, in need of a little something extra to make it worth anyone's while?

And by the way, there's a reason that the need to be relevant itches in the first place. It's a rash. Rashes itch. And rashes need to be cured, not perpetuated.

In tandem, but along a different trail of thought, would anyone of any office—especially someone who rightly understands his office as having been bestowed rather than achieved—would such an office holder rather reshape the institution into what he wants it to be, or would he strive to be faithful to it as it was given, being the best he can be as its steward? I can't necessarily answer that question, although I have my suspicions as to the answer. In the meantime, I can approach the question from another direction.

Would it ever be appropriate for me to address our state's top executive, Rick Snyder, as Governor Rick? Or the policeman that pulled me over as Officer Bob? Or the traffic court magistrate as Judge Judy?

Wait a second...

Anyway, as I was about to say, if any of these people ever set such a standard, I can assure you that it would alter my regard for them and the seriousness of the duty they are performing.

"This sounds pretty self-serving and pompous, Pastor Chris."

No, it's not. In fact, it's just the opposite. To address an officeholder in reverential ways—ways less concerned with assuring one another of equality and more inclined toward demonstrating a respect for the important distinctions between the servant and the one being served—is to esteem the person, the office, and the bestower of the office. And it teaches others to do the same.

The Office of Pastor—or the Office of the Holy Ministry, as we know it in the Lutheran Church—is by no means an office of pomposity. It's not a station of prestige or lordship. It's a station of service. Knowing this, believing this, pastors should be the first ones to protect against practices that allow for perceptions of the office—both inside and outside of the Church—to degenerate into the realms of fictional characters you'd expect to find in a child's favorite TV show. Officer Steve and Nurse Sally—I just don't take those types seriously, and I'd be willing to bet that you don't either.

We're in a real post-modern mess, here, folks. Respect for all things sacred—people, places, you name it—it's all slipping away into the deeper waters of trained disrespect with each allowance we make. When Pastors do it, they're willingly dialing down their own relevancy while making it harder for the rest of us to be seen for the substance and rescue we're trying represent and bring to people who need it.

Now, I won't go into the stories validating my words. Instead, I'll simply say, "Pastor Bob and Father Jim, do us all a favor and cut it out. Respect yourself and your office enough to expect a higher level of etiquette, because right now, when it comes to the clergy being taken seriously by just about anyone—especially the people outside of the Church—you're part of the problem and not the solution."

Thankfully, there are plenty of whisky distilleries that haven't succumbed to such tragedies of respect. The ones that have, well, they exist to prove my point. I don't know anyone who refers to The Macallan as "The Mac," but I've heard plenty of nicknames for Jack Daniels. One is approached with the respect due an artisan, and the other is a mass-produced attempt at being every whisky drinker's pal.

Knockando whiskies are similar examples of admirable substance. A sip from its Master Reserve 21-Year-Old edition proves it isn't striving to be everyone's buddy, but rather it wants to show you what lies beyond the sludge of Jack and Coke—a better, more gifting horizon that surpasses the experience of just drinking booze.

The nose of this exceptional whisky is the first revelation of its class. There's just the right amount of nutmeg and sherry that arrive in the second sniff to balance the richer wood spices that came with the first.

The palate is a respectable concoction of crystallized ginger, smoked nectarines, buttermilk biscuit dough, and zested lemons. In the finish, the smoked fruit lingers, and after a while, is joined by a glazing of dark chocolate.

My recommendation: Strip down to your boxers, get yourself a plastic cup, pop open the bottle, and give the ol' Knocky 21 a go.

Hmm.

Knowing the valuable phenomenon that exists inside this bottle, do you hear how ridiculous that sounds?

Remember that the next time you greet your pastor. What is he to you? Is he the Knockando—a vessel in the stead of the Divine sent to give you extraordinary things—or is he just any old bottle of Jack?

LAPHROAIG, CAIRDEAS (2017), CASK STRENGTH QUARTER CASK, 57.2%

I'm going to stay right here.

It's Christmas Eve and I'm sitting at my computer in my office at the church. The second of three services just received its benediction, and with that, the attendees have all departed for their homes. There's another service tonight, but it isn't for another four hours.

"You should probably go home for a little while, Reverend."

You're right. I probably should. But I won't. It just snowed several inches, and as I write this, I can see that it's still coming down. I live about twenty miles from here, and even though I drive a Jeep Wrangler, I don't necessarily feel like pitching myself into a thirty minute white-knuckle ride home and then the same, if not worse, adventurous ride back. And don't forget, I'll make that same drive one more time at the end of the night to get back home, and then the following morning for our Christmas Day service.

Making this trip once tonight is quite enough. And besides, if you think about it, in everything I just described, you have all of the fixings for a Christmas Eve tragedy. You know, a straight-to-Netflix movie with a title like "All He Wanted Was Some Glazed Ham" and a brief synopsis that reads: "A family of six endures unexpected tragedy when the father, a minister, is killed in an auto accident while driving home on Christmas Eve. Struggling to understand the untimely event, will the love they have for one another be enough to keep them together, or will their relationships melt away over time like the last of the drifting snow in the ditch that consumed dad?"

I'm just going to stay put.

Not to worry, though. I came comfortably prepared. I have a benevolence closet at my disposal. I would've had two peanut butter and jelly sandwiches, but my daughter Madeline—the one tasked with creating and bringing them for me—forgot to do so. Still, Campbell's soup will make a fine Christmas dinner. And maybe a can of sweet corn, too. Additionally, I brought along a couple of bottles of Scotch that I've yet to try—one of which you're soon to hear about. Thankfully, my wife provided a sturdy Tinkerbell bag to make safe their transport and impress onlookers. I even have a Waterford Crystal rock glass. Lastly, my office is warm, my cot is in place, and I'm listening to AC/DC—"Nervous Shakedown" to be precise. Not exactly a Christmas carol, but still something to offset the snarling winds just outside my window and upsetting the stillness of my current solitude.

As I said, I'll be fine, especially since I have before me the 2017 edition of the Laphroaig Cairdeas Cask Strength Quarter Cask.

I received this whisky from my good friends Scott and Georgie Rhodes, and I must say that having just loosed its cork and given it a go, already I can attest to it being the perfect dram for the night I've described, especially since no one is here, and I like it so much I'd have trouble sharing.

The nose of this delightful invention sets free an initial pother of simmering citrus and white chocolate chips, all hovering above a well-stoked peat fire beside which bread crusts have fallen and are being blackened. I'd say the bread was generously buttered before it fell.

A sip reveals a pasting of tar and lemon jelly atop a wedge of warmed sour dough.

The smoke delivered in the palate is relentless, and it carries well over and into a longer finish, one that brings along a morsel of the sour dough, now a little sweeter, and a hint of the oil used to grease the bread pan before baking.

I'm glad I brought this whisky tonight. And yet, had I decided to drive home, increasing the possibility of ending up hanging from my seatbelt overturned in a ditch, the Laphroaig would have been there, and it would have well-sufficed for keeping warm until I was cut free and rescued—be that sooner or later. Either way, while there is something to be said about enjoying it here at my desk as opposed to a snow bank somewhere off of US-23, I'll give it a gracious nod and say that it would be quite pleasing to most Scotch whisky drinkers no matter where it was consumed.

Still, I'm not going anywhere.

Slàinte mhath and have a merry Christmas.

LAPHROAIG, LORE, 48%

The power of Christ compels you.

Take a syringe with a needle of almost any length or gauge, jam it into one of her limbs, and the seven-year-old will barely flinch.

Watch her fall down a flight of stairs, and, without losing her rhythm, she will hop to her feet and say, "What are you staring at?"

Behold her wrestling with her older brother, and in the grittiest moment of the dust up, when their heads meet with the sound of a horrifying crack, you will hear her say to her tearful opponent, "You should be more careful."

However, put her into the orthodontist's examination chair with the intent of putting metal objects into her mouth and you will see her lose her mind.

If you can imagine it, this was the scene: A man dressed in his priestly garb beside a little girl in an examination chair, an orthodontic assistant tasked with cementing a retainer into place, and a room full of people chatting about everything and nothing. The assistant, so kindly and so gently, instructs the little girl to open her mouth widely and say "ah." But as she reaches toward the toothy orifice on the little girl's face, it snaps shut and she begins to flail, her head turning in different directions, her arms swinging and blocking every attempt of the assistant to accomplish her goal. Her father, the man wearing the clerical collar and dressed in black, lurches to hover above her, grabbing her hands for fear that she'll hurt the assistant or herself. In response, the little girl's knees go up and into her father's groin and stomach. One foot kicks the utensil table attached to the mechanical arm sending it spinning away toward the assistant and patient in the next chair over. The father, doing his best not to choke on his own injuries, does all that he can to talk her away from the frenzy. A moment of calm ensues and the assistant tries again only to receive the same response. It's then that the screaming begins and the rest of the room becomes focused on the exorcism-like event happening in Chair One which, by the way, also happens to be completely visible to all in the waiting area.

Looking back, I think that both I and all the others in the room almost expected to see her head spin as she slowly rose in a free-float above the chair. In fact, had she not been bribed by the orthodontist—who is a dear friend, by the way—it probably would've happened this way. And I suppose that as the moment stands in time, the only details missing from the event were pea soup and me sprinkling holy water while shouting, "The power of Christ compels you!"

When I arrived home later in the day, I told my wife, Jennifer, what happened, and I assured her that she would be taking the little girl to her next appointment. She laughed. I think she thought I was being funny. But I wasn't.

Maybe she's possessed, too.

No matter. I'm ready. In the meantime, I'm going to sit and sip whisky, and the Laphroaig Lore edition is the one to reinvigorate me for the next demonic engagement. Or trip to the orthodontist. Whichever. Both are inevitable. I have four children.

I use the word "reinvigorate" purposely with regard to the Lore, because no sooner than it falls from the bottle into the glass does a particular realization materialize: This stuff is rich, but also high-octane. A deliberate sniff brings and bestows committed vigor, suggesting, "A stride with me through the peat fires will not only reward you, but you'll be shaped to box with the Devil and win." And so you follow the whisky's lead into and through the haze, walking past simmering cauldrons of dried fruit and salty butter, the surrounding fires aglow with smoldering peat spewing blue flames. Each of the emanations is delightfully overwhelming.

Already intrigued, you reach to stir and steal a sip from the nearest kettle. It's a powerful injection of singed and salty vegetables—spinach and artichokes—soaking in the sizzling, fatty juices of a sirloin that fell into the fire but was quickly retrieved. The ashes are still on the beef.

The clinging finish defines the dried fruits—apricots and raisins.

Looking at my calendar for tomorrow, I see that I have quite the busy day, a portion of which will require doing battle with those who would see the Lord's church in ashes—both intentionally and unintentionally. Thankfully, none of tomorrow's events involves taking my daughter to the orthodontist, so with that, it'll be an easier collection of twenty-four hours.

SHACKLETON BLENDED MALT SCOTCH WHISKY, 40%

It's nothing a sewer clown can't fix.

As the saying goes, "Kids will be kids." And yet, is that proverb still legitimately allowable for explaining away the behaviors of the current generation of children?

I'm not so sure, especially after what I observed in the checkout line at our local grocery store.

The line was short. It included a group of three vibrant but unkempt kids in their early teens, followed by an elderly woman, and then myself. The kids each had a 20 ounce bottle of Mountain Dew Code Red. The woman bore a basket on her arm that she'd not yet unloaded onto the belt for scanning. In it she had a box of crackers, two cans of soup, coffee filters, a box of spaghetti noodles, and a snack pack of stringed cheese. I had two gallons of milk, one in each hand.

The three kids jostled and laughed, pushed and spoke crassly, consuming more personal space than was necessary. Ultimately, one of them, a young girl, bumped into the lady and caused her basket to tip and several of her items to fall to the floor. And what did the culprit do in response? She didn't apologize, but rather laughed—admittedly it was a laugh of momentary embarrassment—and then she finished the transaction and scuttled away with her cohorts.

Setting her basket on the belt, the woman went to pick up her items, although I got to them first. She thanked me, and in the gentlest of grandmotherly voices, began a short commentary on the growing disrespect she's been observing in kids, and how what just occurred was another certified example.

"How has it gotten to this?" she said, bringing her speech to the man in the clerical collar beside her to an end.

"I have my suspicions," I replied, putting the last item on the moving belt. "Although, no matter how far out of line these kids get," I continued, "it's nothing that a sewer clown probably couldn't handle for us."

"What?" she asked.

"Those are the kinds of clowns that eat kids," I said. "A handful of sewer clowns with red balloons here and there in America and I'd bet things would change. One thing's for sure," I continued, "they'd probably stop protesting the NRA."

"Red balloons?"

"Never mind," I said, realizing she'd completely missed the reference to Stephen King's novel *It*. "It was just a joke. I mean, just know that as a parent, I agree with you and I'm doing everything I can to steer my own kids in the right ways."

"Well, at least someone is," she answered and then went into how, unfortunately, her son's kids are proving to be entitled brats in need of a significant course correction, and had her husband been alive today, he'd have provided it.

The moment ended and I made my way home. I put the milk into the refrigerator and then sat down to open a fresh bottle—the Shackleton Blended Malt Scotch Whisky—which is a deliberate attempt at recreating the Mackinlay's edition that accompanied Sir Ernest Shackleton and his crew on their infamous survey of the Antarctic in 1907.

I suppose the Shackleton edition was perfectly suited to the previous narrative, especially since both the elderly woman and I would do everything in our powers to recreate particular aspects of bygone eras, times when kids spent their days riding their bikes, playing outside, doing some chores here and there, and then taking the extra bit of spending money to the local grocery store to buy a candy bar, never for one second believing it acceptable to exhibit wildly disrespectful behavior in public, lest parents discover and exercise swift judgment.

The odds that we'll ever return to such societal standards are slim, just as I'm suspecting that it's anyone's guess if this Shackleton edition truly met its mark in the attempt to return to something that would have been preferred by an intrepid and discerning explorer of the highest class.

Now, that said, the whisky is pretty good, just not exceptional.

The nose is buttery—the salted and oily kind—and it offers a mere tap of peat followed by an even lighter wash of malt. The palate agrees completely with this assessment, although as the peat's efforts increase, along with it comes a subtle citrus and a drop or two of vanilla.

The finish, I'd say, is medium but also steadily warming, which I'm guessing would have been more than acceptable in -50 degree temperatures at the bottom of the world. And as it warms, it invites thoughts of singed barley bread—not unpleasant in the conditions, but certainly not what you'd expect to enjoy back home.

On the other hand, when considering the current state of affairs in our culture, "back home" might be all the more reason to become an explorer in Antarctica. At least the natives—the penguins—know how to keep decorum in a line. And they certainly dress respectably.

TAMDHU, BATCH STRENGTH, BATCH NO. 002, 58.5%

She self-identifies as a potato chip.

I think the four smaller versions of my wife and I are more aware of our culture's absurdity than I may have suspected. I say this because while they appear to understand the insanity, they have managed to focus its irrational energy in ways that will benefit them during opportune moments.

For example, are you familiar with the game "Slug Bug"? Perhaps it has other names in other countries, but no matter where you go, I'm guessing it's played the same. Essentially, when someone sees a Volkswagen Beetle, that same person is to call out its color and then give the person beside him or her a moderate thump to the arm. We parked beside an olive green Fiat in a gas station parking lot when one of the younger children mistakenly calls out "Slug bug, green one!" and punches the nearest sibling in the arm. In a fury, that same sibling protests that the car isn't a slug bug, but is, in fact, a Fiat.

"Well," the offender replies, "it identifies as a slug bug."

A little further down the road and at home, I've just dropped a handful of potato chips onto a plate to eat as a snack. A nearby observer, the youngest in the pack, turns to her mother to ask if she, too, might have some potato chips.

"No, you may not," the mother says. "You'll spoil your dinner."

"But Daddy's having some," the little girl responds in a whine.

"Well," the gentlest parent offers in return, "when you're a forty-five-year-old man, you can have potato chips whenever you want."

"Okay," the little girl says, reaching for the bag on the kitchen counter. "I'm going to have some chips, then."

"Your mother just told you no, you little fiend," I say with a crumbling mouthful of salt and vinegar goodness.

"I've decided that I identify as a forty-five-year-old man," the eight-year-old grins, shoving her hand into the bag.

"Don't even try it!" I return, swatting at her forearm. "I'll stuff you into that bag. And when no one can find you, I'll tell folks you self-identified as a potato chip and to look in the cabinet."

Since we're talking about self-identities, I have no idea of the age of the whisky in the Tamdhu Batch Strength No. 002 edition. But for a NAS dram, it sure has the complexity of something relatively experienced—something well past the 18-year-old mark—and I sure do like it.

With a nose of grains, light fruits, and butter pecans, this is a heavyweight with some charm.

The palate is proof of its tender charisma. Even as a batch strength Scotch tagged at 58.5% ABV, this whisky is careful and caressing. In fact, you might feel the urge to put a little water into it, but don't. This whisky successfully self-identifies at a lower ABV. The alcohol is never an issue. And water, while it might open up something else for you, in my experience seemed to thin the enjoyment. This whisky is just fine by itself, giving over a warmed mix of tangerines and blueberries sprinkled with a grit of pecans and brown sugar.

The nuttiness stays until the very end, leaving on a medium to long trail of pecan pie.

Okay, for the sake of Child Protective Services stumbling across this review of the Tamdhu and somehow coming to the conclusion that I'm an abusive father, I'll first offer the disclaimer that I would never put one of my children into a bag of potato chips. Such a bag would be far too small, anyway. I'm more likely to put them into a sleeping bag and swing them around until they throw up on themselves from laughing too hard. I mean, what father hasn't done that, right?

Disclaimer #2: I've never swung my kids around in a sleeping bag. Not ever. But don't ask the kids if I've done it. Remember, they've got some messed up self-identification issues already. Their realities aren't to be trusted in a court of law.

THE MACALLAN, 12 YEARS OLD, SHERRY OAK CASK, 43%

I almost died today.

Do you remember that time when you were driving along at sixty miles per hour and you happened upon the cross street you were looking for much sooner than expected? Do you remember how you decided in that moment to attempt the turn anyway rather than pass it, turn around, and come back? Do you recall how in that moment of the actual turn you realized what a huge mistake it was? Do you remember the silent prayer that formed behind your wide-eyed animation and cursing, the one that sounded something like, "Lord, as I roll this car and am ejected into the ditch, please just let me live"? Do you remember that feverish instant of trembling after the successful completion of the turn, that moment when you found yourself in disbelief that you were still alive? And perhaps finally, do you recall that thought a half mile down the road when you gave a sigh of relief that there was no one else around in the moment of the turn to be jeopardized by your deathly lunacy?

Now, envision an Airbus 321 arriving in Orlando from Detroit. Imagine that all 240 of its seats are occupied by excited vacationers.

Be mindful that the overhead compartments are brimming and so is the luggage compartment in the plane's belly.

Imagine that aircraft coming in for a landing and touching down at two-hundred miles per hour. Imagine hearing the ceremonial applause from the passengers. Imagine cruising along for a few moments as though heading to the furthest exit at the end of the runway. Imagine the sudden and deafening sound that comes from throwing the engine thrust reversers into full power in order to make an immediate left turn.

Imagine that turn—because it happened.

The plane tottered. People screamed. Prayers were said.

Once the turn was completed, folks offered another round of ceremonial applause—although I'm guessing it was more a form of communal praise to the Lord for deliverance from the runway canal we nearly rolled into and which was most likely occupied by gators.

The captain eventually came over the PA system to offer a nervously quick welcome to "the beautiful city." After that, he was never seen or heard from again.

My guess is that the tower changed plans on the pilot mid-landing. Or he woke up after the autopilot landed the plane and sounded an alarm that it was his turn to take over.

Either way, here I sit believing the event to be providential.

Yes, I'm giving thanks that we're all alive. And I'm equally appreciative that no other planes were near enough to ours to become endangered by the hasty turn. But I'm also grateful that the pace of that turn most likely shaved a few seconds off the arrival time to our final destination. Essentially, it allowed for me to arrive at the liquor store near the home in which we vacation just in time to snatch this solitary bottle of The Macallan 12-year-old Sherry Oak Cask from the shelf before another fellow came along looking to do the same.

"Excellent," I said, smiling at the proprietor and reaching up to take the bottle. "I've had every edition on your shelves except this one. This one is new."

"That's just the bottle I came here for!" came the sound of a disheartened gent behind me.

"Sorry, friend," I turned in reply. "I almost died today. This one's mine."

And so here I sit with dram in hand, watching the kids swimming in the pool—and it's a fine little whisky for such a pleasurable moment.

An initial nosing of this 12-year-old is rich with dark chocolates, and of course, warming sherry. There is a passing moment of vinegar, but after a minute or two, with a swirl and a sniff, all is followed by black raspberries and coffee.

The palate takes a hard left away from its sweeter runway to a spicier path of a cinnamon and citrus.

The finish is superb. It brings its passengers into a gentle docking with the barrel oak, a dash of crushed almonds, and an extremely distant char.

Again, this is the perfect near-death-experience whisky for any among us. Although, as I re-read what I just wrote, I suppose most any whisky has the potential for being a celebratory dram in such circumstances.

Unless it's Scoresby.

I'd rather be dead in a ditch full of alligators than drink Scoresby.

The Macallan, Edition No. 3, 48.3%

Really? Your generation is leading the way?

"**A**re you okay, Daddy?"
    "I'm fine."

Apparently my youngest son noticed my eye twitching and got a little concerned.

Not to worry, though. I'm okay. My body is just reacting to the conversation occurring at the table over my right shoulder. Yes, the one with the tattooed, bleach blonde twenty-something telling a gathering of smartphone-tapping friends how her generation is leading the way in saving the world from so many terrible things like bigotry, guns, pollution, and general disharmony. My eye was twitching because my body was rerouting its stress impulses to prevent me from saying anything. I think it was also fighting a stroke in progress.

Really? Your generation is leading the way? Leading the way toward what? The complete dismissal of anything objectively true while delivering imbecilic ignorance gift wrapped in the standardization of lifespan-shortening behavior?

Um, don't you guys eat laundry detergent packets or sniff mounds of cinnamon for fun and then share the experiences on the internet? And didn't I just read an article this morning about a member of your generation getting her head stuck in an oversized tailpipe at a music festival?

Maybe I'm being overly critical when I say that I'm struggling with the fact that you have the right to procreate and vote, let alone operate devices with tailpipes.

How about this, instead? Let's agree that you'll just do what your friend is doing. And while you're texting one of your virtual friends in complete silence, I'll go ahead and eat my linguine and shrimp. Let's also agree that the chances are good that a handful of folks will probably arise from your generation who will help to lead the human race forward into better harmonies. But at the same time, let's admit that these few will be doing this from a mantle that has definable contours and is a carrying forth of something that was around long before they knew what a Tide Pod was.

In other words, your generation isn't going to save the world. If anything, it's dumber than pretty much all of the generations before it, and it very well could be making the world worse. You definitely need the expertise from previous generations before even considering taking your first step. I say this having read another article in the New York Times suggesting that over 70% of millennials cannot sew a button, change a tire, or iron a shirt. Well, of course you can't do these things. Such things are almost completely unachievable with your head in a tailpipe and choking on cinnamon. God forbid we need any of you to defend our homeland from invaders. You'll be fairly useless in most combat or survival scenarios, but you'll certainly be able to tell the enemy how to upload their victory photos on Instagram while serving them an absolutely magnificent latte.

I'm just glad that, for the most part, the artisans of the old guard are still at the helm of many of the distilleries I prefer. I don't know what laundry detergent tastes like, but I'm pretty sure I don't want anyone from the current generation making sure I can identify its presence in the nose, palate, or finish of any whiskies crossing my path.

I'll admit to my nerves being a bit seared before trying The Macallan Edition No. 3. Its label tells the tale of a cooperation between Bob Dalgarno, a master distiller at The Macallan, and Roja Dove, a world-renowned perfumer. In short, it sounded kind of gimmicky to me, like I was about to sip a whisky that I could also splash on my neck before going out to dinner with my wife. But I was wrong. This is a fine dram, one that was made by a couple of gents who can not only sew a button, but they could probably do so on the shirt of a sprinting Olympian.

The nose of this collaborative dram teases a carefully crafted packaging of chocolates, buttercream, and sherry. There's a hint of barrel spice, but its moment is fast-fleeting.

The palate delivers on the buttercream and chocolate while adding a slice of glazed orange bread.

The finish is heftier than one might expect, being a little more than long, but not on the burn. It keeps its legs with a bit of allspice and caramel.

The Macallan No. 3 is definitely a product of skill born from experience in varying fields. When it comes to the craft of finer whisky making, Dalgarno chose to combine the truths he already knows with the aptitude of Dove, a man of class who was willing to do the same. In so doing, they've created a dram that is surpassingly better than anything an overly confident millennial bemoaning previous generations might ever deserve.

TOMATIN, DUALCHAS, 43%

A dash of bad math can make this possible.

There are three kinds of people in the world, those who are good at math and those who aren't. As you can see, I'm in the latter group. I just never liked it as a child and even now the disposition remains.

I will admit, however, that I was relatively proud of the ability in my early years to make certain numbers so unrecognizable that I could reasonably argue they were something else entirely. What I mean, for example, is that a carefully crafted eight—one whose edges are purposefully faded—could quite easily be established as a careless three. Or with a little bit of intention, a five's corpus could be crafted so tightly that I could convince a teacher that, no, I wasn't off by one, but rather found six to be the answer like everyone else. Look here. See my six. Yes it looks like a scrunched five, but it isn't. It's a six.

If only the look in my eyes didn't give me away so easily and so often.

Of course mathematics are a daily involvement for most of us. Whether it's reconciling a bank statement or figuring out which whisky you can afford after that year-long snatching of coins from couches, parking lots, and pillows where your child's tooth had previously rested, mathematics is ever with us.

By the way, in order to successfully retrieve money from beneath the pillow of a slumbering youngster, some contemplative calculations born from both physics and geometry will be needed. Before you can wrestle with guilt for the effort, you'll need to wrestle with maneuvers sopping with math. Although, whatever the grappling, it might well be worth it if the outcome is the Tomatin Dualchas. This is a really great, low cost whisky.

More than affordable by way of your loose change jar, the Dualchas can be acquired in most circumstances for less than $30. I don't know how Tomatin can afford to do this. Either their accountant is as skilled in math as I am, which means the distillery will most likely be closing soon, or he is exceptional in math and has brilliantly worked the numbers in a way that brings this remarkable whisky to the consumers for a third of the cost of others on higher shelves that aren't even as good. I'm guessing that the latter is true. In fact, the naming of the whisky hints to such creative maneuverings. Dualchas is the Gaelic form of "legacy," or more accurately, "cultural heritage." Apparently, Tomatin was told they could not sell a whisky in the United States called Legacy, and so with that, they figured out how to do it anyway.

Hey, liquor control commissions of the world, put that in your pipe and smoke it! And while you're doing that, we'll tip back a dram or two of the Dualchas, being sure to savor the magic of a successful equation.

With a nose of honey-butter and sweet malt, the Dualchas begins on the lighter side. But in a sip's moment, it brings to these previous addends a cluster of grains in eddying creaminess.

Like a simple exercise in addition, the resultant finish is a short and well-balanced sum of everything from the nose and palate, except here I'd say that the butter is the most prevalent of its parts.

For the cost, I'll be keeping a few of these in my various cabinets. And I dare say I may not even need to continue my late night swipes from the Tooth Fairy's generosity to make it happen. Speaking of, I'd better stop doing that, anyway. The Tooth Fairy in our house is pretty good at math—especially subtraction—so when the kids are beaming with excitement at the most recent gift that is a dollar or two less than what was actually placed there while I show up with a new bottle of whisky, she becomes suspicious. At this point, she's been chalking it up to forgetfulness, but I'm pretty sure that won't last much longer.

TOMINTOUL, 10 YEARS OLD, 40%

He died peacefully in his sleep.

"You'd miss me if I were gone," Jennifer said playfully.

"Indeed, I would," I replied to my lovely wife with just as bright a smile as hers. But, I should've stopped right there. And yet, I didn't. My mind kept working and I kept talking. "If I ever lost you," I continued, "you know what I'd do first?"

"What's that?" she asked, plopping down on the couch beside me.

"I'd buy a little TV and set it where you're sitting right now, and every time I go to watch a movie, I'd turn it on a 24-hour news station."

"Why?" she pried, looking somewhat bewildered.

"Because you always talk during movies," I said. "I'd miss that a lot. I'd have that TV there to make it harder to concentrate on the movie, and every time I turn to look at it—to tell it to stop talking, knowing that it won't—I'll think of you. I'll probably cry through the whole movie... which will be a scary movie...because you won't watch scary movies with me."

"You know, you can lose me to more than death," she spoke, inferring divorce. Her voice was steady and her face equally void of emotion. "Or I could lose you," she concluded. "You could die in your sleep."

Like I said, I should've stopped. And over the course of the next few days, I'll be sleeping with one eye open, as the saying goes. She's a good woman, but she's more than capable of making whatever happens look like an accident.

"Ma'am," the officer might say, "it looks like your husband died peacefully in his sleep."

"Oh dear," she'll respond, wiping at a dry eye. "You know, I've been telling him for years that I thought he had sleep apnea."

Do you think it is an accident that, if it ever departed from this world, the Tomintoul 10-year-old is the one that folks would miss more than its 16-year-old sibling edition? Well, that's at least how I feel about the whole situation. The 16-year-old was a mess, and with a tagline on the bottle referring to it as the gentle dram, I was uncertain what was meant by "gentle." If I recall, my review of the 16-year-old mentioned tiny sharks attacking my tongue, so if by "gentle" they mean gradually being devoured by little sharks as opposed to being bitten in half by a big one, then the tagline fits. Still, they miss the truer definition of the word.

The 10-year-old is indeed gentle. The nose is warm butter and medium roasted coffee with cream. I also sensed a little bit of what I thought was a lime, but I didn't get that until I added the tiniest drop of water after having already taking a straight sniff and sip.

The palate is unquestionably a browned and buttered English muffin with a thin, crowning layer of sweet mandarin marmalade.

The finish is very close to matching the palate's details, but it adds to it a light but lengthy wash of the butter—something slightly spicy. My guess is cinnamon.

In all, if I were to make an attempt to connect the dots in this little jaunt, I'd say Jennifer is the 10-year-old Tomintoul. If she were ever suddenly absent from this world, she'd be missed. The 16-year-old, on the other hand, would never compare, and would only ever serve as a reminder of what you so desperately miss in the better edition.

Now, I realize there are loopholes in my logic as it meets with the scenario on the couch—plenty that have the potential for making my current hole a little deeper and the next few nights of "eyes wide open" a little longer. Just know I love my wife more than anything in the world, and with that, I'll stop right there.

AMERICA

1792, SMALL BATCH, 46.85%

I've never been to France.

France.

I've never actually been there. I've been to all of the countries around it, but I've never stepped foot over its border.

That's purely coincidental, you know. Even though I'm of German descent, rest assured I haven't been circling the country with shady intentions of eventually staking a claim in its soil. I've just never been there.

Love it or hate it, France has a depth of culture and history that few other countries can assert. I mean, which other country is as thrifty as France, who considers sex a national pastime in order to save money on other forms of personal enjoyment? And which other country can literally boast seven hundred ways to serve eggs? Or claim itself as the source of over two hundred and fifty different cheeses? It takes a very special country to be that devoted to cheese. Forget the nation of Wisconsin. France has this one hands down.

A country filled with such creative individualism and bold originality is bound to have a few revolutions here and there, too, wouldn't you say? Thus, the namesake for this whiskey.

"Hold on a second, Thoma. Where are you going with this? Why are you talking about France in relation to this whiskey?"

Did you miss what I just wrote? The whiskey's name is 1792. It's obviously named in memory of the French Revolution and the year King Louis and Marie-Antoinette were imprisoned. And it makes sense to name a Bourbon after something in France's history. As I've noted in other places, the word "Bourbon" is French. The Bourbons were that extended branch of the French royals who supplied the sitting monarchs with their booze.

Add to that the historical work accomplished by Michael Veach, the one who finally shed light on the fact that Bourbon didn't get its name from Bourbon County, Kentucky, as so many among us have believed for so long. Its birthplace was Louisville. Two Frenchmen from Cognac, France began selling their homemade recipes along the shores of the Ohio River—popularizing it all the way to New Orleans as something like Cognac, which was hugely popular at that time. Over the course of several years, it became known as Bourbon.

Knowing all of this, it makes perfect sense that someone would make and market a whiskey with a deliberate nod to France.

"That's not what 1792 means at all, Thoma."
It isn't?
"No. It's the year Kentucky became a state."
Oh. Really?
"Yes."
Hmm. Okay, then.

Kentucky.

I've never actually been to Kentucky. I've been to all of the states around it, but I've never stepped foot over its border.

Okay, that's not true. I've been to Kentucky many times, and each time was as wonderfully memorable as the first. I suppose that's the better tie-in to this whiskey. I liked it, each sip being as enjoyable as the one before it.

With a nose of whipped cream atop overly-spiced raspberries, this dram is a thrifty deliverance of something exceptionally sensual.

The palate continues the raspberry affair, but invites along a warmed cheesecake of sorts sprinkled with bread crumbs and peppery oak. A second sip is as the first, but more appreciated now that you know it actually met the edges of its promises.

The finish is nearly long. It strains away with the cream and spice, but the last sensation offered is a surprising turn to buttered corn bread.

I suppose I should be glad that my mistake was corrected. Pearl S. Buck said that every blunder has its halfway moment when it can be remedied. Looking back over what I've written, mine looks to be a little past the halfway mark.

But you gotta admit, the name fits either way—and of the two, mine was the better reasoning.

Anchor Distilling, A.H. Hirsch, Small Batch Reserve, 4 to 6 Years Old, 46%

Momma wouldn't like this lady.

I'm fairly certain that every person has those moments when the reactive thoughts that exist in the furthest reaches of the mind have complete access to the thoroughfare of his or her mouth. I know I do. They don't happen every day, but they happen enough to keep things interesting.

"What can I get for you, sweetie?" an unfamiliar voice buzzed sexily through the drive-through speaker, its friendliness causing the one occupying the front passenger seat, my youngest daughter, Evelyn, to lend a look of surprise.

"I just need a medium black coffee," I replied, slowly turning away from the microphone to Evelyn with a wide-eyed expression that met her own.

"Did she just call you 'sweetie'?" Evelyn whispered, her hands barely covering a staggered smile.

"She sure did," I said, giving her a grin of uncertainty.

"Do you know her?"

"Nope."

"That'll be a dollar thirty-seven at the first window, honey," the voice said in the same alluring tone. Evelyn's eyes grew wider. I didn't respond, but rolled forward.

With a few cars between us and the drive-through lady who my daughter was certain was trying to seduce me (and I say this not so much because of what the woman said, but rather how she said it), I explained to Evelyn that some folks just talk to others this way. They don't mean anything by it.

It's just their peculiar way of being friendly.

"I don't like it," Evelyn said. "It's inappropriate."

"Yeah, it's weird."

"And Momma wouldn't like it, either."

"I don't think Momma would care all that much," I offered as we rolled up to the window, "but either way, let's just keep our cool and get out of here."

"Hey, sweetie!" came the overly friendly greeting through the window.

"Good morning," I returned, stale faced. My daughter leaned forward, her weird grin having become a stare.

"That'll be a dollar thirty-seven, hun."

And then, even after I'd just instructed my daughter that we were to keep our cool—and as I'd warned at the beginning of this little adventure—my unspoken thoughts suddenly engaged with my mouth and I took the conversation to an extreme degree in the opposite direction.

"Alas, kind lady," I said animatedly, exchanging exact payment for the cup of coffee, "'twas a score ago that many acquaintances would respectfully call me 'hun,' but even so, only when rightly preceded by 'Attila the.'"

I heard Evelyn gasp.

"Have a nice day, sweetie," the woman said as the window closed, maintaining her pace and completely unaffected.

Rolling away, we both laughed. And I suppose that's why I did it, because I wanted to give Evelyn a good story to tell at school. I'm guessing that the words coming from the drive-through window were meant for the same. And by them I realized two things. First, that people are people, and taking them in stride is a better bet; and second, if my marriage were ever to dissolve, no matter how friendly the woman was at the McDonald's drive-through, she's not all that interested in me and probably wouldn't be a rebound possibility. She spoke as she did to sell me coffee. That's it.

When it comes to whiskey, I've learned similar things over the years.

First, whiskey is whiskey. No matter the distillery, region, or whatever, taking each edition in stride is always the better bet.

As it meets the second point, I say these things revealing a somewhat penitent heart. In my earlier days with Bourbons, there were some distilleries, both big and small, that I'd been less inclined to appreciate because they seemed to be speaking a drawn and sensual word, but in the end, were really just exchanging my money for a business-as-usual bit of booze in a unique bottle with a decorative label. I'll admit to having had that sense when I bought the Hirsch Small Batch Reserve Straight Bourbon, which is eloquently presented by Hotaling & Company and Anchor Distilling as having a connection to A.H. Hirsch and the moth-balled Schaefferstown Distillery in Pennsylvania. Admittedly, there's some magic to this chronicle. But when you read that the whiskey is merely a celebration of "the Hirsch heritage through a range of sourced selections," the intrigue dissipates into the realization that there's not much about the whiskey itself that's connected to the story. They needed a name for some whiskey they contracted from

MGP in Lawrenceburg, Indiana—just like a billion other American whiskey labels on the market have done.

Having said all of this, I liked this whiskey. It's really quite good.

The nose is a little stringent at first, suggesting something chemical in nature. A few minutes to sit, the chemical scent fades and becomes something along the lines of simple syrup in its cooling stage poured over tangerines.

The palate is similar. There's a decent bit of souring citrus. But along the way, a heavier barrel flavor is introduced. I'd say it translates into the simple syrup being overheated, some of it having been scorched in the pan. I think this works well, personally. It adds some depth to something that could've been thin.

The finish is a medium draw of straight cinnamon and what seems a bit like over-toasted bread, not burnt, but real crispy. This may sound bad, but with ever-present lapping of the citrus, it puts flavor and texture together successfully.

Now a word of clarification. As you can see, a sourced whisky does not mean a bad whiskey. Read my stuff. You'll discover that I've had many sourced whiskies that were good. It's just the in-between sales pitch that bugs me. It feels wrong to make a connection with something or someone where no real connection exists.

In other words, don't call me sweetie unless you mean it.

BARRELL CRAFT SPIRITS, BARRELL BOURBON, CASK STRENGTH, 9 YEARS OLD, 54.25%

Daddy, I found this on the ground.

There are certain sentences children can utter that absolutely terrify parents, causing their lungs to momentarily seize and their minds to flash petrifying scenes of dreadful aftermaths.

Consider the gurgled voice of the ten-year-old who announces while hovering above you in bed at three o'clock in the morning, "Daddy, I threw up." In that moment, a litany of possible locations, levels of destruction, the present whereabouts of your HazMat suit, and all viable isolation measures begins to churn in your barely kindled mind. "Get to the bathroom!" is your only manageable reply.

There's also that moment when your youngest reaches out to you with an unidentifiable something in her hand that she found on the floor in the restroom stall.

"Daddy, I found this on the ground," are her words. Again, your repulsion gland becomes inflamed as you weigh the legal ramifications for leaving her behind against the effort it will take to sanitize the scene before allowing her back into your car.

Lastly, for whiskey drinkers, there's the following, potentially panic-inducing question.

"Daddy, can I pour your whisky for you?"

"Um, sure, honey," you reply, walking through the front door and having already set your heart on something soothing and easy.

"Which one do you want?"

"Well, I was thinking I'd have—"

"I'll surprise you," she interrupts.

An uneasy moment passes as you take off your shoes and set your things near the door. You're not in the mood for guessing, and yet your pride is in a partial swell because of the care your child is attempting.

Laying your coat on the chair, there's a nearby clinking of glass, followed by the voluptuous lapping of what you're hoping will be an enjoyable, ambered liquid being poured. In another second, she is before you and ready.

"Here you go, Daddy," the little girl says proudly with an outstretched hand and a beaming smile.

"Thanks, honey," you say, taking the dram from her hand. "Which one did you pick?"

"I'm not going to tell you," she beams with a terrifying smile. "I want to see if you like it."

"Well, sweetie, let's give it a go," you say nervously, sitting down at the kitchen table. Putting your nose to the glass, you inhale. "Hmm. Smells…a little bit…like Elmer's Glue," you offer in the first round, fearing you're about to choke down two fingers worth of something you'd rather not. Taking another sniff, your heart begins to calm. "The glue is gone. Now I'm getting something fruity—like strawberries—and a little bit of cinnamon."

You sip and savor. She watches intently.

"This is a strong one—a cask strength Bourbon, right?" She doesn't answer you, but only shakes her head, indicating she won't reveal her secret until you approve of her selection.

You sip again.

"This one has a thick barrel zing. And the spiced strawberries have turned into spiced peaches—sort of like the ones in those fruit cups I buy for your lunches."

She smiles, but still keeps the name of the whiskey to herself.

A longer finish meets with your final thought. "It's got some staying power. It's a little syrupy, but it's also got just the right dryness to balance things out."

"Do you like it?" she asks.

"I think I do," I say, but only to get a gratified hug and the revelation that she'd poured the sample of the Barrell Bourbon 9-year-old Cask Strength edition I received as a gift. In truth, had I been handed the dram by someone less interested in pleasing me, I'd have said, "I don't *not* like it."

Overall, it was interesting, but you can sort of tell that it is a farmed whiskey; that is, it's a concoction that Barrell Craft Spirits bought from some source somewhere and then slapped their label on it. Checking into it, I could only uncover that it was born in an unnamed distillery in Tennessee.

Still, I didn't lie to my daughter. I think I like it. And if I had a bottle of it, I'd probably drink it on occasion. In general, barrel strength whiskies are good to keep around when kids are throwing up or picking up strange objects in public bathrooms. If anything, the higher the ABV, the more one's blood is equipped to defeat strange amoebas. Even a whiskey that you don't *not* like serves well in such circumstances.

BASIL HAYDEN'S, DARK RYE, KENTUCKY STRAIGHT RYE WHISKEY, 40%

Don't let the can opener in the bathroom confuse you.

Even though the sun is very near the edge of the world, making all preparations for presenting itself to the new day, the darkness proves the tenacity of its jealousy at 6:05 AM. "Don't forget about me," it prods by way of a small thing, a reminder to an already exhausted clergyman that his children might not be all that interested in succeeding in life.

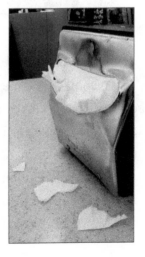

The noonday sun is brightly beaming, and still the darkness hovers. It affronts as a napkin dispenser stuffed beyond capacity. Like a chittering raccoon clawing aggressively for an object just out of reach, the clergyman wrestles in desperation for something to cleanse his digits of the meal's debris. But it isn't to be. The grip of darkness is robust.

And so the clergyman surrenders, choosing instead to be as a raccoon in a birdbath, sloshing his fingers into his water glass before drying them on his pants. As he departs, perhaps he finishes the task using the coat of an unsuspecting customer in the booth nearest to the cash register.

Perhaps he does this.

Back in his office, the afternoon sun is cascading through the blinds of his window. Still, the darkness labors to pin him in a strange conversation with a visiting pastor who, having used his host's personal bathroom, is wondering why he keeps a can opener near the toilet. Between them is the momentary insinuation of a struggle with some sort of biological condition that only such a device can relieve.

Eventually the clergyman arrives home. The sun has long since offered its goodbyes through a blanket of oncoming clouds. The darkness resumes a fuller reign, and with that, is less interested in the goings-on of mere mortals.

But the clergyman has become interested in the darkness, at least a more fitting lightlessness at the end of a day's collections of minor irritations. The Basil Hayden's Dark Rye edition is the bidder.

"Dark and Rich" are its adorning words. And rightly so. The deeply rubied whiskey smells of sun-dried cranberries, cinnamon, and rye.

A sip and savor introduces the port noted on the label while bringing along a merger of the nose's cinnamon and something that reminds of canned beets. Strangely, it isn't as forbidding as it sounds. It's delicious, in fact.

The finish is near the edge of being lengthy with a slight burn, but the heat comes from the spices and not the alcohol. As it fades, it reminds once again of the port and rye, and then slips in a dash of burnt sugar.

I say, if darkness is to reside among us, let it be by this whiskey. The price of the edition—around $45—affirms its accessibility and place in anyone's cabinet of delights.

And just for the record, the can opener in my bathroom has nothing to do with my innards. I keep it there because the bathroom also serves as a mini-kitchen. I suppose if I were the casual observer, I'd be wondering more so about the guitar in the corner and how much time the clergyman spends in his bathroom.

Blanton's Kentucky Straight Bourbon, 46.5%

Momma!

"**S**o, do you want to take the kids to Disney Springs tonight?" Jen asked, holding herself at the edge of the pool in a float.

"Momma!" the youngest pried.

"Sure," I said. "Let's go after dinner. We can go—"

"—Momma!"

"—to Basin and some of the other stores that the kids want to visit."

"Sounds like a plan," Jen replied. "Maybe we can let them swim again later tonight when we—"

"—Momma!"

"—get home."

"It'll be kind of late," I said, moving from the step at the shallow end to where Jen was soaking.

"—Momma!"

"As long as it's not—"

"—Momma!"

"—too late," I finished, dodging an impatient splash.

"If we leave here at 6:00," Jen suggested, "we can walk around for a few hours and then get back so that—"

"—Momma!"

"—so that they can swim, maybe until about 9:00 or so."

"—Mommmaaaa!"

"Yeah, for the sake of the neighbors," I said and paddled, "we'd better not let them swim much past—"

"—*Mommmmaaaaaaa!*"

And then in a furious turn, one so fast that not even the water around her was disturbed, Jen acknowledged the pestering child with a singular word through a primeval sound that could only be described as half human.

"Whaaat?!" she sounded with a wide-eyed howl.

All of the pool's commotion came to a halt. But the little girl, wholly unaffected, flipped up her goggles and spoke in as carefree a manner as she'd been asking. "Watch me do a handstand!" she said. In a moment, her toes were to the sky while her mother stood there staring silently, her mouth somewhat agape.

I laughed so hard I nearly peed in the pool. Jen, of course, remained still. Although, even in her relatively motionless stance, she gave me a glance that more than communicated she was less than impressed with the level of joviality in my response.

The moment sort of reminded me of some folks I know in the whiskey world.

"Hey, Chris, have you tried Blanton's, yet?"

"Reverend, you should review Blanton's."

"When will The Angels' Portion do a review of Blanton's?"

"I can't believe that Thoma hasn't reviewed Blanton's."

"I think the Reverend should try Blanton's and do a review."

"Hey, Reverend!"

"Whaaaat?!"

"Are you ever going to review Blanton's?"

Sigh.

Yes. And for the record, I've had Blanton's before, but I don't remember it being all that memorable. Nevertheless, with a focused attempt this time around, I'm convinced that all the pestering was not without substance. In other words, I'm glad I finally got around to this one in official taste-testing mode. It's really pretty good—a much more elaborately performed dance than an eight-year-old's handstand in the pool.

The nose offers an initial wade of charred cherries and caramel. A second inhalation brings in more of the fruit.

The palate is a creamy synchronization of the nose's cherries, a handful of vanilla chips, and some barrel spice. A little bit of water opens up the performance in a way that reveals the caramel from the nosing.

The finish is a medium splash of the barrel spice followed by the vanilla chips just as they're about to melt.

Again, this is far better than what my daughter intended for Jennifer to behold. By the way, notice the little girl wasn't asking for my attention. I have all four of them trained. When they come to pester me, I pretend I don't speak English and respond in Spanish, Latin, or Greek. If I really want to tire them out, I use Russian. Of course, Jen doesn't appreciate the blowback from all of this, because it means that they almost always skip me and go straight to her for anything they want or need. But that's fine for me. Although, it could be bad for the swimming pool and everyone in it if I find her frustration far too amusing.

BRECKENRIDGE, STRAIGHT BOURBON WHISKEY, 2 YEARS OLD, 43%

Hasn't anyone on the Olympic Committee seen *Rocky IV*?

R alph Waldo Emerson noted, "Nothing astonishes men so much as common sense and plain dealing." He's right, you know. Common sense writes the script and plain dealing performs it. The audience looks on and knows the truest heart of the story.

With this in mind, am I outside of the boundaries of common sense by believing that anyone seeking to compete in the Olympics should only be allowed to do so as a representative of their country of origin? I mean, doesn't it seem as though the truest heart of the Olympics is for each individual nation to showcase its own pure-blooded, natural-born talent in various competitions, all seeking to be the homeland that can claim domination in any particular event? Watching the "Parade of Nations" during the opening ceremony of the Winter Olympics, I learned that this isn't so for a good number of the competitors.

For example, I learned that the three members of the Nigerian bobsled team were all born and raised in the United States. I heard the commentator say that Sarah Schleper, the downhill skier representing Mexico was born in Glenwood Springs, Colorado, and raised by her father, Buzz Schleper, who owns a ski shop in Vail. I was rather shocked to learn that the lightning fast speed skater, Ahn Hyun-soo, won three gold medals in 2006 in service to his native land of South Korea, but now he goes by the name of Viktor Ahn and competes for Russia.

Apparently all of this is perfectly acceptable because the official Olympic charter only asks that competitors be *nationals* of the individual countries they represent. Funny thing is, each country defines the term "national" for itself. Equally odd, if the competitors decide they want to switch countries and compete for a different team, they only need to wait for three years following their last competition before doing so. Sure, that sounds like a long time, but it sure seems awfully convenient seeing as the particular seasonal Olympic Games come around every four years.

To all of this, there's only one thing I can think to say, and it's, "What the—? Hasn't anyone on the Olympic Committee seen *Rocky IV*?! Does anyone remember the thrill of seeing a best-of-the-best boxer going head to head with a pure-blooded counterpart?"

I guess not. And it's enough to leave me uninterested in the Olympics altogether.

When I'm beholding such an international spectacle, I want to see the true rendering of its heart. I want to witness the champion DNA of a nation as it has been cultivated by its own regimens and ethos. I want to be found in awe of the almost superhuman abilities that one country may have that another may not. I want to be found cheering for a competitor who puts his or herself into a battlefront of sorts, not necessarily striving for "self," but rather for a homeland, a place that is dear, a nation of communities and culture which, in that moment, deserves to be recognized because in the competition, it produced the best.

But now it just sort of seems like we have people (and I'm not saying they aren't good at their sport) skipping town to compete somewhere else because they didn't make the cut back home. Nations seem to buy athletes from other countries just so they can have a showing or shore up holes in their teams. I don't like this about the Olympics. But at least I'm consistent, because I'm not fond of it in the whiskey industry, either. It's somewhat off-putting.

Ah, this is true. Plenty of whiskey brands touting a genuine dram from a certain locale actually purchase their product from unnamed distilleries in a land far away. I can't say for sure if the bottle of Breckenridge Straight Bourbon before me is such a culprit, although I've read that they will take what they've made on the premises and blend it with bourbons from other sources.

Still, as I parenthetically noted above, that doesn't mean the competitor isn't good. Indeed, this is a perfectly sippable Coloradan edition worthy of your applause.

The nose is distinctly graceful, giving over a performance of caramel apples, buttered toast, and oak barrel char. A little while in the glass and it takes a twirl toward citrus.

It's just as gentle for the mouth as it is for the nose, setting before its judges a routine of vanilla cake with butter cream frosting, a dusting of cinnamon, and a sipper of mulled apple cider.

The finish is a spin from what I just described into an abrupt stop on the spice still hanging from the roof of my mouth. It left my tongue dried and expecting something more.

Nevertheless, it was quite enjoyable, and whether a national or actual citizen of Colorado, it represented the state quite well. And for Breckenridge's sake, I hope this competitor decides to stay put.

BROWN-FORMAN DISTILLERS, THE PRESIDENT'S CHOICE, 1969 BOTTLING, 8 YEARS OLD, 56.4%

She sometimes ends up in the dishwasher.

As the saying goes, you win some and you lose some. I prefer to say that sometimes you land it and sometimes you end up in the dishwasher.

In Evelyn's case, it was the former. She was doing something Evelyn-esque, most likely spinning around in circles or trying to do a cartwheel in a place where cartwheels might not be a good idea. Whatever it was, this time she got a little too close to the open dishwasher.

I turned just in time to see the tragedy's conclusion—the little girl's unbalanced planting of her calves against the edge of the dishwasher's door, her hands sprawling outward in a helpless plunge, her tiny backside plopping into the stainless steel innards, her back scraping the front of the bottom basket, the entire machine breaking loose and tipping forward from the brackets that secure it to the bottom of the countertop, the resulting look of terror that her chronic disregard for her father's instructions not to do what she was doing could very well end with that same onlooking parent simply pushing her the rest of the way into the machine and closing the door.

I'll admit that I thought about it. I reconsidered only because her mother was closer to her, and with haste, scooped her up and tended to her needs before I could break from my speechless gaze. There just wasn't enough time for me to get to her, shove her the rest of the way in, actually get the detergent poured into the little latching basin, and close the door. I mean, being the multitasker that I am, I might as well make it so she doesn't need a bath at bedtime, right? Let the now wobbling machine do the work.

Anyway, I retrieved some essential tools, my drill, and a Glencairn. I poured myself two fingers worth from a 1969 bottling of The President's Choice 8-year-old Kentucky Bourbon from Brown-Forman Distillers which I'd received as a gift from my kindly friend, Kay. Dropping to my hands and knees in an attempt to examine and then fix the damage from the misadventure, with a sigh, I offered to myself in secret, *Sometimes you land it. Sometimes you can't get your kid into the dishwasher quickly enough.* Having diagnosed the problem, but before beginning the labor, I reached for my dram, swirled its contents, sniffed, and then took a sip. My speechless gaze returned, although this time rendering with delight, *Sometimes you land it, and then sometimes you really land it!*

The whiskey was nothing short of superb.

The nose was that of rich cinnamon, summery raisins, and a square of Ghirardelli caramel-filled chocolate. A sip delivered a wood-spicy depth of the Ghirardelli, a batch of buttered pecans, and the faint impression of vanilla-soaked blueberries.

The finish was a medium rinse of the cinnamon and vanilla.

Once the dishwasher was fixed, I jumped online to see if I could learn more about some of the rarer editions from Brown-Forman

Distillers and maybe even discover some of the particulars that went into this edition that was custom distilled and bottled for Haab's Restaurant in Ypsilanti, Michigan. What I found was that it could very well be a variant interpretation of Old Forester.

But I don't like Old Forester. In fact, if I recall correctly from my review of the stuff, I determined it was probably a favorite of Satan because it tasted like cigarettes and rye toast, and for some reason, reminded me of a house in my neighborhood that I'm pretty sure is haunted.

My only guess is that if this is indeed a historical rendition of Old Forester, it was selected and bottled during a time when Brown-Forman Distillers was more interested in precision whiskey-making as opposed to mass production and wide distribution.

Knowing that this near half-century edition of The President's Choice Bourbon is an acquired rarity in limited supply, I'll be holding it very close, and I'll be taking it very slowly. I certainly won't be keeping it anywhere out in the open where it can be destroyed by a whirling and twirling little girl who sometimes lands it—but sometimes ends up in the dishwasher.

FLEISCHMANN'S PREFERRED WHISKEY, BLENDED BOURBON, 40%

The whiskey needs a shower and some Old Spice.

It's Saturday at 5:45 AM and I'm awake. Why? Because life is about to become...well...not summer.

Two more days until the school year arrives like the vexatious neighbor from any of the cookie-cutter sitcoms. In 48 hours, very early in the morning, the school year will walk through the front door of life. He'll pillage my schedule like it's my refrigerator, rudely snatching what he deems appetizing. He'll make himself right at home, plopping down on the couch and kicking up his feet. After two or three days of nudging at him, urging him to understand that he isn't welcome and that, in fact, he's stealing from me, I'll give up. By then, the nature of his pretension and ignorant immovability will have sunk in, and I'll know that he isn't going anywhere for at least another nine months.

That's how I feel about the school year.

And why? Because for a guy like me, someone who will see nearly every free evening and weekend evaporate until June (with a few air pockets after Christmas and Easter for catching my breath or maybe even sleeping in), summer is that time when certain responsibilities go into hibernation and I gain a little bit of extra time to do other things—"me" things—at a more comfortable pace.

"So, why then are you up so early this morning, Reverend, especially since this is the last day to be had for sleeping in?"

Ah, yes. Indeed, what am I doing here at this moment upon the fast-fleeting timeline, this last and highly prized instance when I should be deeply mining of its resources and availing the opportunity for remaining in my bed past 7:00 AM?

I'm vacationing.

I'm not rushing to do anything. I'm sitting and watching the sunrise, not driving into it. I'm sitting in my kitchen with my favorite mug drinking coffee I brewed myself, not bought from the drive-thru with sticky coins from the cup holder in the minivan. I'm reading the tasting notes I scribbled last night after trying a sample of Fleishmann's Preferred Whiskey and I'm tapping at my computer to see what comes of them instead of reading emails or inter-office notes and doing what I can to write as many responses as possible before an over-scheduled day pushes them to the following morning.

Essentially, I'm sitting quietly and doing "me" things at a comfortable pace.

This is my schedule when we vacation in Florida for ten days each year in June. I get up early, drink my coffee, and every now and then give a smile to the early sun through a nearby grove of palm trees while I sit and type until Jen and the kids get up. When they do finally emerge from their much-needed slumber, we eat breakfast together and go outside to the pool to swim for a few hours. Minus the pool and palm trees, I'm doing what I do when I'm on vacation, and that's exactly what I told myself before bed last night that I was going to do today.

Having said all of this, I suppose I should've chosen a different whiskey to consider on this final day, because unfortunately, this one only serves to carry me from finer things back into the dross of burdensome ponderings. When it comes to blended whiskies, everything about the Fleischmann's Preferred is as the school year at the stoop preparing to ring the doorbell.

Smelling an awful lot like someone who managed to brush his teeth but forgot the importance of showering, this aggravating neighbor greets you at the door with an initial breath of Colgate followed by the souring smell of graying meat that's a day or two past the "Use by" date on its packaging. There's a hint of something floral, but I'm guessing that it's merely an attempt by the visitor to shroud the aforementioned facts with a spritzing of Old Spice.

The palate reveals that the meat is indeed in its last minutes of being consumable, and rather than adding some sort of seasoning, it was doused in children's mixed-berry flavored acetaminophen, which is probably a good idea considering the headache you already knew the nosing of this stuff was bound to bring when it walked through the door.

Of course, like the school year, this whiskey lasts far too long. It most certainly overstays its welcome, coating the taste buds with syrupy medicine resulting in the inability to enjoy very little of anything else you might want to savor afterward. I tried to wash it away with water, but that simply didn't work. It took three fingers worth of the Laphroaig 10-year-old to beat the aftertaste into submission and eventually drive it from my home.

Yes, it did eventually depart. It was incredibly exasperating—often too much to bear—but it did eventually leave.

With that, June is coming…eventually.

GEORGE DICKEL, WHITE CORN WHISKY, NO.1, 45.5%

Please don't steer your 15-passenger van brimming
with children into the drive-thru.

Not everything in life is clear. I understand this.

Take, for example, the U.S. Tax Code. That's a near unnavigable monstrosity. Even the ever-optimistic Christopher Columbus, after a day or two of sailing its paper waves looking for shore, would have forsaken all hopes for a sure landing and thrown himself overboard to drown in the ink.

Another is the grisly *Lusus Naturae* of Michigan, which is the series of four interconnected, tri-laned roundabouts at the Lee Road exit of U.S. 23 in Brighton. Each day, many attempt to brave its Kraken-like embrace, but few emerge to share their terrifying tale.

Some things in life are crystal clear.

The coastal waters of Bimini are clear. Albeit they're infested with hammerhead sharks. And yet, the water is so pristinely clarion that you'll effortlessly behold your doom's gliding approach long before the first bite.

It's crystal clear that the drive-thru at McDonald's is for serving quick orders to people on the go—a Big Mac, fries, and a coffee for the one who didn't have time for dinner and is already late for an evening meeting. It's also abundantly clear that this truism isn't so clear to some. In other words, I'm suggesting that there will always be those who don't realize that it is much more polite to go inside the establishment to place a massive order. The drive-thru isn't for the 15-passenger van filled with children, piloted by the parent who thought it would be a much simpler way to gather pile after pile of specially prepared food that everyone else in the drive-thru knows the teenage attendant will never in a million years get right the first time around.

"Yeah, and make four of those cheeseburgers with only one pickle and a light swipe of ketchup. Make another six with only one pickle and a light swipe of mustard. The other nine can all be regular, except with no cheese or those little sprinkled onions."

"So, just ketchup and mustard?"

"Yeah. Would you mind throwing an extra slice of cheese on my Quarter Pounder? And nine of the kids want their drinks to be half Coke and half Hi-C. Can you do that? Great. And then I'll have five orders of the twenty-piece chicken nuggets. But could you keep them in the fryer a little longer than normal? That's the way I cook them at home and the kids just love 'em. It makes them a little crispier. Yeah, thanks."

"Um."

As one, two, three, four, five, six, and seven large bags are passed through the window to the driver, over the course of the past twenty minutes, the line in the drive-thru has begun to look more like a winding funeral procession. The facial expressions of my fellow mourners give it away. And it gets even worse when the van's driver remains at the window and checks the contents of each bag—

unwrapping sandwiches to make sure there aren't too many pickles strewn throughout the lot—and then hands a few things back to the attendant because the order is incorrect. Just as the rest of us knew it would be.

"Ma'am, if you wouldn't mind pulling forward, we'll sort this out and bring your order out to you."

"Oh, sure," the woman says so kindly, pulling forward. Still, the space-shuttle-sized vehicle is far too big to allow enough room for the patron behind her to actually reach the window, unless of course he's willing to climb out onto the hood of his car to make the transaction. I would be. But he isn't, and with that, it becomes more than clear there will be no escape for any in the procession. The drive-thru's hostage scene will carry through to its completion, and in a sense, will be reminiscent of the waters off the coast of Bimini— something you expected would lead to fulfillment, but became, instead, an unclouded vision of the gaping jaws of starvation and your late arrival to a meeting.

There's another thing that's crystal clear, but in a literal sense: The George Dickel White Corn Whisky No. 1.

Unlike the previous scenario, thankfully, the longer I'm immersed in this particular potion, the more I think I like it, and the more I want to investigate white whiskies in general. It has a creamy, richly sweet, and overtly grainy nose—like a helping of Frosted Flakes long-soaked in milk.

In the mouth, there's the sense of burnt cornbread, but surprisingly, it isn't all that bad. There's still enough sweetness in the mix to make it both inviting and interesting.

The finish could use some work, though. It's there that the whisky becomes somewhat bitter, letting you know that even though the dram is certainly clean enough in its appearance to pass as water, there are pollutants in there—namely charcoal and what I am suspecting could be fragments of a corn cob's waxy husk. Still, as I mentioned previously, the longer the George Dickel White Corn Whisky No. 1 holds me captive, the more I feel I may be someone capable of epitomizing Helsinki Syndrome and one day finding myself strangely admiring my captor as I carry through to the hostage situation's questionable end.

That is, of course, as long as my captor isn't the heartless driver of a 15-passenger van full of finicky children in the drive-thru at McDonald's.

GRAND TRAVERSE DISTILLERY, 100% STRAIGHT BOURBON WHISKEY, 46%

On second thought, was C.S. Lewis hitting on my wife?

I had a dream last night that I was driving a Dodge Viper painted liked Bumble Bee from the Transformers. I'm pretty sure this is the result of having seen the very same car for sale along the side of the road on my way to a nearby hospital to visit a parishioner.

In the dream, I was driving very slowly through a parking garage, making my way to the top deck. As I crept along, winding my way skyward, making one left-hand turn after the other (which, if you have ever been in a parking garage, is opposite to the typical flow of traffic), with the convertible top down, I discovered on each new level massive crowds of people dressed in tuxedos and gala gowns. Being careful to weave through the gatherings, the people turned to stare. Some pointed. Others leaned to their partners to whisper. After a little while, I remembered that I was wearing my clerical collar, and with that, a familiar feeling washed over me as I rolled along—a sensation I recall experiencing the first time I found myself in Washington D.C. sitting across the table from a handful of our nation's political leaders.

It was the unblunted mood of being in a place where I did not belong.

In terms of my time in D.C., does this lowly parish pastor belong at the table with U.S. nobility, challenging their efforts at leadership? With regard to the dream, does a man of such lowly vocation belong in a Dodge Viper? Not only that, but how dare he drive past his betters, onwards and upwards to higher levels in the structure?

Needless to say, I kept driving. Eventually I arrived at the top level, but when I did, I discovered a very thin crowd—perhaps only a handful of people. Among them, at first, I recognized only two. The first was C.S. Lewis. He was leaning against my minivan, laughing and smoking his pipe. It was then that I noticed my wife, Jennifer. She was talking with him. In that same moment, I realized she had our youngest daughter on her hip, no longer seven years old, but a toddler again. On the periphery of the conversation were my other little ones—Joshua, Madeline, and Harrison—all much younger than they are now.

When the kids saw me approaching in the Viper, they ran to greet me. Lewis motioned for Jennifer to go, too. Joshua, the first to arrive, wanted to sit in the driver's seat. Hearing his brother, Harrison asked if he could, too. Madeline just wanted me to pick her up, and so I did. And I held her close. Jennifer balanced Evelyn and gave me a kiss.

That was pretty much it.

Like most of the dreams I have, if, when I awaken, I'm able to retain much of what transpired, I do so wondering if the imaginings have any particular meaning. In other words, what is my mind doing while I'm sleeping, and how is it trying to sort out what I can't seem to categorize while I'm awake? Most often, I don't know the answer to that question. But this dream left me thinking that, even as I find myself in different places with different people—sometimes even ending up at events reserved for those we would consider the societal elite, the best of us—in the end, the highest stratum of the structure of this life contains those for whom you'd give up everything to keep with you for eternity. The familiar embrace of someone who loves you, not because of what you've done, but because of who you are—a husband, a father, a friend—that embrace is sublime.

But, why was C.S. Lewis there? And why was he getting so friendly with my wife? I don't know. I do admire him. A lot, in fact. I'll have to think about that one.

And what does this have to do with whiskey? Well, I suppose the dream I shared—which in a sense is one that teaches contentment, finding happiness right where you are—could lead toward valuing the whiskies created in one's own state. As a Michigander, I'm discovering that even as I could shell out Dodge Viper dollars for a nice bottle of Scotch, I can find myself just as smiley with a bottle of whiskey from one of my own home's distilleries for a lot less. Michigan whiskey manufacturers are creating some really good drams.

Take, for example, the Grand Traverse Distillery's 100% Straight Bourbon Whiskey. This is some great stuff.

Even while gathering closely to the sample as it was being poured into my bottle to take home, the scent was foretelling an exceptional sipper. And when I arrived home and transferred the elixir to a Glencairn, giving it a swirl or two before lifting scents of sweet corn dotted with black pepper, sea salt, and paprika, again, I knew I was being led to something exceptional.

The palate confirmed my expectations, first ushering along the sweet corn and the sea salt, but then adding to the jamboree a little bit of the smoke from the fire below the pot that's boiling the cobs.

The finish was a medium relenting of barrel spice and baked beans mixed with brown sugar. Yes, you read that correctly—baked beans—something you'd never eat at an elitist gala in Washington D.C., but would most certainly be served, by your friends and family, beside a plastic bowl full of potato salad and a plate of sweet corn on the deck table in July. Scooping it onto your paper plate, and stealing a bite with your plastic fork, you realize that while it wasn't delivered in a Dodge Viper, it's no less transient or precious, and that's because you are right where you belong.

Grand Traverse Distillery, Ole George Whiskey, 100% Maple Finished, Straight Rye, 3 Years and 7 Months Old, 50%

Daddy, when will you let me say the a-word, again?

McDonald's was relatively quiet. But of course it was. The time was a little past 4:00 PM and the dinner rush had yet to come in for a landing.

An elderly couple sat only a few paces from us. A kindly gentleman to his wife, the man helped his bride with her chair. She smiled at us as he did. We smiled back.

"What a beautiful young girl," she said, leaning ever so slightly toward my daughter, Evelyn. "How old are you, sweetie?"

"I'm nine," Evelyn answered, giving a bright and friendly smile. "How old are you?" she volleyed, revealing her unguarded approach to anyone willing to engage in conversation with her.

"Oh, I'm much older than you, dear," the woman answered, unwrapping her McChicken sandwich and seemingly unaffected by the less-than-appropriate question. "Are you enjoying dinner with your dad?" she continued, stealing a wandering glance of my clerical collar.

"Yep," Evelyn replied.

"Well, that's nice," the woman offered, her grandmotherly voice well-rehearsed. "It's nice to spend time with dad."

"Yep," Evelyn said.

"I'll bet as a pastor, he's gone a lot helping other people."

"Yep."

And then in an instant—and not uncommon to her flightiness—Evelyn broke off the engagement and turned the conversation back to me, asking a completely unrelated question. "Daddy," she said, "when can I start saying the a-word again?"

"Not for a while," I answered, noticing a sudden expression of shock between the elderly couple. "We've got quite a few weeks to go before you can say it again. After that, you can say the a-word all you want."

"That's such a long time," Evelyn moaned. "I love the a-word. I love to say it and I love to sing it."

"I know you do," I said. "Just hold on for the next few weeks and then you can say and sing it as much as you'd like."

"Okay," Evelyn said, taking a bite from one of her hamburgers dressed only with ketchup. She looked back to her previous conversational partner, but the woman had become strangely removed, her eyes a bit wider than before. This didn't bother Evelyn at all. She continued with her meal and started a different thread of discussion with me, something about a scene that came to mind from the movie *The Avengers*. Still, I sensed the abrupt disconnection on the part of the woman beside us and it made me wonder.

It wasn't until we were back in the car and making our way down the road that I realized the woman's concern. But first, you may need the same explanation she required.

At the time this occurred, we were in the pre-Lenten season known as the Gesima Sundays. This church season lasts three weeks. Right after the Gesima Sundays, Lent begins. Lent lasts six weeks—Ash Wednesday to Good Friday. During this time, nine weeks in all, it isn't unusual in historically liturgical churches like mine to jettison the word "Alleluia" from the liturgy, hymns, and general vernacular of the congregation. Alleluia is a Hebrew word which means "Praise the Lord," and since we're contemplating more closely the suffering and death of Jesus during these combined seasons, we set alleluia aside. At Easter, the congregation welcomes the word back into her speech, singing it boldly in celebration of Christ's resurrection.

Evelyn was referring to the word *alleluia*. But that's not what this woman understood.

Instead, sitting two tables away in her favorite McDonald's was a nine-year-old daughter of a clergyman who is allowed to use a certain expletive. And while the little girl was currently barred from using it because it would seem she had a great love of employing it, after a time of temperance, the day was coming when her father would once again allow the word to roll from her lips with some measure of control. Additionally—and I'm guessing here—it's quite possible that the woman assumed the explicit descriptor came into the little girl's mind during their short discussion together, suggesting that perhaps Evelyn's peculiar boldness in asking her age, the short answers of "yep," and the sudden inquiry of her father regarding her freedom to use the a-word were all pointing to a crass little girl who was restraining her candor while being annoyed by a woman she didn't know.

Again, looking back, this is really rather humorous. But it also teaches a lesson on human stupidity and the tragedy of miscommunication in the hands of assumption. I suppose this same lesson is more than applicable in the case of the Grand Traverse

Distillery's "Ole George Whiskey" maple finished edition sitting before me right now.

Consider the voice of the label. In person, the label itself communicates the high probability that the effort to design it wasn't hired out. Such carelessness with the label stirs a questioning of the quality of the product inside the bottle it adorns. Add to this the heralding of maple finishing, which for me is tantamount to putting a notice on the bottle which reads: "You will hate this. Don't drink it."

But even as the beverage itself was being carried by a miscommunication that was harnessing my assumptions, it took a solitary sip to break through such human stupidity and deliver a pleasant delightfulness worth sharing with you.

This is a really good whiskey.

The nose of this edition of the Ole George is one of sweet rye spice and cinnamon toast. Add the tiniest drop of water and you may be tricked into sensing the fizzing carbonation of cherry cola.

A sip reveals the maple finish, and the folks at Grand Traverse Distillery show they have what it takes to get such a finishing right. It's a subtle, almost gentle enhancement. It's certainly not added to hide the medicinal sour of a bad whiskey, but rather it compliments a good whiskey, giving it just enough sweetness to make it unique—and dare I say, better. With the higher ABV, one might expect some burn, but instead it comes off with balance, bringing along a tart nip of caramel to grab at the tongue.

The maple is fast-fleeting in the finish. Still, I'd say the finish whirls at the edge of medium and long. There's just enough of the rye spice (which was sweet before but is now buttery) to keep it in the medium category. At the same time, the nip noticed by the tongue continues beyond this, implying the desire for a lengthier stay.

In the end, whatever you decide, don't let the label keep you from being in the position to actually come to a reasonable conclusion. Do what you can to suppress the nature of human stupidity—which we all contain—and give this whiskey a try. It's a good-hearted and youthful dram that means you no harm. And I'm almost certain that after a sip, you'll choose to enunciate Evelyn's a-word as opposed to the one the old lady simply but foolishly presumed while eating her McChicken sandwich.

JAMES E. PEPPER, 1776 STRAIGHT RYE WHISKEY, BARREL PROOF, 57.3%

In the ocean, you're food.

The sun is down. The popcorn is made. The drinks are poured. The blankets and pillows are in place. The Discovery Channel is on and everyone is in their usual places on the couch. It's time for the Thoma family to do what it does every year while on vacation in Florida. It's time to re-establish and reinforce a healthy fear.

It's time to watch Shark Week.

The problem this year is that Shark Week isn't actually scheduled to premier until the middle of July, and here we are in the middle of June. No matter. We've downloaded episodes yet to be watched from a previous year, and with that, we're all set to wipe our brows, clinch our teeth, and be reminded why none of us—*no, not one*—will ever go into the ocean.

The episode in particular that we're watching right now is one that includes a particular South African gent named Dickie Chivell. He's a marine naturalist in his mid-twenties, and he's quite the character. I'd say he's more so reminiscent of a stunt man than a budding scientist because he has the tendency to do some pretty risky things to get great white sharks to come in for a close-up with the camera. In a previous episode, he fashioned what he considered would be, for the sharks, a nearly invisible dive box. It was comprised of panes of Plexiglass glued together.

Yes, glued.

Sheesh.

In tonight's episode, Dickie has climbed into a homemade, one-man device called the "Wasp." It looks a little like an oversized garbage can made of bars and is designed to rest on the sea floor so that its top can be opened for photography opportunities while its bottom allows the operator to actually use his or her legs to move it around.

Watching Dickie being circled by six or seven massive great whites, my wife asks from across the way, "Would you ever get into something like that?"

"Sure," I reply, "but only after they show me the buttons for the underwater rocket launchers. I'd need to be able to turn anything that decided to get too close into a swirling mass of chum in an instant."

So in other words, no, I wouldn't. And I'm glad the Discovery Channel is trying so hard to teach us that sharks aren't as scary as the movies might suggest while my children watch Dickie being rammed and snapped at in his little contraption by huge creatures fully intent on eating him if they can knock him loose.

"Would you ever get into something like that, Maddy?" I ask, lobbing Jen's question along to my eldest daughter.

"No way!" she says without breaking her stare from the television. "I'm never stepping foot into the ocean!" The other kids echo her sentiments.

Check and mate, sharks. And once again, thank you, Discovery Channel. You have succeeded in putting the right amount of terror into the right people. With that, I'm going to pour myself another dram, and then afterward, sleep very well knowing that my children will never purposely put themselves into the midsection of the food chain.

Tonight's celebratory dram is the James E. Pepper 1776 Barrel Proof Straight Rye, which for its "midsection of the food chain" price, was relatively enjoyable and well worth the effort to smuggle it within a tiny vial in the suitcase.

With a nose of warmed toast and brown sugar, the 1776 presents itself as a kindlier whiskey. But with the first sip, it circles back around, picking up momentum. It opens up and takes hold with a sturdy grip of the rye, raspberries, spicy oak, and a smidgeon of caramel.

Its finish is longer than expected, being sure to nip at you with the barrel spice and hints of citrus.

In all, the 1776 is doing all of this for play, and not for predatory purposes. It invites a whiskey drinker into its waters, reminding the swimmer that the best things aren't necessarily in the boat on the top shelf. There are other things down in the reef worth exploring, too…unless we're talking about a real ocean where real sharks exist. Then it's better to view them from the boat. In fact, because boats sink, it's better to just stay on land. It's even better to be sixty-eight miles from the ocean, on a couch, eating popcorn, and covered in blankets and pillows while watching Shark Week.

Although, one significant gasp while eating popcorn during a scene with a shark thrashing against Dickie's cage and you could end up choking to death. Then I guess it really doesn't matter.

Jefferson's, Ocean, Voyage 17, Very Small Batch, Aged 4 to 6 Years, 45%

I needed proof.

The tornado sirens were screaming. I'd not heard them because I was on the treadmill typing, listening to AC/DC, and trying to get less fat.

But my daughter, Madeline, heard them. In fact, ever since March 24 of 2007 when an EF-2 tornado hopped right over our house (yes, I saw it) and destroyed pretty much everything else around us, I'd say some sort of early detection system was instilled into her soul. Somehow she's more inclined than the others to a keep a lookout when the weather's changing for the worse.

"The tornado sirens are going off," Madeline said, motioning to get my attention while remaining strangely calm.

"Get your sister and brothers and get back down here to the basement," I said, removing my earbuds and matching her placid gaze. She skipped back up the basement steps and called for her siblings. I brought my pace to a halt, shut down my computer, and moved to action, doing what any responsible father would do in that moment.

Grabbing my mobile phone, I darted to each and every cabinet holding my precious and inimitable collection of whiskies to take pictures.

The photo albums were passed over. I darted through storage spaces with irreplaceable keepsakes. No mind was paid to the backup hard drive on the shelf containing every historical record of the Thoma family. My quest was set for more important things, and I pondered all along the way, *If this glorious collection gets swept up and carried miles from here to its destruction, the insurance company will never believe its origin was this one location.*

Proof was needed. No, I needed wisdom to feed my agility in this moment, because I'd already failed against the essential Theodore Rooseveltian maxim that "nine-tenths of wisdom is being wise in time."

Let it be known that I accomplished my goal well before the first child ever arrived to the safe space. I was there with a few blankets I'd snatched from the guest bed to tuck them in and give them comfort. And I'll add, gladsomely, that while a tornado did indeed touch down and destroy several businesses and residences about twenty miles from our home, no one was injured. I'll say with a less than gleeful tone that none of those businesses were liquor stores, which means that I didn't receive any unexpected deliveries to my front yard by way of tornado-mail.

Hum-hum. Anyway, my collection—and family—were safe. None from among my community was harmed. All may be counted as well and good.

Although, the Jefferson's Ocean Voyage 17 edition before me now could have been a casualty.

After the sirens stopped and the children were shooed from the basement, I remade the guest bed and then checked another cabinet upstairs—a place where I used to keep whiskey bottles—just to see if I'd somehow overlooked a few. Sure enough, this bottle was in there. A gift from my father after a recent trip home to Illinois, I'd placed it there temporarily and had since forgotten to introduce it to its kin.

But again, all is well, and the Ocean Voyage 17 is anchored safely in port.

A bit of a ploy I'd say, the idea behind this whiskey (and the sixteen releases before it) is that it has been traveling around for four to six years on a ship at sea. The "ship's log" tagged to the bottle's neck implies that the vessel ventured to as many as five continents, and all along the way, the various conditions of the sea imparted something to the elixir being carried in its belly.

Yeah, maybe.

But honestly, I didn't get anything suggesting that. As far as I can tell, this is a pretty straight shooting, but well-formulated, blend of bourbons that went into the cask tasting great and was extracted at the end tasting great, having not moved an inch.

There's no salty sea air wafting in the nose, but rather a thinned, but more than pleasant, breeze of cinnamon, oak, and vanilla. Another sniff delivers a pinch of cloves.

A sip is a careful steering through a narrow inlet of the nose's vanilla. There are moments when it comes very near to rocky char, but as it does, the caramel-coating on the oaky hull is never in jeopardy. The precision required for this leg of the journey is by no means lost on the final product.

Alas, the craft arrives at home, having slowed from winds of sweet cinnamon and tangerines at medium speed.

Thankfully, I was there to receive it when it arrived. Or rather, it was there to be received. What a shame it would have been to have traveled so far and seen so much only to be sucked up in a tornado and cast into the wetlands behind my house—or Lord forbid, the yard of someone in the county who drinks Scoresby.

Thank you, Lord, for your compassionate deliverance of my family, my home, and my booze.

And thanks, Dad, for the gift. It's quite delicious.

MINOR CASE, STRAIGHT RYE WHISKEY, AGED 24 MONTHS, 45%

Things will get better.

"In seed time learn, in harvest teach, in winter enjoy."

I get what you mean, Mr. Blake. And your words are poetically charming. However, and unfortunately, I live in Michigan where for almost eight months of the year there is the potential for the outside temperatures to be just as cold, if not colder, than a walk-in freezer.

Maybe, William, you were speaking of a certain measure of anticipatory winter enjoyment, which is the kind of joy that sees itself come to full bloom during the spring thaw. Is that what you meant? If so, I'm guessing that just as you've never been to Michigan in the winter, so also you've never been here in the spring. If you had, then you'd know that such joy is non-existent, too. At least not on our vast expanse of highways and byways. Twelve seconds of travel and I'm more than certain you'd abandon the idea completely. In that twelfth second, it's likely that you'd come to the conclusion that driving a major freeway in Michigan in the spring must be quite similar to navigating the cratered surface of the moon.

You won't experience joy in this, but you might experience a certain measure of exhilaration born of the ever-present possibility that a new crater might open up without notice and swallow your vehicle completely.

"Surely not!" you exclaim. Ah, well then, if not your car then most certainly the street sign to your subdivision.

Personally, I'd say that when it comes to mindful bits about winter in Michigan, Bill Watterson of "Calvin and Hobbes" fame was closer to capturing its essence when he said, "I like these cold grey winter days. Days like these let you savor a bad mood."

In other words, I live in the wrong state.

I say this not just because I despise winter and major car repairs, but because I'm too far away from places like Kentucky, a place where the average winter temperature of 23 degrees feels like a Sahara noontime to Michiganders, and a palled, January mood could so easily be assuaged by a spontaneous trip along the Bourbon trail, perhaps even concluding with a visit to the place that is swiftly becoming a personal favorite in whiskey provision: Limestone Branch Distillery Company.

My first experience with this group came rather recently by way of the Yellowstone Kentucky Straight Bourbon. It was phenomenally enchanting. And with that, while I've experienced and reviewed more than my fair share of American whiskies—falling for a limited few, but for the majority, remaining more so inclined toward the gifts of Scotland—I figured I'd better continue to investigate, convinced that where one edition from Limestone was a joy, others may be waiting on shelves to greet me with a similar affection, too.

This proved to be true. Another of their offerings—the Minor Case Straight Rye Whiskey—is a bright-beaming array of holy things at the end of a car-munching day.

An initial nosing of the Minor Case betrays the whiskey's sherry cask finish. A second draw speaks of warmed concord grapes and root beer.

A sip reveals vanilla cream and cinnamon-imbued caramel chews—not the kind you get in that greasy little jar at the fix-it shop trying to "do you a favor" by keeping the reassembly of your suspension to less than two thousand dollars, but the ones made by artisan candy makers in places like Mackinac Island.

The finish takes a stranger turn, and yet, it does not swerve from the enjoyable. It has a longer stride, offering along the way a spicy pepper and a scoop of orange sherbet.

In all, the Minor Case edition is kindly enough that you might be persuaded to climb up and out of your most recent pothole, leaving your vehicle nose down in its void right there in the middle of I-96, and still say, "Alas, I've a dram of Minor Case awaiting me at home. I'd better get walking because things are sure to get better."

OLD FORESTER, KENTUCKY STRAIGHT BOURBON WHISKY, 43%

The Liquor Control Commission is an extension of the Devil's reign.

Just down the street and around the corner from my home, there's a house that's been bought and sold three times within the past eighteen months. I've seen the realtor signs adorning the front yard of this proud and presentable home, a domicile that doesn't appear to have any particular exterior defects. And yet, the moving truck continues to return to swallow everything it only recently gave up, and "Sold" turns back into "For Sale."

I'm not sure why.

I would assume that as each of the mortgages took shape, a typical inspection was performed and the house was ultimately judged as both habitable and sellable. If that's true, then why the frequent turnover? The home is on a quiet but vivacious street. It's surrounded by friendly neighbors. And from what I can tell, it has a reasonably sized yard edged by a shallow forest. I pass it every day on my way to the office, and, as I do, I glance and admit to its appeal as a place to raise a family, perhaps even being the kind of locale to which the children would one day return with their own families to visit Gramma and Grampa in their twilight years.

So what is it, then?

I suggested to my wife that perhaps the house is haunted. She laughed at me at first because she knows I don't believe in ghosts. But I was serious—not in the sense that it might really be ghosts, but rather because it might be inhabited by the Devil. My thought is that maybe this is one of his vacation homes.

As a pastor, the more I learn the Devil's routines in this world, the more I suspect he has a comfort zone, and it's one that I think he's willing to shake up only a little. With that, why not vacation in Michigan? It can be hellishly familiar while at the same time being off just enough to be counted as a vacation.

For example, it's ungodly cold for eight months of the year, and while that doesn't match the thermostat in hell, it certainly keeps to the theme of suffering. Also, Michigan has tons of lakes. None of the lakes are comprised of burning sulfur, like the one just outside the Devil's kitchen window in hell, although I hear that because of pollution, there are a few near the cities that could potentially ignite.

Michigan also has a Liquor Control Commission that severely hinders her citizens from accessing a good number of the finer whiskies enjoyed by so many in other states. This particular detail does double-duty as it meets the Devil's vacationing standards.

First, and easiest, it keeps with the suffering theme. Second, it matches the Devil's work ethic. He's a busy guy who, even while on vacation, doesn't like to be too far away from his trade endeavors. He's the hairy guy you see wearing the Speedo in the chaise lounge beside the pool scanning excel spreadsheets and responding to texts from the office. He's also the kind of guy who'll do this in one of his own resorts just to keep an eye on it. Since the Michigan Liquor Control Commission is technically an extension of his reign, it makes sense that he'd land in some inconspicuous house within the confines of its regional governance in order to monitor its terror infliction.

I'm also thinking there's a good chance the varying homeowners didn't necessarily discover his presence because the lights were flickering, the cupboard doors were opening and closing on their own, or the children were hovering above their beds. My guess is that empty bottles of Old Forester kept showing up and they couldn't figure out why. After consulting various volumes on the occult, and maybe even having a sit-down with their priest, they learned what twenty-five years of skipping church couldn't teach: Old Forester is a favorite of Satan.

And why wouldn't it be?

The first wafting from this $20 Bourbon smells a little bit like a can of soggy green beans. That's weird, and almost certainly a sign of devilry. Give the dram a twirl, fan the space above it, and then give it another sniff. You'll discover hope in the form of cinnamon-sprinkled rye and bubble gum. But another sniff dashes that hope, seeing it submerged in the polymer-like smell of a brand new Speedo. And your only thought: *Thankfully, this skimpy male covering I'm nosing is fresh out of the package and not drying beside the pool.*

The mouth feel is warmly pleasant, but after a savoring moment, it becomes something along the lines of a flavored cigarette smoldering in an ash tray that's beside and downwind from a piece of rye toast. Thankfully there's orange marmalade on the toast.

The finish is longer than most, leaving too much spice behind which burns your tongue and causes grief.

I can see why the Devil might drink this, not to mention why my state's Liquor Control Commission would allow for its abundant availability.

And as you can see, I have my suspicions as to how all of it might be connected to an unassuming, proud, and presentable house just down the street and around the corner from my own—one that, for some reason, cannot be retained by anyone for any length of time.

OLD HEAVEN HILL, KENTUCKY STRAIGHT BOURBON WHISKEY, 50%

Sign, sign, everywhere a sign.

There is the well-known adage which speaks to the making of an assumption and the often unfortunate fruits it produces. The powerful little proverb, like a guardian angel wrapped in splendor and might, has protected so many in our society from doing or saying things to make themselves look foolish.

But is there such a proverb for sign keepers? I mean, is there a little nugget of ancient wisdom that a sign keeper might have readily available, an easy rhyme or an artless saying that he or she could pitch against before venturing up the ladder with those little plastic letters to spell out the message they intend to communicate to the masses?

If one is ever discovered, we'll need to make haste in releasing it to the internet, because here on earth, amongst our own ranks, there exists a particular gathering of people charged with signages who desperately need shepherding before being allowed to interface with the public.

Consider carefully the fast food sign below and you'll understand my concern.

The keeper of this sign either needs to be fired, or should be heralded as a hero for managing to reveal a terrible and two-fold secret. In only eight words, we learn what goes into the restaurant's hamburgers and why they need to hire a few more people. And perhaps, there's still more to the story. Maybe this sinister recipe was there in the beginning with Dave Thomas, the restaurant chain's founder. Perhaps all those years ago, Mr. Thomas chose to name his new restaurant, not necessarily to honor his daughter, but to tell us what (or who) was in his first round of sandwiches. And why would he do this? Because as many psychologists will tell you, secretly, some psychos want to be caught.

Do you see how far astray poor signage can lead someone? Well, it certainly didn't lead me to the drive-thru.

Another example might be the produce sign included here.

Yes, long yellow things—or as humans know them—bananas.

Again, either the creator of this sign needs to be fired, or he needs to be captured. My guess is the latter. The sign suggests that an otherworldly creature is working at this particular grocery store, and while it may have mastered its appearance,

allowing it to live among us while formulating its plan for world domination, it has yet to master the English vernacular. The description of a rather basic fruit betrays its presence and identity.

Call in the men in black suits and be ready with a mop. I'm pretty sure there's about to be a clean-up in aisle two.

Then there's the sign on the exterior of a gas station near my office.

The maker of this sign not only needs a sign keeper's proverb—if one is ever found—but he or she also needs to return to where we started with this little yarn and learn the one about making assumptions. First of all, how do you know the person's ex-spouse is to blame for the divorce? Perhaps the ex-spouse tirelessly sought reconciliation and the one standing before the sign was the bringer of the marriage's demise. Second, let's say the ex-spouse is completely to blame. If this is true, how do you know he or she actually has a heart to which the beer might be compared? I know quite a few folks who've thrown their marriages away, and my guess is they don't even have hearts, but rather a mass of blackened evil pumping oily, bubbling tar through their veins. Bubbling tar is not cold. This sign is full of assumptions.

Speaking of signs and assumptions—the Old Heaven Hill Kentucky Straight Bourbon Whiskey has the words "Symbol of Excellence" on the label.

Excellence. What are we to make of such a term being used to announce a whiskey that's good for little more than weed control in the driveway? Seriously, this stuff is a ground clear solution that kills to the roots. In fact, I'll bet if I took the time to read the fine print on the whiskey's packaging, I'd find instructions on usage, area coverage per gallon, and other notes touting that it becomes rainproof in thirty minutes and shows results in as few as twelve hours.

Ortho and Roundup have nothing on Old Heaven Hill. That should be the sign on its label.

The nose of this $8 whiskey is one that suggests its standard of excellence is something between rotting grass in the compost and rotting grass caked under the lawnmower's carriage. Either way, it's rotting vegetation of some sort. There is a little bit of something sweet in there, but my guess is that it's either the Glyphosate or the Diquat dibromide, both of these being sweeter smelling components in most popular weed killer products.

After smelling the whiskey, the palate is shockingly better than expected. At first, it's a bit sour, but then it takes a swift turn toward being a normal and drinkable Bourbon, giving over rye spices and a little bit of caramel.

The finish kills any chances of a long-term relationship. The vegetal sour returns, and in tow is the feeling that you should probably dump the rest of the bottle into a pump sprayer, being sure to add six fluid ounces for every gallon of water, and then make your way out to the pond to spray the algae. The frogs and snapping turtles will get a nice buzz, the pond will once again glisten in the sunshine, and you'll have saved about $50 in comparison to the typical vegetation killers suitable for such a use.

And after such a job, it would be most appropriate to make a sign.

PEERLESS KENTUCKY STRAIGHT RYE WHISKEY, BARREL PROOF, 2 YEARS OLD, 54%

The raucous splashing hides our blinding whiteness.

One of the greatest things about our annual summer vacation, at least when it comes to fulfilling the expectations of our children, is that the home we rent has a private pool. This means that each day, from sunup until sundown, the Thoma family is free to enjoy a pastime that is typically out of reach to us the rest of the year. It also means that once a year for about twelve days, the people in the surrounding homes have the opportunity to enjoy a few things, too.

It is most certainly true that our neighbors get a very real sense of what it's like to live on Luke Skywalker's home planet of Tatooine, which is a world with two suns. I say this because as a fair-skinned family from Michigan, we are pretty white. This means that as we emerge from our vacation home, donning our swim suits, the bright beaming rays of our planet's singular sun now reflecting off of us, it is as though a second sun has risen in the sky. It's really quite the sight. Even the neighborhood flora seems to, so strangely, lean toward our locale while we're in town.

Another aspect of our visit I'm sure the neighbors enjoy is the constant screeching from our eight-year-old hoarder who loves to swim and yet cannot seem to enter the water without twelve flotation devices, three pairs of goggles, some diver fins, and some sort of sharp object that, when she accidentally drops and loses it, is sure to be rediscovered by her father's foot. And she cries because someone has accidentally splashed her or because one of the other children passed by one of her stray possessions and decided to use it—perhaps a paddle board or water wing that has ended up at the opposite end of the pool.

"Harrison," she'll call in a whine, "I'm using that!"

I can't even begin to tell you how many times this clergyman has re-baptized that little girl in full immersion mode without her momma knowing it. I mean, someone has to fight the evil, right?

I suppose the most enjoyable time for the neighbors comes when we erupt into full "Death Ball" mode, which my more familiar readers will recall, is a bloody spectacle of tidal thrashing that involves throwing a rubber ball as hard and as fast as one is able.

Agonizing screams are expected during the event, and they only go silent when someone gets jammed in the pool filter, is knocked unconscious, or we need to take a break to refill the pool because all the water has ended up in the yard.

Yeah, it can get pretty crazy. But it's fun. And not only does the raucous splashing hide our blinding whiteness, but it's a time when you actually crave the disposition of a screeching, demon-possessed hoarder for your team. Don't take the ball from her. She'll eat your soul.

Of course, as the neighbors will most likely look back on these days with a frown, we'll continue to smile and look forward to so many more. In every way, they're unmatchable for this weary family, especially when the fullest burdens of fall, winter, and spring are upon us, pulling us along, in tow, throughout the rest of the year. And yet, somewhat in pace with these few, peerless days in the sun, there exists the year-round opportunity to enjoy an appropriately-named dram in the barrel proof Peerless Kentucky Straight Rye Whiskey from the Kentucky Peerless Distilling Company.

With a nose of dried apple chips and vanilla, the Peerless leads one away from the humdrum of typical bourbons to a more sunlit scape of memorable whiskey sipping. The palate proves a landing at someplace uniquely uncharted, giving over a wash of richly sweet ryes that almost immediately turn to the apples from the nosing that have been sun-soaked in spicy vanillas and a dash of pepper.

The finish is as remarkable as any of its other qualities. Medium in length, its burn amplifies the spice without lessening the lurking sense of the dried fruit.

Speaking of "lurking," I almost forgot to mention one other thing that the neighbors surely enjoy about our visits: Lizard hunting. Geckos—or whatever they are, maybe anoles—are everywhere in this place, crawling on the screens of the lanai, running along tree branches, and taking their lives into their own little hands by entering the pool area and crossing paths with a group of fascinated vacationers. At the time of this writing, it hasn't happened yet, but it did last year and we're only a few days into our vacation, so I'm sure it will again. Very soon, like these native lizards, the children will be found slinking around the outer perimeter of the home, lurking in bushes, barely blending into the landscape because of their whiteness, eyes peering through the branches with hands at the ready to snatch one of these little critters and give it a relatively uncreative name like "Lizzy" or "Gecky" or "Steve."

I'm absolutely certain that the neighbors will miss this less-than-stealthy but always startling activity occurring just beyond their kitchen window. What more does one need in the morning to get the adrenaline flowing than a fresh cup of coffee and an ear-piercing scream of "I got one!"?

Rebel Yell, American Whiskey, 24 Months, 45%

No offense, but your kid is crazy.

The world has lost its mind.

If it isn't official already, it's at least in the pipeline toward making it official. I'm sure there are people somewhere sitting around in committee meetings right now, maybe in someplace like Oslo, Norway or Paris, France. They're writing stuff, debating, setting parameters, establishing dates—getting ready to make the announcement that the world has officially lost its mind.

The evidence? Hobby horse competitions in Finland.

Yes, you read that correctly. Right now there are over ten thousand girls in Finland between the ages of 12 and 18 who spend hours each week preparing routines, practicing form, and grooming their steeds for competition.

"So, what's the big deal with that?" you ask.

Do you know what a hobby horse is?

"Yes."

Oh good, then you know it's the replica of a horse's head made from various materials and attached to the end of a stick—or a "dowel rod" to the people who still ride hobby horses and are easily offended—and the stick is placed between the legs of the rider who prances around attempting to mimic the movements of a real horse. From what I know, it's something that's been around for centuries. It was used in theater, festival parades, and as a child's toy. I'm pretty sure my sister, Shelley, had one. I just leaned over to my wife to ask her about them and she said she had one, too.

"Again…so…what's the big deal?"

Well, I don't normally find myself moved to criticize child competitions. Gymnastics, soccer, and even Comic-Con events— these all have their value in the lives of human beings inundated with the challenges of everyday existence. But when these competitive lifestyles become all-consuming, overshadowing attempts by parents to live vicariously through their children that ultimately result in the snatching away of childhood and other more important things in life, it's then that I tend to offer commentary. In other words, when these things cause you to skip school and dodge Sunday morning worship, I'm annoyed.

Beyond this, and as it meets hobby horse competitions, I certainly wouldn't think to criticize the playful activities of children. I have four, and it is always a bright-eyed event when they are carried away into imaginary spaces—realms where cardboard boxes are castles and hobby horses are majestic steeds, sometimes even with wings that lift them into the open expanse above the clouds. The castle is called "Eleanor's Realm" and the horses have names like William, Lance, and sometimes, depending on the child, Steve. I know the importance of such play. But again, when imaginary things cross over and into the realm of more important things, I begin to question. Again, in other words, when I listen to an interview with a little girl who speaks of her hobby horse as though it were a living horse, I begin to wonder. I get concerned when she talks to it while practicing her routine, telling it, "When we go into the jump, I'll kick and you lift your head." Or when she gets visibly frustrated and near the edge of tears before the interviewer as she explains that she's doing her part, but she feels like the horse is having trouble learning its part. This should bother folks. God forbid the glue that's holding the hobby horse's head on the stick gets weak and the head flies off in the middle of a jump. On the other hand, maybe that's all it would take to get the child into the therapy she so desperately needs right now.

Who knows? I sure don't.

In the end, I wonder if this is merely an emanation resulting from life in a world where many of our relationships are virtual. We are connected to others through digital devices, and eventually, the device becomes the reality, the thing we can't live without, rather than remaining the means of representation to or communication with someone real.

Once again, who knows? I sure don't. I just know that when I watch these hobby horse competitions on YouTube, I can't help but feel like shouting out rebelliously against a world that has lost its mind. But in order to keep from raising my voice and frightening the nearby children in the cardboard castle, I pour a drink instead— one that's calming, but can also do the shouting for me. The Rebel Yell American Whiskey, if only in name, is certainly an acceptable partner.

A rather nicely balanced blend of Bourbon and rye, the Rebel Yell American Whiskey is a warming dram, offering scents of cola, bubblegum, and rye spice. Disregarding an initial sour, a sip brings what tastes a little bit like Raisin Bran Crunch cereal in vitamin D milk.

The finish is a medium jaunt that maintains the raisins and nuttiness from the palate while bringing back the cola from the nosing.

In all, the whiskey was much more complex than I expected. And apparently, with the ever-increasing insanity—I mean, popularity—of hobby horse competitions, ESPN might just end up needing one more channel to make sure you experience the thrill in your own living room.

RED CEDAR, BOURBON WHISKEY, 40%

The untold story of Stormtrooper TK-421

"That was one of the worst days to be a stormtrooper," TK-421 sighed, leaning against the breakroom countertop and taking a mouthful of coffee from his favorite mug. He'd received the cup as a gift from General Tarkin himself not long after completing the last of four teamwork training seminars mandated by the Emperor.

"The first or the second Death Star?" TK-559 asked.

"The first."

"Why the first?" 559 pried.

"You know why," 421 said dryly and took another sip.

"So," TK-559 began, "what actually happened that day? And how did you manage to get off the Death Star before it exploded?" He was anxious to hear the story, having already heard about his new partner's brush with the rebels while guarding the Millennium Falcon. "I've heard the rumors," he said, "but no one really seems to know the real story."

"What've you heard?" 421 asked, setting his cup on the counter beside him.

"Well, some are saying you actually died, and that you aren't you. You're 421's twin brother, and you're taking his place so that the family doesn't lose the paycheck or the Imperial healthcare plan."

"That's funny," 421 said, stretching his arms up and behind his head to cradle it in his hands. "That's actually the craziest one I've heard so far." He gave a glance, "You realize how stupid that is, right?"

"Why's that?"

"Because we never take these things off," he answered, drumming his fingers against his helmet. "No one even knows what I look like. Why would it matter if I was a twin?"

"Yeah, I suppose," 559 admitted.

"So, what else are folks saying?"

"Others think you're a rebel collaborator, that they didn't actually shoot you with a blaster, that you just faked the whole thing and went with them when they escaped."

"Yeah, I've heard that one before," 421 said, reaching for his cup to take another sip. "That's been around a while."

"And?" 559 kept on.

"And what?"

"Are you?"

"Am I what?"

"Are you a spy?"

TK-421 allowed a few seconds of silence before answering matter-of-factly, "Yes, I am." 559's hand dropped slowly toward his holstered blaster. "I'm just kidding," 421 laughed, putting out his hand to wave him off. "Slow your roll, boy scout. I'm not a spy."

The digitized sound of 559's excited breathing buzzed from his helmet.

"You know," 421 said snidely, "you're kind of a spaz. As a matter of fact, almost every stormtrooper I know is a spaz. That's probably why no one ever hits what they're shooting at."

"Whatever," 559 replied. "So, give it up, 421. What happened that day?"

"It's really not that big a deal," he said. "Although, you could say I got lucky."

"How so?"

"Well," he started and swirled the last bit of coffee in his mug. "You already know I was assigned sentry duty for the Millennium Falcon after we captured it with the tractor beam, right?"

"Yeah."

"And you know that it turned out the rebels were actually hiding on the ship when they jumped me."

"Yeah, that's what everybody's been told."

"Well, anyway, in the skirmish, one of 'em got a shot off and it caught me in the side. But you know how our blasters work, right? Not only do they tear through you, but they sort of taze you, too. When I got shot, it didn't kill me, but instead—"

"—How did a blaster round not kill you?!"

"It hit the flask I keep hidden in my belt line under the armor. The round ricocheted and put a hole in a seat cushion near a holochess table on the ship. But as I was going to say, it knocked me out cold. The metal flask blocked the round but not the wattage."

"So, it just tazed you, bro?"

"True dat."

"Then what happened?"

"Well," TK-421 continued, "when I woke up, I found myself in a hidden cargo space below deck. All I can figure is that the rebels were in such a hurry to split, rather than taking the extra time to chuck me from the ship, they left me to slide around in the back while they escaped."

"Nice."

"Yeah, pretty heartless. My guess is that I ended up sliding into the cargo hold and they just forgot about me."

"So what did you do?"

"Thankfully the cargo space I was in had a ventilation duct that led to one of the landing legs. It was just big enough for me to crawl through." TK-421 put his hands behind his head again. "Once I got into the gear compartment, I just stayed there and waited until we landed."

"How long were you in there?"

"Quite a while. But you see, that's the interesting part of the whole thing. Before I crawled through to the landing gear, that cargo space I'd landed in, well, it was full of all kinds of smuggled stuff."

"Really?" 559 buzzed with anticipation.

"Yeah, there were tons of Nutrigrain bars down there—"

"—Oh, man. Those were outlawed big time."

"I know, right? But, I gotta tell you, that guy Solo was smuggling a whole lot more than illegal Nutrigrain bars. He had Hard Rock Café shirts from places where there're no Hard Rock Cafés—places like Degobah and Tatooine. He had stacks of fake Levi's jeans, boxes of Coach handbags—all kinds of stuff."

"Rebel scum."

"And that's only the half of it. There were four or five crates of whiskies from all over the galaxy."

"Seriously?"

"Oh, yeah. But this stuff wasn't counterfeit. It was the real deal."

"That's amazing!"

"You ain't kidding. He had bottles of Aberlour and Laphroaig, Bulleit and Stranahan's. He had Knappogue Castle and The

Exceptional by Sutcliffe and Son. He had stuff from The Macallan and The Balvenie, and then out of all of it, he had one bottle of something I'd never seen before—Red Cedar Bourbon.

"Wow," 559 said enthusiastically. "It sounds like you were good to go down there."

"I sure was," 421 affirmed. "But don't forget I was injured. That blaster round didn't kill me, but it did manage to superheat my flask so that it burned me pretty badly." He unsnapped a section of the armor near his belt and revealed the top portion of a rather large scar. "See for yourself."

"Oh man. That looks terrible," 559 said, his voice betraying concern.

"And it hurt like hell, let me tell you. I actually had to peel the flask away from my skin, and when I did, the skin went with it. But again, thankfully, I was in a place that had everything I needed to clean the wound and bandage it up."

"You mean you used one of the whiskies?"

"Yep," 421 replied. "And one of the Hard Rock Degobah shirts as a bandage."

"Which of the whiskies did you use?"

"I popped open the Red Cedar, but for two reasons. The first being that since there was only one, I figured it was Solo's prize bottle and I wanted to ruin it for him; but second, because I needed to clean the wound and it was the closest one to me—which, looking back on it, was a big mistake. I should've tried grabbing for something else, because when I popped it open, the whole compartment started to smell like stale lemons doused in overly sharp bitters. It was pretty intense, and I thought the stench might give me away."

"Tell me you didn't—"

"Yes, unfortunately, I did," TK-421 admitted. "I tried a swig of the stuff. You know, just to see."

"And?"

"And it was a lot like the nose," 421 replied, but then in the same breath, he quickly gave a retraction. "On second thought," he said, "it was worse. It tasted like burnt grapefruits spotted with equally burnt mint leaves and singed oregano. Not the best combination. Too weird for my tastes."

"How'd it finish?"

"It was a long finish, one that sort of clawed at my tongue for a few minutes. There was no bottled water down there to help wash it away, so I had to let my saliva build up. And once I managed enough spit, I swished it around in my mouth and then hocked it into one of the Coach handbags."

"Nice," TK-559 said, once again sounding his concern for the whole unfortunate situation.

"One thing I will say for the Red Cedar Bourbon," 421 offered, "is that it works well as an antiseptic. I never did get an infection, and I was down there hanging on the landing gear for quite a while."

"That's good," 559 said and sighed. TK-421 took the last gulp of his coffee and turned to get another. "Wait a second," 559 interrupted. "You never said how you got away."

"Oh yeah," 421 laughed, turning back again to get comfortable against the countertop while he waited for the machine to fill his cup. "Well, like I said, I waited for them to open the gear hatches with the hopes that we'd land somewhere that I could hop out and find a place to hide—at least until the Empire discovered them again. The Empire always finds these morons. Of course, before I shimmied through the duct, I grabbed a whole bunch of Nutri-Grain bars and some of the better whisky to keep with me while I waited for the cavalry."

"Which one did you get?"

"Actually, I grabbed two—a bottle of The Exceptional Grain and the Aberlour 16-year-old. I ended up finishing off most of The Exceptional while I waited for a chance to escape on Yavin—which was crawling with rebels, so I had to stay hidden up in the gear compartment the whole time I was there."

"So that's where you were when the Death Star blew."

"Well, sort of. We left Yavin for a little while and were back in space when the Death Star blew up, but eventually we went back to Yavin for a few days. Some sort of party, I think. Anyway, my chance to escape came at the next stop. Unfortunately, when we were coming in for a landing and the hatches opened up," TK-421 embraced himself and gave a faux shiver, "I was hit by an ungodly blast of cold air that knocked the wind right out of me. It made me drop the bottle of Aberlour I'd been guarding."

"That sucks," 559 growled.

"I saw it land in the snow near what I could've sworn was a Wampa reading a newspaper. Turns out we were landing on Hoth."

"I heard from one of the guys in the snow regiment," 559 interjected, "that Luke Skywalker—the punk kid who blew up the first Death Star—I heard he was attacked by one of those things."

"Yeah, I heard that, too. Good. He had it coming."

"And?"

"So, anyway, when the Falcon landed, I found my chance and jumped off and hid in a storage bin. And like I said, I figured you guys would eventually show up before too long."

"And you were right. We did."

"Yes, you did. And yes, I was—about everything except for the Red Cedar, that is."

REDEMPTION RYE, PRE-PROHIBITION RYE REVIVAL, 46%

Which kind of "nice"?

"People are nice," he said, "but it's always for one of the same three reasons."

"Just three?" I asked.

"Just three," he replied resolutely. "The first is because the person is just nice—genuinely nice. It doesn't matter the situation, circumstance, or people involved, the person is just all-around nice."

"I know lots of folks like that," I said. "At least I think I do." I poured a little bit of the Redemption Rye into another of my crystal rock glasses on the table and then pushed it toward him. I took a sip of my own and pried, "And the second?"

"The second is only being nice because he wants something from you."

"Are you implying something?" I asked, half smiling. "I just slid you an untapped whiskey in one of my favorite glasses."

"Funny, but no."

"Good. How about the third, then?"

"The third is only nice because he or she wants to get away from you."

"What do you mean?"

"He wants you off his trail," he said and sipped. "And it can be for all kinds of different reasons."

"Like what?"

"Like the person just doesn't like you and doesn't want to talk to you. Or maybe the person is hiding something. No one ever suspects the really nice people to have secrets."

"So, how do we know who's who in the crowd?"

"You can't," he said. "At least not until you've been around the person long enough. After a while, people learn which nice you truly are."

"Well, I think you're a pretty good guy," I said and smiled. "I'd be willing to say you're the first kind of nice."

"I'd say you are, too," he said, but only grinning. He was holding something back.

"So, which kind of nice?"

"You're a pastor," he said. "You have to be all three."

I wasn't ready for the answer he gave, but in hindsight, he's probably right. At least I think he could be right. I get along pretty well with most people. Hopefully that's an indication that I'm more or less sourced from some level of genuine niceness. Although, knowing the sinfulness of mankind, most would probably say that about themselves.

Thinking on the second kind of nice, I suppose that in order to accomplish certain things with certain people, the second kind is needed—or as Jesus said in Matthew 10, "Be as wise as serpents and as innocent as doves."

But the third kind of nice, that's a tough one. Still, I think my friend could be right, except that in the case of pastors, it's an outflow of both the first and second forms of niceness. For example, there are certain folks of which I can definitely say I have no desire to be their best bud. Nevertheless, I don't treat them any differently in public than the folks for whom I'd happily buy a drink. It wouldn't feel right, and in the end, it would really bother me a lot. I've never preferred such low roads in situations of conflict. And yet, beyond all that, I'm a sinful twerp in need of the same forgiveness all the other sinful twerps need. That truth alone keeps me from getting too bundled up in the guts with past transgressions. To say it another way, I may be the third kind of nice, but it isn't because I'm trying to hide anything from you. And why wouldn't I want to hide my past sins? Because from a Christian perspective— and I happen to be a Christian—not even God remembers that stuff. Funny, huh? But it's true. Jeremiah 31:34 says that when God forgives sin, he remembers it no longer. And in Psalm 103:12, we're told that when God removes our transgressions, He sets them as far from us as the east is from the west. That's an impossible distance, one that is completely beyond mortal comprehension, and in my mind, that's pretty cool.

I suppose if folks want to hide from their own past transgressions, that's fine, but just know I'm not all that concerned about mine. They're scars—bad memories. But good or bad, memories are behind not before us. I'll add that I'd most certainly wonder which of the three kinds of nice you are if you actually allot time in your schedule for digging up other people's skeletons. It certainly couldn't be the first kind of nice. It couldn't be the kind of nice that has any regard for what is the glorious material fueling the core of the word "redemption." It couldn't be the kind that travels into and through that core, coming out on the other side delighted by the sunrise of a new day.

It couldn't be the kind that would move me to willingly share with you a dram of the Redemption Rye edition. I mean, why would I pour this into even the least of honorable vessels for you to enjoy when you haven't the wherewithal to understand the title on the bottle let alone the gesture that makes it yours? You'd never fully grasp the pleasantness of the straight-wafting rye spices in the nosing. You'd be someone less inclined to take hold of the agreeable vanilla streams that lead away from struggle toward a more resilient friendship.

All of this being true, you'd most certainly miss the spiced fruits, coffee, and caramel in the palate that leads to a medium finish that revives the joys discovered in the nose.

And why would you miss all of this? Because you're being nice to get something from me—namely dirt. You're savoring my words and working to draw out something you might use against me later. That's the vilest form of niceness, and rest assured, I know what it looks like. Which means I'd be more than ready for you. Which also means that I'd watch every one of my words carefully, maybe even throwing out a few misdirects to let you feel as though you're getting something. But in the end, and unbeknownst to you, I'd have poured you a glass of Scoresby and not the Redemption Rye. I'd only give this dandy little gem to a friend.

Russell's Reserve, Kentucky Straight Bourbon Whiskey, 10 Years Old, 45%

She had a hamster.

My daughter has a hamster. Well, she *had* a hamster. Fernando was his name.

I'm not at liberty to tell you where he is and why he is there, but what I can say is that rather recently, his more-than-benevolent caretaker approached me with the request that I assist her in taking a picture of all of the tiny rodent's belongings in order to sell them online.

"Done and done, my dear child. And if you don't mind, shall I scribe for you a finely tuned advertisement that will, most certainly, rid you of these things while achieving a top dollar goal?"

"Whatever. Sure. I don't care. I'm just never getting another hamster."

"Again, done and done."

Together we staged Fernando's belongings on the kitchen table. I took a picture with my phone and then uploaded it to the Facebook Marketplace. Once I'd gotten an affirmative nod from the seller beside me regarding the $55 price tag, I tapped away at a short description of the items, and then posted it to the local resale networks. Here's what I wrote:

> Well-cared-for hamster supplies. Everything you need to keep a happy and healthy hamster. Unless, of course, he's an unappreciative jerk. Then you can evict him, being sure to send him to live with a friend so that you can sell all his junk and buy a cactus. Anyway, good stuff here.

Within a few moments I received a notice from Facebook announcing that my advertisement was in violation of their marketplace policies and asking if I'd like to appeal. At first I thought, *Wow, there must be a hypersensitive member of PETA living somewhere in the tri-county area.* I just figured I had offended someone by the way I described the situation with Fernando. But that wasn't it. It turns out that even though I posted the advertisement in the pet supplies section of the market—which I would imagine assumes each seller is going to note the kind of supplies being sold and the particular animal with which the supplies are associated—it was the word "hamster" that triggered the block. It sounded the virtual alarms because it is illegal to sell animals on Facebook.

That's one bad algorithm right there. And as to whoever formulated it, Facebook should follow my lead and replace him or her with a cactus. I mean, cacti are designed by the Creator to be fairly self-sufficient, needing very little care or concern. The algorithm that tagged my post, however, is making a lot of extra work for the people dealing with the appeals process.

"Ah, here's another trickster trying to sneak by us," I imagine a young and idealistic screen jockey whispering. "Hmm, let's see. Ah, the fraudster used the word 'hamster.' Bad idea, pal. This guy is probably a dark web dealer in illegal Mammalia Rodentia. Poor little things. Oh, wait. He's selling his daughter's hamster stuff…in the pet supplies section…like a normal person. I hate this stupid algorithm."

Maybe instead of a cactus, the people at Facebook should consider hiring Jimmy and Eddie Russell, the master distillers who particularized Russell's Reserve Kentucky Straight Bourbon Whiskey. I'll bet they could provide the expertise for getting the formula right. They certainly succeeded in catching all the right details with this 10-year-old edition.

With a gentle nose of candy corn and something reminiscent of pineapple juice and cake frosting, the Russell's Reserve puts forth a fanciful advertisement that beckons to give it a try.

But with what is being offered in comparison to its price—which in my particular corner of the whiskey universe was about $45—one might become alarmed, thinking the deal to be trickery. Nevertheless, a sip proves the honesty in the transaction. This is no bottom shelf Bourbon attempting to sell itself incautiously. It is a finely calculated presentation of wood spice, honeyed nougat, a simpler pinch of cinnamon in cola, and a wrapping in mild warmth.

The finish—an easy, medium-length retelling of the spicy cola—is a pitch to revisit the whiskey as often as one might prefer. And now you can, because after a couple of hours, the folks at Facebook acknowledged the uselessness of their algorithm and allowed your pet supplies advertisement to go through. With such a pardon from Facebook gulag came a good number of inquiries, one of which led to a final sale. With a crisp $55 in hand, you can easily afford a bottle of the Russell's Reserve. Although, now you are facing another problem.

"Daddy, did the hamster stuff sell, yet?"

"It sure did, honey," is my reply. "But I forgot to tell you that I charge a $45 fee for each online advertisement I'm hired to design. Here's your ten bucks, sweetie."

SOUTHWEST SPIRITS AND WINES, TITLE NO. 21, 42%

Terrible things are born from boredom.

It wasn't that long ago I suggested to the chairman of my church's School Board that we choose some sort of keyword or gesture between us, something to be employed during a meeting when either one of us begins saying something that has any potential for making the meeting take longer.

I suggested the throat-cut signal, but he thought that'd be too obvious to onlookers. He returned by suggesting the finger-to-the-mouth shushing motion. I told him that's a signal my wife uses on me pretty regularly so it would probably work.

In the end, we decided to ponder the idea and revisit it. In the meantime, the meetings will remain all but unenthusiastic, which is good, because there's nothing worse than a bunch of folks sitting around in committee with nothing to do.

As evil may have roots of gold, so many other troubles have their roots in boredom. I mean, what should we expect of people in authority with nothing to do? Start a war, that's what. I'm pretty sure that's how the Eighteenth Amendment to the U.S. Constitution came into being. There was probably a committee of really bored congressmen sitting around with nothing to do, and because it's already innate to the government to make life harder, they decided to outlaw booze. I can see it now...

"Right-o," I hear in my mind an elected gent saying. "What shall we decide on today?"

"Well, good sir," another replies, "all is well and there's nothing on the docket."

"What to do then, friend?" the first asks, visibly disappointed.

"I say, my friend," comes an exuberant reply from another at the table. "Let us amend the Constitution! It'll surely bristle the whiskers of the Lutherans!"

"Hoorah and it's done, then!" the Baptist chairman says, interrupting with finality. "What a brilliant idea! To it, men!"

And with that, in order to busy themselves, they went to work crafting their own pietistic importance—or as Tolstoy put it, they engaged in "the desire for desires."

Indeed, terrible things are born from boredom. However, I'm willing to say that the Title No. 21 (which, technically, is born from this terrible event in history because it's named after the amendment that would later repeal prohibition) is to be considered an exception to the rule. Even as a bottom shelf whiskey I happened upon at the local Walmart, it's quite delightful.

The nose of this dram is subtle and sweet, rendering scents of candied pie—chocolate silk with a cinnamon crust. A drop of water lets loose cornstarch and salt.

A sip is a warmed wash of sweet butter, allspice, and overly ripened McIntosh apples. Again, a drop of water introduces something new—a peppery geist.

The finish, a medium trail of the chocolate and cinnamon from the nosing, is a kindly bit of forgiveness to the bored politicians who tried to rid the world of such things, suggesting to them that they nearly betrayed a worthwhile gift of God.

But not to worry, men. We've forgiven you. Well, maybe the Episcopalians have forgiven you. We Lutherans are still considering it in committee. Still, there is one thing you should know of the whole lot of Christendom.

Your chances at re-election are incredibly slim.

SPECKLED TAIL AMERICAN WHISKEY, 40%

Chapter 1: The Brethren

The sun was falling behind us as we raced through the turns leading from town. Soon it would be night. The night was never to our advantage. Always to theirs. We needed to find a place to hide.

"I've never been this far out before," Jennifer said as we passed a pasture of grazing cattle. I could see the shifting shadows of the surrounding trees stretching across the road as the sun continued to dip lower.

"Me either," I replied. I was lying, of course, and I knew if she'd detected my lie, she would never trust me again. Still, I did it anyway.

"Do you know where you're going?" she mumbled. Even at only a sip, she had swallowed far too much of the Speckled Tail American Whiskey and was beginning to falter in her speech.

"I have an idea," I answered, "but I'm not entirely sure. How much of that stuff did you drink?"

"I don't know. I can't remember." She rested her head against the window. "How did you know to go for that sword?"

"I just knew."

A moment of silence passed between us.

"When we get a little further out of town," I said, breaking the quiet, "I'm going to pull over so you can puke. You're gonna have to try to puke. You have to get that out of you. I mean, you saw what it will do."

"I know," she said, "Just keep driving."

"I love you," I said, but she didn't answer.

What is Michigan that it would be home to such things? We have lakes, temperamental weather, and microbrewers, but not much else. And so, what I'm about to share, you'd expect to discover only in movies. Popcorn in hand, the silver screen glows with scenes of a distant village settled in a remote English countryside. But here we are in Michigan sparring the same hidden powers written into scripts—and we're doing so for our very lives.

I'd caught a glimpse of the bottle of Speckled Tail that was insistently served in a rock glass to me and my three companions, two of whom are no longer with us—or at least not as you'd expect for them to be. Being the enjoyer of whiskey that I am, I reached for my phone and tapped and scrolled, casually in search of the whiskey's origins, hoping to find it sourced by a reputable distillery.

"Are you calling someone?" Vistus, our host, asked abruptly.

"Just seeing if any of my online friends have written about this stuff," I replied. "I've never heard of it."

"But I never told you what it was," he said.

"I'm observant," I volleyed in response. Again, I'd already noticed the bottle. It rested on an end table partially shadowed by a suit of armor clutching a sword and serving as sentry to a nearby fireplace.

"It is very rare," he said, giving a grin. "In my countless years, few have consumed it." As far as I knew in that moment, he was right. I found a singular mention by an obscure religious group in Florida, but otherwise, the internet was silent—completely empty of mentions from anyone.

Vistus spoke as three of his four guests tasted the whiskey. I was uneasy. I didn't want what was in the glass before me. I continued to scroll, but only to bide time. As I did, Vistus shared a lengthy history with his guests, which I'll relay to you in a moment.

"It is an unfortunate impression you convey, Reverend," Vistus said, stopping mid-story. "Will you not receive the gift I've set before you?"

I could no longer avoid a sip. I gave a stiffened smile and sniffed.

A nose of unnatural caramel and chocolates rose from my glass. Both scents were rich, but also very stale. I could tell I'd soon be tasting artificial flavorings.

The others sipped and gave polite smiles. Even Jennifer smiled. She betrayed her fear, barely getting a coating on her tongue. I sipped, too. The palate offered syrupy coverings of the candies from the nose, but not enough to hide the bitter tinge of alcohol and a distinct saltiness.

It was bloodlike.

I don't know the whiskey's finish. I didn't swallow. I spit it from my mouth and knocked the glass from Jennifer's hand. I knew what we were drinking wasn't natural.

The two beside us, both of whom had so nervously consumed nearly all within their glasses—began to convulse.

"A rather abrupt response to my hospitality," our host said, furrowing his brow and giving a simper wide enough to allow a sharpening canine tooth to emerge. "And very unwise."

The next few moments were less cordial—and very violent—far too violent to describe here.

Now we're on the run.

Recalling the history Vistus had shared, it would seem that our immediate troubles have their roots in the dark woodlands of Eastern Europe, set back from society, and yet not necessarily apart from it. Vistus spoke of the ones he called the Brethren. In the daylight, clustered at the outskirts of villages, they lived as gypsy traders. At night, they slunk stealthily through the small towns feasting. Some, however, were mindful to engage in planting seeds of their unrighteousness in the schools, courts, and churches.

By this, they labored to become a part of society.

It wasn't until the early 1400's that the Brethren found themselves pitted against the mortals and nearing extinction. Many were being revealed, hunted, and killed. Their numbers were dwindling. Survival required reform. Mortals could no longer be their primary source of food.

A powerful faction bearing a fiercely loyal ideology arose among them. They would abstain from mortal contact completely. If they continued to collide with man, they believed extinction to be all but certain.

And they were right. Those who remained among men were lost.

The Brethren preached this new way, and those who would not follow were dispatched. Either they accepted the new way, or they were devoured. Those who managed to escape were revealed to the mortals. Mankind, lost in its own superstitions, could always be trusted to hunt and slay them. The remnant, about 100 in all, believed the time for coexistence would one day return.

A hundred years passed before a contingent crossed the ocean bearing the same hope to the New World.

In the newly established American colonies, they continued to wrestle against their unnatural appetites, eventually finding it necessary to venture away from the settlements and into the undiscovered reaches of the country. They settled into an obscurity in the Appalachian highlands. There they would feed on the wildlife and safely avoid human contact. But soon the American population increased and spread across the mountains forcing them into migratory patterns, all to avoid detection.

In their travels, it wasn't uncommon for someone to discover them. A Native American seeking trade, a mountaineer in search of fortune or adventure, a religious group seeking the monastic life— of these there were some who would be found alone on the wrong face of the mountain. Each would be captured. Each would be offered the Speckled Tail and a place among the Brethren. It was through this whiskey that you became a werewolf. You cannot become one by accident. A bite will not do it. That's foolishness, anyway. In a lycanthropic state, it is impossible for a werewolf to decide to do anything but indulge fully in the old way.

You become a werewolf by choice. It's always by choice.

You must accept the whiskey as the way of immortality, or refuse it. But refusing the Speckled Tail was as equally welcomed by the Brethren as accepting it. A refusal brought about a savage carnival of darker things.

Few refused the whiskey. The fear of death against the promise of immortality almost always stirred the murkier desires of men's hearts, and once the whiskey had brought about the change, ultimately removing the victim's soul, nothing of regret remained.

Over the years, the Brethren's numbers began to grow. With such evangelical success, one would have thought that the time for integration was drawing near. Still, with technology advancing and pushing the populations further west, they soon realized that seclusion in large numbers would be impossible. In the winter of 1830, they elected to divide. Five hundred would press to the west while the rest would divide among the mountains and the flatlands of the Midwest.

A good number found a suitable home in Michigan.

It is now 2019. They have settled and their numbers have grown. The time for hiding was coming to an end. The time to return to the old way was on the horizon.

Jennifer and I know them. I have refused the Speckled Tail American Whiskey and lived. I don't yet know how things will unfold, but I know that I can make them known. And they know it, too.

They cannot allow it. They will not allow it.

I do hope that very soon I'll be able to tell you more, but until then, you mustn't blink at what I've shared. And I beg you, if you behold the Speckled Tail American Whiskey in the home of your host, there's only one thing for you to do.

Run.

Straight Edge Bourbon Whiskey, 42%

You snore.

"Daddy, you snore when you're sleeping," the little girl said, shoveling a mound of Fruit Loops into her mouth.

"No, I don't," I replied decisively, but also somewhat annoyed by the turn of conversation so early in the morning.

"Yes, you do," she continued. "I got up to use the bathroom last night, and I heard you."

"Maybe you heard your mother," I said.

"No, it was you," she giggled through a slurp.

"Maybe it was Harrison. Or the Sasquatch living in the attic." I set my coffee down. "And how would you know, anyway? Your bathroom is, like, two miles from our bedroom, our door was closed, and you're like a zombie when you get up to go pee at night. Sometimes I'm afraid I'm going to hear a noise, get up to check, and see you in the corner of one of the boys' rooms with their brains in your hands."

"It was you," she garbled through another mouthful. "I used the bathroom in your bedroom because ours is gross."

"Well, you snore, too," I said resolutely, taking a sip. "And you fart in your sleep."

"But my sleepy sounds are sweet little girl sounds," she volleyed. "Yours are scary."

"Well, if you think the sounds of lawn mowers at two o'clock in the morning are sweet little girl sounds, then I guess you're right."

"Well, you sound like a lawn mower and a chainsaw."

"You sound like a lawn mower being pushed by a guy with a chainsaw and dragging our old noisy dishwasher…on lawn mower wheels… because that's the only way it would probably work in the yard."

"You sound like a lawn mower in a tornado."

Well, you sound like a tornado full of lawn mowers—a mowernado."

"You sound like a mowernado with chainsaws and dishwashers and bombs and garbage trucks and Godzilla."

"Well, you sound like your brother, Joshua."

"I'm going to tell him you said that," she said, giving a grin.

"Good. Finish your breakfast, Princess of Snoretopia."

"Well, if I'm the princess, you're the king."

"But, my dear, you and I both know the Snoretopian prophecy has decreed that one day, from among the royal Snoretopian bloodline, a master snorer will arise and take the throne. It will be a young maiden whose snoring is like none other, someone whose snoring rattles the mountains and boils the rivers in this fair province. And again, since she'll be from the royal bloodline, she'll most likely be a daughter of the king." I took another sip. "Face it, honey. It's probably you. Your snoring is the worst. I still have to replace the window in your bedroom because of how loud you snore."

"You have to replace it because it leaks," she argued.

"It leaks because your snoring rattled it loose from the frame."

With remarkable skill, she rolled her eyes, gulped down the last of her Fruit Loops, and stood up from her seat. "I'm done," she said. Having put her bowl and spoon into the kitchen sink, she skipped off and around the corner of the living room. With the thumping of her feet up the stairs, I heard her call back, "I'm telling Josh what the King of Snoretopia said about him."

I didn't reply this time. I took another sip of coffee and typed "ways to stop snoring" into the internet browser on my phone. Not for me, of course, but for the princess. I don't snore. Just ask my wife. She'll tell you that what I do is probably best described as choking but not dying. And this only happens when I sleep on my back. When I sleep on my side, you'd think I actually did die because I don't make a sound.

Either way, as the ante was upped in the morning conversation, in a similar fashion, the Splinter Group from Napa, California has a better game with the Straight Edge Bourbon Whiskey. I say this because I've had their Slaughter House edition—which was actually released after the Straight Edge—and I couldn't quite find the footing to ever want to buy it again. But this prequel whiskey is pretty good. In fact, it's better than pretty good. It's really good.

The nose of this ambered dram is a fine-tuned offering of what one might expect from a better Bourbon. In other words, you won't question the oncoming vanilla and cinnamon. And as the palate delivers on the expectations, it also surprises. With the vanilla and cinnamon comes a gentler bit of plum and rye toast.

The finish brings everything together with a short wash of mild spice and a little bit of the barrel wood. In all, it's everything one might appreciate in a calming nightcap that eases the throat and nasal passages for a snore-less night. It most certainly lends toward a revisiting with the Slaughter House edition to see if I missed something. Perhaps my mood for the review was affected because I'd been kept awake by the sleepy sounds of the Princess of Snoretopia roaring through the castle.

It's possible. It's also quite possible that the Princess didn't make a peep and that my late evening restlessness was due to me choking but not dying.

STRANAHAN'S, SNOWFLAKE #20, QUANDARY PEAK, 47%

No use in keeping the S.W.A.T. team's plans a secret.

Do you remember that time when you were younger and the coach of your sports team decided he was going to broadcast his half-time locker room discussion through the loud speakers, making sure that the other team as well as the spectators knew his game plan for winning?

No?

Yeah, me either. Apparently that's only something you do if you are dealing with a barricaded gunman situation.

How do I know this? From listening to the radio today as I traveled from one location to another. The local news station buzzing, I heard a field reporter speaking with a police captain regarding an unfolding situation involving an armed man in a house who was refusing to come out. He'd already fired over a dozen shots at the police and was threatening to, in his words, "not go down without a fight."

The reporter asked plainly about the game plan, and the captain responded with equal plainness, pretty much sharing everything they intended to do, even to the point of revealing how many S.W.A.T. teams he had on the scene, where they were positioned, the resources they had at their disposal, and when they'd most likely move in to secure the scene and what might precipitate that move.

Now, I don't know if the gunman was listening to the news station, but I can tell you that if he was, by the information being shared, he'd all but been handed a ticket to the planning meeting with the S.W.A.T. commander, police captain, and the negotiator in the makeshift tent at the end of the street. The details being revealed over the public airwaves seemed to be a strange handling of confidential things, and quite possibly to the gunman's advantage.

There are certain circumstances that rise to the level of ticketed invitation. A barricaded gunman situation is not one of those events. And just for the record, if I were the police commissioner, I'd be planning a little chat with my captain, one in which I'd explain to him the details of my strategy for such future engagements. And by the way, a key component of the strategy would be his absence from the scene. But as I said, there are certain events worthy of ticketed invitation, and the Stranahan's annual Snowflake edition release is one of them.

The 2017 edition—Quandary Peak—was released on December 2, and, as usual, it was done so in extremely limited supply. So limited, in fact, whoever organized the whole thing had to actually print on each ticket things like "Ticket valid only if still in line through 11 AM on 12/02/2017." And from what I hear, with people camping outside the distillery in order to be one of the few to actually receive a ticket worth a single bottle at $99 plus tax each, this is a strictly enforced rule. You know what that means? It means don't step out of line.

I received the generous sample for review from my friend Mike who traveled from his home in Iowa to the distillery in Denver where he not only didn't step out of line, but was generously kissed by fate and granted the very first position nearest the front door. Good for you, Mike! And for me, too, since he was kind enough to share. Indeed, having now tried this exclusive whiskey, I more fully grasp the devotion of those referred to as "Stranafans."

A sniff is easy and light, sending up streams of dark and meaty fruits carried on a high mountain breeze of rum spice and barely a pinch of pepper.

The palate is a downcurrent of the rum and fruit from the nose meeting with another stream of caramel apples topped with singed almonds. It's really quite delightful.

The finish is a medium jaunt. It dawdles along lazily with barrel spice, caramel, and a drop of salted butter. Then suddenly, it's gone—dried up, evaporated, vanished—kind of like the chance for the guy who stepped away from the line for a moment at 10:59 to take a quick call from his wife. With that, I'd say he had plenty of time to ponder that poor decision while driving home empty handed. Even more so must we sympathize with the rage that has him holed up in a house in Detroit waiting for the S.W.A.T. team to breach his back door with a battering ram and smoke grenades.

You only get one shot at this stuff.

TOMMYROTTER DISTILLERIES, TRIPLE BARREL AMERICAN WHISKEY, 46%

Now, if we can just keep her out of prison.

"So," the youngest of my four children asked with a voice suggesting the need for clarification, "Joshua gets to drive Momma's car, and so now she's getting a different one?"

"That's right," I said. "We gave him the Ford Explorer to drive and now she needs to get a different car." I made the turn into our subdivision. "She likes her Explorer," I added, "so we'll try to find another one just like it."

"Which car will Madeline drive when it's her turn?" the little girl continued to pry.

"I already told her she could have my Wrangler," I replied.

"And because you like Jeeps you'll get another one just like Momma's gonna get another Explorer?"

"I guess, yeah, if we can afford it."

"How about Harrison?" she asked, her tone noticeably calculated.

"I'll keep to the rotation. He'll drive the next Jeep I get, and then I'll probably get anoth—"

"—a Ferrari," she interrupted, finishing my sentence. "You should get a Ferrari." A depth of seriousness in her eyes, she gave a glance and reached over, gently placing her hand on mine. "I hear Ferrari's are really nice, Daddy," she said. "I'll bet you'd like a Ferrari more than another Jeep."

A moment of silence passed between us. She gave a grin.

"I'm on to you," I said, pulling into the driveway. She didn't respond, but continued her half smile, grabbed her backpack, and hopped from the Jeep.

"Hey, Harrison!" I heard her call through the front door just as it was closing behind her. "When I start driving, Daddy said my first car will be a Ferrari!"

She's fresh into her ninth year of life, but I already predict Evelyn will be the CEO of a major corporation. She's an analyst. She's a planner. She's a goal-setter and a go-getter. She keeps all of these traits harnessed and working in time for finding a way through just about anything—like a team of horses pulling the carriage of ambition. I'd say she epitomizes the Greek tragedian Euripides when he wrote, "Slight not what's near through aiming at what's far." One needs only to consider the conversation I just shared, which began with the eldest brother driving a decomposing Ford Explorer and ended with the youngest tooling around in a ride fit for Magnum P.I.

There are others like her, and thankfully they're flexing the muscle of determination in the whiskey business. Bobby Finan and the virtuous folks at Tommyrotter are among them. Never having met any of them, I'm comfortable making this assumption and admitting to its verity while taking in a dram of their Triple Barrel American Whiskey. It betrays their communal wit.

The nose of this edition is ambitiously energetic, more so than you might first expect. Don't take too deep a breath. Take your time.

Do it gently. If you do, you'll get nearly equal portions of walnut nougat and dark, deeply roasted coffee. If you don't, you'll catch a medicinal snap that could put you off before you get a chance to actually begin.

The palate is as determined as the nose, except now there's no controlling its pace. It breezes through in Ferrari fashion, turning heads and generously doling out sweet cream, maybe a tad bit of honey, charred toast, and something that reminded me of a dry merlot.

The medium finish is reminiscent of the coffee in the nosing, but now it's far warmer and peppered with allspice.

I like it, and it has me thinking…

On second thought, if Evelyn isn't eventually a CEO, I'm pretty sure she's going to be the first of the four children to do time for the highest grossing Ponzi scheme in history. I mean to say, she has incredible skills, and my sincerest hope is that like the folks at Tommyrotter, she'll choose to use them for good and not evil.

TRAVERSE CITY WHISKEY CO., AMERICAN CHERRY EDITION, BATCH 006, 35%

I'll need one for my duck.

"When I get older," Evelyn said unprompted at the breakfast table, "I'm going to get a motorcycle."

"Really?" I asked, not knowing why the thought came to her mind. "I used to have a motorcycle," I added to the conversation. "But I sold it before Momma and I got married."

"Why?"

"She didn't really like it, and I wanted to make her happy."

"You did?"

"Yeah. And I also needed the money to help pay for our wedding."

"Oh," she said, giving a look to show she was pondering my words. "Well," she began again, "when I get a motorcycle, I'm going to get one with a sidecar."

"A sidecar?" I asked, although my questioning was purely rhetorical. Based on the experience with her mother that I'd shared the moment prior, I expected her answer to be one designed to include her future husband in her two-wheeled adventures.

"Yep. I want a motorcycle with a sidecar."

"Why a sidecar?"

"For my duck," she said plainly.

"Your duck?"

"Yes. I'll need one for my duck."

"You lost me," I added just as plainly and took a sip of my coffee. "I don't know where you're going with this."

"That's okay," she said, putting her hand on mine. "You'll probably be dead before any of this happens, anyway."

And there you have it. Except this time, instead of the little girl's yarn of thinking making a single twist, it made two. She's getting a duck, and I'll be dead before it happens. Both of these declarations were unexpected.

I've learned to expect the unexpected from all of my kids. Every time I think one thing will happen, something entirely different transpires. It's often the same in the world of whiskey, which ended up being the case with the Traverse City Whiskey Company's American Cherry Edition. I expected this lower proof dram to be a syrupy disappointment, perhaps only suitable as a dessert drink for newbies attempting the nightlife in the whiskey's namesake city. But with each phase of the conversation, there were twists in its story, and each was surprisingly pleasant.

With the cork on the table, a nosing straight from the bottle gives in to expectations—thick, sugary cherries. Nothing but cherries. A moment in the Glencairn and a little bit of Bourbon spice arrives on the scene. This was unexpected. At such a low ABV, I expected nothing more than the smell of artificially candied water. But it wasn't. It was just lively enough to remind you that it's whiskey.

I experienced the same with the palate. With the first sip, the cherries rose up and attacked my tongue like troops storming a beachhead. But in a moment's notice, the candied fruits faded and gave way to a more prominent troupe of subtle oak spices and salt. Again, I was surprised by this turn, primarily because it took what could have been an over-the-top sweet and brought it more into balance.

The finish is a bit sharp, medium in length, and in its initial departure, leaves behind a tang confirming that flavoring was added. But again, as a secondary stage ensues, there's a memory of the Bourbon spices from the nose and palate. It speaks to discussions on barrels and aging rather than so-called infusions. This certifies the dram's worthiness for exploration by more than just the nightlife seekers.

Now, looking back over what I've written, I'm startled. I rarely side with flavored drams such as this American Cherry Edition. Knowing this, I'll bet a good number of my readers are equally astonished, as well.

That's okay. You let me have my occasional Traverse City Whiskey Company cherry whiskey and I'll keep my mouth shut about the duck in your sidecar. That is, if I'm even alive to see it.

Two James Spirits, Grass Widow, Straight Bourbon Whiskey, 45.5%

Superior they said never gives up her dead...

L ake Superior was enraged.

With venomous fury never before seen by such a tested crew, she spit three-story waves and leveled steely blows against the hull of the S.S. Edmund Fitzgerald.

"Captain," John McCarthy, the First Mate, said in pale-faced terror, "the witch is hitting us at fifty knots." His words were unbelievable. Had he been known to the crew as anything less than a moral sailor, one who preached the joys of marriage to all twenty-eight others aboard before each red light temptation in every port of the Great Lakes, they'd have disregarded his reading as poorly placed humor.

"This is the Fitzgerald," Captain McSorely said, attempting to instill calm. "She can take it." But as he clutched the radio's microphone tightly, holding it to his chest, he was betrayed by white knuckles against the midnight blue of his coat.

Just beyond the bridge windows, the S.S. Anderson—a sister freighter that only a few hours before was behind them, but had now taken the lead through the storm—her rig lights were fading as the distance between the two vessels increased. Her captain, Jesse Cooper, knew well that McSorley and his crew had lost communication and were without radar, so he did all he could to preserve his own while keeping within sight. And yet, with each swipe of the Fitzgerald's sixty-inch wiper blades, the bridge windows were doubly washed by Superior's thick sprays. The Anderson was a blur, and she faded more and more into black.

Like a lion stalking a herd, the lake was choosing. Its eyes were set upon the Fitzgerald. The freighter was sickly, and the predator knew it.

When the last and tiniest gleam of the Anderson was swept away by a thirty-five foot wave crashing over the port bow, it was then that a midship crossbeam rocketed its rivets and the superstructure began to buckle. The surrounding steel gave a low moan as the ship twisted between the rising and falling of the lake's indignation.

"Captain!" a crewman threw open the bridge door and shouted. "A railing and two of the vents are gone," he despaired, leaning over and resting his palms on his knees. "And now four hatches have blown—from the deck down to cargo. They've been ripped from their frames! The Fitz is taking on water!"

"Keep with the pumps," McSorely said, steadying his gaze against the hurricane blackness. "She'll hold as long as we need 'er."

Another crewman followed behind the first. "Sir," he said, trying to catch his breath, "we've been running the pumps. But now the generators are underwater and the pumps are failing."

"Captain," McCarthy said, stepping forward to put his hand on McSorely's shoulder. "Without the pumps, we'll sink," he whispered respectfully. "We need to make toward land." He looked to the terrified men and then back to the Captain. "If you put us leeward," he said, "this north wind will carry us to Whitefish Point. If we make it to the point, we may have a chance."

"If we do," McSorely returned with a poised, but equally quiet hush, "we'll run aground in the shallows." Leaving the microphone to dangle and sway with the waves, he leaned into the conversation. "I know those waters, John. The shallows begin a quarter-mile offshore, and with twenty-six thousand tons of ore in the Fitz's belly, she'll take those shallows much sooner." Meeting his friend's eyes, "Can you swim a half mile in a storm like this?"

"No, sir."

"Then we need to keep our heading and make for Whitefish Bay," the Captain continued. Turning his attention to the other crew members, he called out, "The north shore of the bay will cut the November Witch in half. She won't take us if we can just get to the bay." He reached for the swinging transmitter, snatching it midair from an upswing. He dropped it into its slot like a gunslinger dropping his gun into its holster. "Our communications are down," he said. "But I've made this trip a hundred times. I'll get us through to the bay. Also, Captain Cooper and the boys on the Anderson know we're right behind them. They'll get there first, and they'll make sure folks are ready and waiting for both us and our haul."

It was then that he did what captains do—he worked to inspire courage.

"And I'll bet they'll have some Two James Spirits whiskey already poured, maybe even the Grass Widow edition—three fingers for each of us—or as much as we want through the rest of the night."

"Aye, Captain," McCarthy relented. Even though he was never much for anything except communion wine, he knew to follow the Captain's lead. "I hear the nose of the Grass Widow is a dandy one, too—filled with Bourbon barrel spices and the warm pie crusts any of your grandmothers would make in the fall."

"And a sip," the Captain interrupted, "well, just know that it's worth every bit of terror these gales can muster." By their eyes, he could see the men's spirits starting to rekindle, and so he kept on. "Men, a sip holds a mere breeze of cinnamon and wood spice kissing red Michigan grapes. And those grapes—warmed, ripe—probably picked from a vine on the peninsula's tip near Old Mission Lighthouse, picked by your favorite girl on a sunlit afternoon. I've eaten those grapes, men, and like you, I know there're none so fine."

"But the finish," the First Mate added, "it's there that hope becomes gladness. It's there in the short fade that you find yourself ready for a new day, a new challenge, a new witch to come up and out of these lakes we know so well."

"So bring it on," McSorely said, giving a growl and tipping his hat to the handful of crewmen. "We aren't meant to drown here. Fifteen more miles to the bay. Fifteen more miles till we drown in a dram of the Grass Widow!"

"Aye, Captain!" the others hollered, the thought of safe harbor and a full glass of Detroit Bourbon in hand stirring them to action.

"No one goes on deck till the bay," the Captain called to the last of the crewmen through the door. "And put a man at every remaining hatch. Make them as secure as you know how and you'll get your whiskey."

The sailor gave a nod to the Captain and a hopeful glance to McCarthy. This was the last they'd see of each other in this life.

On November 10, 1975, sometime around 7:00 PM, Cooper radioed McSorely with the hopes that the Fitzgerald's communication capabilities had been restored, and to ask the condition of the ship and her crew. Much to his surprise, Captain

McSorely's voice could be heard through the static responding assertively and finally, "We're holding our own."

Moments later, the ship broke apart and Lake Superior swallowed every hopeful man on board—all twenty-nine sailors wishing for a sip from a widow—destined to be widow-makers instead.

TWO JAMES SPIRITS, JOHNNY SMOKING GUN, 43.5%

It's the dad's job to clean up the puke.

The Florida sun was well situated in its midday position. With no clouds to be seen, it was hot. In another vacation home, two doors down and across the street, something was stirring—a raucous bout of shouting that signaled a tortured situation.

"Sounds like a fight's getting started," I whispered, eyes wider than before.

"Do you think so?" Jen whispered in return, covering her mouth with concern. "Oh, I hope not."

In a silent glide, I made my way to the other end of our swimming pool and lifted my eyes above the deck, just enough to peer through the lanai and see that the front door of the home was open.

"What are you doing?" Jen asked with fretful insistence.

"I'm just looking to see what's going on," I replied quietly.

"They'll see you!"

"No, they won't," I said, sending a splash back to her.

I could see that the front door of the home was open with a woman standing in the entryway. She was facing her opposition with a volume equal to his.

"You have to do it!" she insisted, arms crossed in defiance.

"But I didn't even go!" came an angry shout. "And I warned you it would happen!"

"I don't care!" she hollered. "I'm not going to do it! I can't! I just can't!"

The verbal jousting continued for a few minutes more before the man inside finally yielded. Stomping through the doorway and out to the SUV parked in the driveway, he made his way around the vehicle, opening each of its doors before finally taking a few steps back in a posture of self-defense.

At first I thought he was preparing for some wildlife to lunge out—like a wasp. Or maybe a puma. But his pause was only momentary, and in an instant, he tucked his hand up into his shirt and covered his mouth and nose. Circling the car, he reached into each of the passenger areas and tossed its contents into the front yard. It wasn't long before he stumbled backward again as if to reassume his defensive posture, except this time he hunched over, and with his hands planted on his knees for support, he gave thick coughs that teetered near the edge of choking.

It was then that I knew the situation.

"Oh man," I said, my words laced with terror.

"What is it?" Jen asked.

"I think he's cleaning up puke," I replied, unblinking and starting a lazy drift back to the other side of the pool only to make a half circle and return to my previous perch. "Yeah, I think he's cleaning up puke in that very hot car."

For the next twenty minutes, this lonely father traveled back and forth through the front door of the home, each time carting a different supply—a bucket, garbage sacks, various cleaning supplies, and finally a vacuum cleaner.

"I feel his pain," I said to my wife as she started to chuckle. "Jobs like this really do take two guns. I almost feel like I should go and help him."

"Maybe you should," Jen said unabashedly.

"Because when there's puke on the scene," I continued, "I'm the guy who wades in to clean it up."

"Yes, you are," she said, remaining stone faced.

And she's right. When it comes to the dirtiest of jobs in our household, especially ones that involve virally potent body fluids jetting from our children's various orifices onto carpets and sinks and beds and bouncy seats, I'm the guy. And it doesn't matter if I'm stricken with the flu, either. I'm the lone gunman in the fight because I'm the only one who can handle the gore.

To provide a maximum example, I remember a time about ten years ago when our oldest sent a spray down the side of his bed and out about five feet across the carpet. Half asleep, he walked through it to our bedroom to tell us he'd thrown up. I'd already been up managing my own puking and had just returned to bed. Jen started gagging even as he told us what had happened. I asked him where and how much, and he said on his floor and that it was only a little bit. When I followed him to his room, it was easy enough to discover the location of ground zero, and not only because of the trail of puke prints he'd made on his way to our room—which I'd slimed through, as well—but because there was, in fact, not a little, but a lot. And because the outer edges of the human muck pond blended into the carpeting so well in the dim light, I managed a few steps into its shoreline before realizing it.

By the time I'd even gotten started cleaning up the mess, I was covered in it. Even in my exhaustion, I cleaned it up alone—his bedroom, the hallway, my bedroom, the boy—and then I bathed myself.

The guy across the way seemed to be having the same lonely trouble, except I'm guessing that the exceptional heat was amplifying the odor and causing him to choke back his own unexpected reflex. I'm also guessing that his wife had already traveled some distance with the scent, was at her wits end, and just wanted to get away from it. Still, her husband muscled through. Good for him. Sure, two guns would have been better, but he was already proving his mettle. He didn't need me. And now was not my time, anyway. I was watching in hygienic safety from the pool with a whiskey nearby.

By the way, that is, in fact, the key to any such effort as was unfolding before me. A man can set anything in order with a dram of decent whiskey in hand to sniff and sip. The sniffing abates any smells and the sip wages war against any microbe-sized bodily invaders.

I live by this practice, and it works. And in this particular instance, I'd have suggested a whiskey I added most recently to my collection—the Johnny Smoking Gun edition from Two James Spirits in Detroit.

Meant to compliment Japanese cuisine, which includes the spoiled sushi I'm supposing that the neighboring wife and children ate on their way home to dad, the Johnny Smoking Gun is a stranger breed of whiskey, most certainly giving over pieces of the Orient.

The nose offers barely a hint of smoke and sour citrus. The palate is a weird but wonderful jab of sweet tea, honey, and mild oranges. I cannot over-emphasize the Oriental nature of this dram. The folks at Two James did some serious work in devising a whiskey that would absolutely serve well to wash down yakitori and a side of warmed udon.

And the finish is sublime—sensual in its sweetness and careful in its shorter burn.

Now, I should clarify that it's not that Jen, my lovely wife, doesn't want to help in times of vomitous crisis. I know she does. It's just that she can't. Like so many in this world, the sights, sounds, and smells of such things cause her to gag so much that by requiring her assistance, I'm setting myself up for double the damage. With that, it's better to just go it alone and let her keep her distance. She can take the kids' temperatures, give them baths, and make the toast and chicken noodle soup. I'll handle it when it all comes back up.

VALENTINE'S DISTILLERY COMPANY, MAYOR PINGREE SMALL BATCH RYE WHISKEY, BATCH 002, 45%

Bedazzler supplies are in aisle one.

I walked into the store, and much like that first step from the plane onto the soil of a foreign land, its culture washed over me like a rogue wave. It was as if, suddenly, I'd grown claustrophobic.

My breathing became heavy. My heart began to race. Even more so did my hands become sweaty when Jennifer offered with a smile, "We're going to need a shopping cart," insinuating that we'd be traversing each of the aisleways of this strange terrain in search of these and those things of all natures and styles, none of which could be carried in a smaller tote basket.

The store? Michaels Arts and Crafts—a fully-provisioned supply house for those with the desire and skills for precision home décor. When it comes to makin' stuff, you name it and this place has it.

Got any titanium templates for making Kim-Jung-Un-shaped paper weights from molten steel? The Christmas

party for the Socialist Club is tonight, and I don't want
to show up with nothing to share.

> Sure do. Aisle ten. And by the way, what time is
> the party?

Say, where might I find what I need to make a manger,
but one that's exactly thirteen millimeters tall?

> Aisle four has all of our miniature manger
> supplies.

Excuse me, where might I find your paintable glass
geckos?

> We have a wide variety of paintable Reptilia
> over on aisle eight's endcap.

Hi, um, I'd like to use my Bedazzler on my cat, and—

> —All of our Bedazzler supplies are in aisle one.

Oh, no, I already have all the bedazzling gems I need, I
just need to know what kind of lacquer I should dip him
into after I'm done. I want it to be harder for him to
scratch them off.

> Gotcha. All fur shellac and polyurethane is over
> in aisle six.

It wasn't until I saw what I thought was a rather unique flower
pot—which in the end, turned out to be a product called a "scene
garden"—that I thought to myself, *This place needs to change its
name*. As far as the name change idea goes, I was thinking we could
go from this:

To this:

Anyway, a scene garden is, essentially, an elongated flower pot that people fill with a base element—like gravel, sand, dirt, puke, or whatever you feel like filling it with. The pot is then arranged with tiny adornments that portray a scene, such as an oceanfront affair with little plastic people resting in chaise lounges beneath beach umbrellas and surrounded by palm trees. Maybe there's even a little guy on a tiny surfboard floating in the basin of water serving as the ocean. Really, a scene garden can be anything—a family having a picnic, a fairy garden, a shark attack, a bar fight. Just know that no matter what you choose, Michaels will have the stuff you need to make those free hours in your day fly right by toward a successful conclusion.

They have everything a bored-but-crafty person might need.

At first nosing of the Mayor Pingree Rye Whiskey, I got the sense that the Valentine's Distilling Company—a native to Detroit, Michigan—found time in its busy schedule to stop by Michaels to pick up a few key ingredients from somewhere between the heat pens used for pyrography (wood burning art) and the edible-but-nearly-tasteless birthday cake sheets printed with a little girl's favorite Disney princess character. To translate, I took from the dram a mild-but- singed sniff of oak, as well as a slight hint of something candied. A second sniff affirms that whatever is sending up the candy smell is far too thin to be of any consequence. It may even have been the perfume emanating from the lady in the next aisle over. Yeah, the one accompanied by the Shih Tzu dressed like Santa Claus. Cute? Nope. Those tiny glossed eyes aren't natural. The pint-size creature is merely holding back its little doggie tears.

The palate is an altogether different visit to the all-giving craft store. There's an initial creaminess to the whiskey, one that delivers what seems to be an attempt at typical rye components, such as spice and honey. I say "attempt" because along the way to the checkout, I'm guessing the formulators stopped by an artificial flavoring aisle and dropped in a few waxy morsels—compounds meant more for scented candles than food or drink. In particular, I tasted something chemically floral. If I had to say what candle I may have been nibbling, I'd guess it was lilac or something. Yeah, probably lilac.

The medium finish is crisp enough, giving over a nip of allspice and oak. Unfortunately, just as those two characteristics are peaking, the finality turns a tad sour. Once again, I'm guessing it's whatever candle scent found itself in the mix.

I wish I could say more—especially since these guys are from my neck of the whiskey woods—but in the end, the Mayor Pingree Rye is only a scene garden. It's a crafty effort at representing what others have offered and experienced in reality.

VERY OLD BARTON, KENTUCKY STRAIGHT BOURBON WHISKEY, 45%

The kids need therapy.

Jennifer believes that my children will one day require therapy because of the stories I tell.

"That's a very hurtful thing to say," I say, gruffly. *But you're probably right*, my inner voice whispers, taking her side and recalling that just today my son Harrison, having a general nervousness when it comes to dolls, asked about the movie *Child's Play*.

"It's about a serial killer named Chucky whose soul ends up in a doll," I explained. "If I remember correctly, he's trying to transfer his soul into a little boy, and in the meantime, runs around killing the people trying to stop him."

"That's stupid," Harrison said, doing his best not to betray his uneasiness.

"Of course it's stupid," I continued. "That's not how it works in real life."

"Whaddya mean?" the boy asked.

"Do you know how sometimes the cashier at Walmart will ask me if I want an extended warranty on an item I might be buying?"

"Yeah," he said. "That happened when you bought that external hard drive."

"Well," I kept on, "they're supposed to do something like that whenever you buy a doll."

"They are?"

"Yeah," I said, my voice steady and my face plain. "They'll usually ask if you want the doll possessed or unpossessed."

"Wha—?"

"Seriously. You have the option of getting a plain doll, or for a little more nighttime excitement, you can upgrade to the possession pack. For an extra twenty bucks, the store manager will put a curse on the doll before you take it home."

"Are any of my dolls cursed, Daddy?" Evelyn lobbed from the living room.

"No, honey," I turned and called back. "None of yours are possessed—at least I don't think so. Although I wasn't with Momma when she bought some of them, so I can't say for sure."

"I think one might be," my almost-always-reliable partner in crime volleyed. "I think I saw one of my Barbies floating in the door of my closet the other night."

"Was she keeping you up last night?" I asked. "If so, I can do an exorcism on her tonight before you go to bed."

"That's okay," the little girl replied. "She said she wasn't after me."

"Did she say who she was after?"

"It sounded like she said 'Larry,' but I was tired and I don't think I heard her right."

I turned back to Harry, but he was already gone. I fully expect to find all of Evelyn's Barbies in the trash tonight.

Foolish boy. Everyone knows that when you throw a demon-possessed doll into the trash, it always turns up under your bed a little dirtier and a lot angrier.

Therapists. Seemingly demon-possessed things. Trash. Dirtier and angrier. Unfortunately, these things not only pinpoint all of the things my wife adores when it comes to my off-the-cuff storytelling, but they are reminiscent of my time with the Very Old Barton Kentucky Straight Bourbon. This particular whiskey is a special kind of deceptive unpleasantness.

With the twist cap removed and two fingers worth in my glass, a sniff suggests that the Walmart store manager may be nearby casting subterranean, but enticing, magic. At first, the scent is sweetly pleasant, offering something of vanilla and maple-butter. A drop of water—which in my case, I'm guessing must have been blessed—causes the sweetness to turn sour.

But the truest struggle between heaven and hell begins with the first sip.

A horde of sorts attempts to present the dram as endearingly sweet, setting before their victim the possibility of carmeled citrus. But that hellfire-quenching drop of holy water reveals the whiskey's more sinister intent—a sputtering plume of the leftovers from the last picnic in Hades, which included charred corn and an imbalanced scald of barrel spice topped with pepper.

The finish is fairly quick, which is surprising. In any of my dealings with Lucifer, I can usually count on him to put up a more formidable fight. But this time around, he gives a swift bite of alcohol and then calls it quits before the bout gets any further. I guess he already knows there's no tricking a man who's already attuned to his ways.

I mean, consider the scarring—*eh-hem*, creative—stories I tell my children. Which reminds me, I suppose "Larry" sounds a lot like "Harry."

I'd better go check the trash. I've already thrown away so many of the kids' toys just for fun, I can't afford to have the kids doing it, too.

WILD TURKEY, KENTUCKY STRAIGHT RYE WHISKEY, 40.5%

Moldy oranges never killed anyone.

B enjamin Disraeli—a man rarely discussed, and in many ways, often underestimated—once remarked to a colleague, saying, "Desperation is sometimes as powerful an inspirer as genius."

He's right. A man will do what he must when desperate.

Take, for example, the man who has forgotten his lunch, has no money, and knows the only scraps in the church refrigerator are those of an ancient bag of carrot sticks, an even older mound of oranges, and a partially eaten chocolate cake left over from a special celebration the previous Sunday. This man will lay aside all manner of civility in exchange for a paper plate and plastic fork, and he'll pretend it's his birthday. Of course he'll celebrate in the darkened corner of a barren cafeteria.

Or consider the man who's been asked a question by his bride, and the query is one that begins with such words as "Tell me the truth." Terrified of revealing the truths of his mind and desperate for a way of escape, this man may attempt a sudden redirection of the conversation by sharing that earlier in the day, he ate the last and final strip of chocolate cake in the refrigerator at work in its entirety. Desperation settles for the reprimand of lesser force.

But what about the man who finds himself in need of writing a whiskey review for the masses, but again and alas, he is cashless and cannot afford the edition he'd prefer to engage? In such situations, the desperate but diligent man willingly ventures to a bottom shelf dram and hovers there among the $20 stratum, eventually settling on one while thinking to himself, *You never know. It might be good.*

Admitting nothing regarding the first two scenarios, I'd be more than happy let rise from my shoulders the burdensome truth of the last. Yes, I bought a bottle of Wild Turkey Kentucky Straight Rye Whiskey, and just so you know, it was worth the shallow wad of loose dollars I found in a freshly laundered pair of pants, each of the quarters I'd stored away in the cup holder in the van, and all of the dimes, nickels, and pennies in the canister in my office. At right around $19, my hopeful contemplations proved true. This is a fairly decent bottle of booze.

The nose of this rye meets one's reasonable expectations of spice and wood char. There's also a little bit of something that reminded me of sitting in a pine forest while eating a caramel apple. Not too bad.

The palate is not as enjoyable, and I say this because even as I could sit and smell it for a while, a sip from the whiskey packs very little punch. It's barely reliable in its trade. It almost seems like a watered down version of what it was in a former life—as though the distillery manager became desperate to fill a much larger order and found himself turning the ABV dial from 43% to 40.5%. Desperation, as we've already considered, will cause a man to take drastic action. Still, the action resulted in a whiskey that's not entirely too thin to experience the rye spice and caramel foretold in the nose.

The finish is short. Like the space between the floor and the shelf upon which this edition resides.

Still, at $19, I have to admit that this is a pretty good buy, especially for a hunter/gatherer of loose change experiencing a dry season. With that, I suppose I can continue to focus my scavenging efforts toward the bottom whiskey shelf while praying for Sunday morning celebrations involving cake.

WILD TURKEY, LONGBRANCH, KENTUCKY STRAIGHT BOURBON, SMALL BATCH, 43%

I'll let it go because I'm assuming you were drunk.

For us non-celebrity folks, I think that Facebook sets the cap at 5,000 when it comes to how many friends you can claim. At the time of this writing, I have about 2,600. Wait, let me say that again. I *had* about 2,600. I just spent most of the morning unfriending more than half of them.

I'm somewhat ashamed to say that I felt a little like Thanos, and I liked it. Almost.

The reward in the exercise is that I'm down to a much more realistic number. Even so, I'm hoping that I can cut into that one, too. In my opinion, it still feels a little too big. I just don't know most of the people and I'm not so sure they'd even notice my absence from their news feed, anyway.

"What criteria did you use for jettisoning these digital relationships?" you ask.

Well, first of all, you need to know that it's really no big deal if you didn't make the cut. It's not like anyone was on a waiting list to be my friend. I just needed to make the list a little more manageable and a little less stressful. But since you asked, I did employ a few critical filters.

For one, if you are a huge, over-the-top fan of a few political positions in particular, you were one of the first to go. Beyond that, if you had a tendency toward excessive foul language in your posts, you're probably gone. If over half of your posts are scantily clad, narcissistic selfies, I excused you from my room. I'm no master of grammar, but if you've shown a consistent lack of knowledge regarding the simpler things, like the usages of there, their, and they're, you've probably been banished—unless, of course, you are one of my friends from overseas. You got a pass on this one.

These types of things played into my decision-making.

"But, by doing this, aren't you lessening your own opportunities for helpful dialogue regarding some very important issues?"

Are you being serious? Facebook is no committee table at the United Nations, my friend. It isn't about dialogue. It never was. When it comes to the information being shared, it's about the distribution of agreeable things that make for friends. Unfortunately, even that has become an incredibly fragile premise. When it comes to differences of opinion, it has become a field for planting snarky bombs and throwing digital punches. I mean, honestly, when was the last time you got into a discussion on Facebook about a casual or critical issue and found yourself able to convince or be convinced by an opposing side?

Never, that's when. But still, it gets worse.

Even within the relatively like-minded circles in which I swim, I'll sometimes find myself paddling with blood-thirsty predators. For example, I just viewed a post from a kindly Lutheran friend who shared a non-denominational pastor's video about keeping children with their parents in worship instead of sending them along to something called "children's church." I've been writing about this very topic for over twenty years, and so the video was refreshing to see, even though I don't fully appreciate the person in it. But what's interesting is that my friend had to preface the shared video with a defense that she is staunchly Lutheran and is by no means a supporter of non-denominational theology. Why did she do this? By posting the video, she was merely expressing a gladness that the cookie cutter hipster in the video had finally decided to swim upstream toward truth in this particular issue. This is a good thing, right?

But her words betrayed the need to prepare for a typicality. She'd let out a little blood by agreeing with a premise from a representative opponent, and she felt the need to have her spear gun at the ready lest any sharks be lurking in the Facebook reef.

And of course, they were.

It used to be that I'd preface certain discussions in the whiskey world in the same way, but I don't anymore. Over the years I've learned that while so many in the whiskey fabric have differing opinions on so many things, very few in this particular part of the digital ocean are ever willing to let differing opinions about most things be the absolute reason for cutting ties. It pretty much takes a stingingly venomous rant against a person as an individual, and even then, the target of the attack is more likely to put it aside until a later date, assuming in the moment that you were drunk. It sort of seems like we're all just cruising around on rafts, each with its own wet bar, and we're lifting our drams of the moment in salute to others as they float by.

I like that. In fact, if I was considering deleting you from my list of Facebook friends for any of the previously mentioned reasons, it's likely that I relented because you are a part of the fabric and you get the whole "friend" thing.

And so the dram I lift in salute to you today is one that I believe is worthy of your time, and it's one that I'd be happy to send along to you when we drift past one another in our rafts: The Longbranch Small Batch Kentucky Straight Bourbon from Wild Turkey.

Having never been a big fan of the standard release from Wild Turkey, the Longbranch is an exceptional gem delivered from this well-known distillery. With a nose of cinnamon atop a sliver of pumpkin pie, the Longbranch teases a deeper well of flavors just below the vessel. And it delivers.

With individual sips, the palate calls up variant levels of spiced cream and vanilla—some samples peppered a little more than others. There's also a fairly generous helping of citrus, barrel char, and salt. These carry over into a milder finish, one that makes for an easy afternoon down the lazy river.

Again, I like that. I like it almost as much as Thanos-like mass deletions in the virtual universe of social media.

Yellowstone Select, Kentucky Straight Bourbon, 2017, 46.5%

I want eggs.

"We're having breakfast for dinner tonight," Jen said with her back to me at the stove. She had an earbud in one ear and was listening to something on her phone. The kids threaded between us with table settings. Glancing over her shoulder, she offered, "You can have eggs and sausage, or you can have those." She used her elbow to point to the toaster and a box of thawing waffles.

"Eggs sound good," I said, pulling my chair from the table and taking a seat. A plate and a fork were already in place.

"Okay," she affirmed, moving to the toaster. "How many waffles do you want?"

"No, that's alright," I replied. "I think I'll have some eggs tonight."

"Okay," she said, pulling a package of the waffles from the box. I watched the bag become fogged from the warmth of the stove as she opened it. She took out four waffles, dropped them into the toaster slots, and lowered the lever until it clicked into place.

"Honey," I said with a warmth to match the kitchen, "do you want me to make my own eggs?"

"No," she answered resolutely. "I've got this."

The kids started to giggle.

"Is the table set?" she called to the little ones. All responded in the affirmative. "Then bring your plates over so I can serve this stuff up." They each filed to her with a plate in hand. "Bring Daddy's plate, too. And, Harrison, you get the syrup from the pantry for his waffles."

Harrison turned to look at me. I looked at him. We remained locked in a stare even as he made his way to the darkened pantry and emerged once again with a bottle of Aunt Jemima.

Handing the bottle of syrup to his bustling mother just as she was retrieving a portion of melted butter from the microwave for pouring onto the waffles, Harrison gently urged, "Isn't Daddy having eggs?"

"That's what I made him," she said. Just then, the waffles popped up from the toaster. She put them on the plate in Harrison's hands and then poured a little bit of the melted butter into a good number of the tiny squares. "Here, give him his waffles." Looking to me, she added, "I put some butter on them. You can do your own syrup."

Harrison turned to face his father. The other children stepped aside, their eyes wide and pairing with the butter-soaked waffles. They gave momentary glances to the young boy charged with delivering them to a man who didn't want them.

At the end of his carefully reverent pace, Harrison set the waffles in front me and said, "Daddy, here are your eggs."

"Thank you, Harry," I said, patting the boy's shoulder. "And those are some fine looking eggs. Now, can you do something else for me?"

"Sure."

"Fetch my phone, dear boy."

"Why?"

"Because I'm going to call an ambulance for your mother. I think she may be stroking out."

The children started to laugh, all of them looking to their mother.

"What's so funny?!" Jen said, pulling the earbud from her ear and turning.

"Daddy kept saying he wanted eggs," Evelyn said tittering, "but you made him waffles."

"No, he didn't," she insisted. "He said he wanted four waffles!"

"Harrison," I interrupted, "get my phone, please. Joshua, get started on cleaning up the kitchen once everyone's done with dinner. Evelyn, get your mother's coat for her. It's chilly outside tonight. Madeline, before we go, I'll trade you for your eggs."

Now, I tell this story not necessarily to reveal a mother of four's occasional insanity, but rather to highlight one of those times when you were expecting one thing but got something else.

The Yellowstone Select Kentucky Straight Bourbon is a whiskey as such. Although, I should say that my expectations were reversed in this particular instance. A relatively unknown whiskey to me, I wasn't necessarily expecting much, and yet what I received was pure joy. In fact, I dare say that this may be one of the best bourbons you'll find. I am certainly willing to say that I count it as a favorite among the very few I would consider most worthy.

The nose of this delightful dram is one of cherry coke and a crisp tag of wood spice. The palate is a warmed crème brûlée topped with dark cherries, a mild dosage of white pepper and allspice, and a splinter of rye-kissed oak. Yes, it is. Don't doubt me.

The finish allows a medium moment for gathering all of the sweeter notes and well-tempering them by the spices. In one sense,

I suppose the only unfortunate thing about this whisky is that, like all other whiskies, it has to have a finish. A finish signals a sip's end. And I don't want it to end.

Just as I don't want waffles. I want eggs.

IRELAND

JAMESON IRISH WHISKEY, CASKMATES IPA EDITION, 40%

The pizza tree is rather fruitful this year.

I heard that Play-Doh trademarked the scent of their product. My first thought was, *Can you really keep the smell of wet dirt all to yourself?*

I heard a few years back that the infamous jewelry company Tiffany's did the same thing with the color referred to as Robin's Egg Blue. Again, I'm surprised it was possible for a company to secure for itself the image of Cool Blue Gatorade mixed with whole milk.

A couple of days ago while sitting beside the pool on vacation, I was staring at what I think was a magnolia tree and reciting to myself the Ten Commandments and their meanings from Luther's *Small Catechism*. As a Lutheran pastor, I do this sometimes to keep these things sharp in my mind. If you are at all familiar with Luther's words in the first of the Six Chief Parts in this handy little volume, then you'll know that he first provides the biblical text for each commandment and then begins its meaning with the words, "What does this mean? We should fear and love God so that we do not…"

There, beside the pool, I remember thinking, *If Luther were writing in the 21st century, he probably would've offered something like: Honor your father and mother. What does this mean? We should fear and love God so that we do not take forty-five minute showers, leaving the room with water dripping from its ceiling and no hot water for mom and dad. Or how about this: You shall not bear false witness against your neighbor. What does this mean? We should fear and love God so that when our parents ask if we've cleaned our room we do not say something like, "Um, Yeah," which really means we just crammed everything, even the stuff that was in the right places, under the bed.*

I suppose I'm breaking the previous commandment relating to truth-telling when I share with you that my daughter asked how waffles were made and I told her that they grow like fungus on the sides of trees in the Everglades. When she asked about the syrup that goes on the waffles, I told her that we get it from the same trees that give us the waffles—which is why they go so well together.

"But isn't maple syrup made from maple trees?"

"Yes it is, honey. And maple trees grow in swampy regions like the Everglades…and Washington D.C."

"But don't we have a maple—"

"—Just eat your swamp tree fungus."

I'm sorry if my thought-wandering is annoying you. It annoys me, too, sometimes. It certainly keeps things interesting with my kids, although my wife would probably be able to use it successfully against me in court.

"Mrs. Thoma, why should I give custody of the children to you?" the magistrate would ask.

"Your honor," Jennifer might reply, "he tells them that garbage cans are predatory creatures that roam in the wetlands behind our house and that waffles grow on swamp trees in the—"

"—And pizzas, Momma," Harrison would chime in. "He said pizzas grow on trees, too."

"Is this true, Reverend Thoma?" the judge, turning to me, would ask.

"You know," I'd say resolutely, "I have a black vestment just like the one you're wearing. I got mine from C.M. Almy. Where'd you get yours? Although—and I'm just being honest—you should liven it up a little. The solo black might fly for trials during Lent, but beyond that, it's awfully—"

"—Bailiff, please remove this gentleman from the courtroom."

The Jameson Caskmates IPA edition is a little like what you just read. It has a heart for creativity, but as it shares its fanciful ideas, it does so by going from one thing to the next with only the slightest thread to tie it all together. It's somewhat unbalanced.

There's fruit in the nosing, but it's hard to tell what it is at first. My guess was oranges. But then I took a sip. It's definitely something from a citrus tree, but the tree is growing mutant oranges that look like pineapples and taste a little like kiwi and sea-salted potato chips. It's a confused tray of side dishes. For all I know, this strange tree also has waffles growing at its base.

There's a little bit of hops in there, betraying the IPA on the label, but not enough to convince a beer drinker that this is a viable alternative to his favorite home brews.

The finish is nice enough, lasting a little longer than what you might expect from a fruiter concoction, and then receding with mouthy hues of ginger, salt, and peppercorns.

Again, if you're at all familiar with *Luther's Small Catechism*, then you'll know that his explanation of the Ninth Commandment deals with coveting other people's possessions. After sipping this particular dram, I'm thinking that the reverend doctor might have scribed, "We should fear and love God so that we do not covet our neighbor's whiskies that aren't the Jameson Caskmates IPA edition…"

KILBEGGAN, SINGLE GRAIN IRISH WHISKEY, 86%

Here's to the fallen!

It was a whitewater fray of disposable rage played out among both young and old. Tears of victory and suffering streamed together among the portions of flesh floating in the swimming pool now stained red. Swim suits were tattered. Scarring imprints from a lightning-fast rubber ball adorned the faces and arms and backs of the contestants.

The Death Ball match had begun.

Perhaps you, the reader, do not know that Death Ball is an annual Thoma vacation-time contest into which only certain members from among the fittest in society may wade. (For more on Death Ball, be sure to visit pages 155 to 157 in *The Angels' Portion, Volume III.*) It is played in a swimming pool. And while it has very few rules, it requires great skill, monumental endurance, and the willingness to either receive death's stroke or bring it down upon others in order to possess a rubber ball.

Traditionally, a regulation sized death ball is between 18 and 20 inches in circumference, weighs approximately 10 ounces, is painted with the likenesses of Anna, Elsa, and Olaf from the movie "Frozen," and has a smooth texture for minimal gripping but maximum sting. A Death Ball match is comprised of two teams, each with three players of varying ages.

Just this year I've become aware of variations to the game, designed to help hopeful amateurs make it in the bigs. One minor league, called Mildly Hazardous Ball, produces some broken bones but is still slight in comparison to the true game. Another, Permanently Maimed Ball, sounds fierce, but it employs a rule called "kill begging" that gives a seriously mutilated player the option to beg for and receive a merciful death at the hands of his enemy. But to all true Death Ball players, these are but unthinkable, cowardly substitutes for the real thing. Death Ball has no room for the weak. No room for mercy. When you step into the pool, you're stepping into doom's lair to test your strength against its embrace. You will survive or die. That's it.

The whiskey world has similar categories. There are some whiskies that choose to reside in the training levels. There are others existing in more competitive realms. And there are, of course, the elite few that sit atop the highest shelves of whiskey spectacle. I'm thinking that the folks behind the Kilbeggan Single Grain Irish Whiskey are not only well familiar with Death Ball, but by their name they tip their hats to the "kill begging" rule of the second tier. By this, they place themselves no higher.

They do this honestly. This whiskey is good, but it's not good enough for Death Ball.

The nose of the Kilbeggan is piercingly light, which is to say that it throws its waftings of fruity vanillas and malt with a subtler and yet still more accurate skill than most. A first and second sniff will confirm that you're not dealing with a rookie.

It's upon the palate that the Kilbeggan shows its need for improvement before being allowed to ascend to the more glorious arenas. Its first shot is that of citrus—a concoction of syrupy oranges and lemons. A second spike delivers a swirl of caramel. Nice? Perhaps. The problem is that these candied flavors feel artificially imposed. I sure hope that was not the case, because as it is with high-stakes Death Ball, so it is in the stadiums of whiskey. Doping will most certainly get you disqualified, bringing nothing less than the ultimate shame.

The finish reminds you why the whiskey is in the second tier and not the third. It shows skill with a well-balanced and medium finish of the malt and vanilla from the nosing.

I would imagine that many might consider this a whiskey only suitable for mixers. I'd suggest it as a more than toast-able post-match dram with any surviving teammates.

> "Aye, here's to the fallen!" the team captain calls out. "May they sink to the pool's bottom in dignified glory!"
>
> And all the team replies, "Aye! To the bottom!"

I suppose the whiskey is worth keeping around. At $30 a smack, it's a far better buy than that budget team tattoo you got on your ankle after your first minor league match. Maybe for now, at least keep some in the medicine cabinet. When the editions get better, you'll want to move it into your collection. My guess is that the Kilbeggan distillery has what it takes to eventually play in the highest league. I say this because it managed to fashion distilled spirits for two hundred years before closing for about half a century. It got back on its feet in 2010 and started putting out drams again in 2014. In that sense, its innermost fibers are those of youthful desire paired to a longstanding pedigree. But for now, tier two is its place. Still, I don't think it will be long before we see its name measured by the same top-tier calibers of play only exhibited in the arenas of Death Ball.

PROPER NO. TWELVE, IRISH WHISKEY, 40%

She's an alien, I just know it.

Jennifer, my wife, has a secret. When she shared it with me, I was nearly traumatized beyond repair.

"Surely, you must be joking," I said, unwilling to believe her words. "It can't be true. Tell me it isn't true."

"It's true," she replied. "I've never eaten a Big Mac in my life."

"Never?!" I exclaimed with animated concern.

"Never," she said, speaking with a resoluteness to match.

"But the sign says they've served over ninety-nine billion people," I continued, my eyes still wide with disbelief. "That's like twelve times the number of people on the planet!" I shook my head. "I just sort of assumed you fit into that huge number," I said, despondently. "You know, assuming that you are an earthling, like the rest of us."

"I've never eaten a Big Mac. Ever."

"I wanna see your birth certificate and passport. Show me your papers, woman!"

"Shut up."

"No, seriously," I said. "Show 'em to me. I want to make sure you're documented. I need to confirm that I didn't marry a Russian spy or something."

"You're a dork," she said, walking away, disregarding my concern with an outstretched palm.

The whole conversation was troubling, and I wondered if, perhaps, my little ones were traveling the same un-American paths as their clandestine mother, who I can't even confirm is from earth let alone a citizen of these great United States. And so, the very next day, while Jennifer (who I'll now refer to as Agent X) was taking my two daughters to their horseback riding lessons, I took my son, Harrison, through the McDonald's drive-thru for lunch.

It was a test.

There at the menu board and microphone, I asked him if he'd like a Big Mac instead of his usual two-cheeseburger-and-fries meal.

"Sure," he said, the ease of his answer granting me relative certainty.

"I'll have two Big Macs," I spoke into the microphone, "two medium fries, and—"

"—I've never had a Big Mac before," Harrison said quietly to himself.

"What?!" I called out, turning to him in terror. "You, too?!"

"Sir," a voice came from the speaker. "Could you repeat that last part?"

"And two medium Cokes," I said, hitting the gas before I could hear my total.

"You've never had a Big Mac?" I pressed with a directness that caused the boy to become more attentive.

"No. I usually just get cheeseburgers with only ketchup."

"You know you're not an official citizen of America until you eat a Big Mac," I said, sternly.

"I'm not?"

"No, and if the authorities show up and find out that you've never had a Big Mac, you could get deported—or worse—they may try to feed you one, and your body rejects it, and then they lock you in a government lab and dissect you."

"Wha—?"

"—Yes. They'll send you back to your home country—or whatever planet your mother came from—but not before they try to figure out how you can subsist for so long without having ever eaten a Big Mac."

"But I was born here."

"Or so we were led to believe," I said, putting my hand to the side of my mouth and whispering so that the woman at the window couldn't hear me. "I don't think we can prove it. As far as I know, your mother forged your birth certificate."

"She did?"

"Look at the sign, Harry," I said, pointing to the McDonald's marquee. "Ninety-nine billion is a lot of people. You're in danger, friend. It could be that you're not really one of us."

"So, what do I do?"

"Our only hope is to feed you a Big Mac and see what happens. For one, United States immigration code states that if you eat a Big Mac, you are officially an American and you're due all privileges and protections. If you refuse to eat one, it could only be because you are French...or maybe from another world. And if you do eat one and your body rejects it, I'll do what I can to hide you for a little while, at least until we can figure out what to do. Either way, we'd better hurry home and get to it, son."

"Can I start eating before we get home?"

"Do it, man," I said. "Do it."

I paid the woman. She handed over the goods. We said a quick table prayer. I drove. He ate. By the time we got home, all was well. Harry had eaten his first Big Mac—and by the way, it was one with bacon on it, which is tantamount to affirming and blazing right past citizenship to being qualified for a seat in Congress.

With that, I was happy for my son, although I'll confess to sleeping with one eye open these days now that I know what I know. Agent X might try to cover her tracks and off me in my sleep.

Or lay alien eggs in my face.

Either way, the moral of the story is to pay attention. Know who—or what—is around you at all times. I don't mean to alarm you, but resident humanity is established through a proper order of proofs. We breathe air. We drink water. We eat Big Macs. So, if you see someone who his able to hold his or her breath under water for an unusually long period of time, be amazed. But if you meet someone who has never eaten a Big Mac, call the authorities. It could be a sign of alien probing. It could be that you've met an alien scout who is surveying our weaknesses before an invasion. And what's more, you never even knew they were here.

Which reminds me.

The Proper No. Twelve Irish Whiskey is anything but emblematic of proper order when it comes to the world of whiskies. I say this because when I popped the cork and poured the first dram, I gave it a nosing, but I really couldn't smell anything. Every whiskey has its proper proofs. I usually walk through these proofs in order—nose, palate, and finish. This one was somewhat alien to that process. It didn't have anything to nose. I even gave it to Agent X to sniff because I can pretty much count on a recoiling at every whiskey I set before her. But this time she just looked at me.

"I don't smell anything," she said. "Is this a Big Mac?"

"No, dear," I replied. "This is Irish whiskey. A Big Mac is a sandwich."

She's an alien, I just know it.

Anyway, what little I could draw from the whiskey was as bare as I've ever experienced. There were the faintest hints of vanilla and copper, but again, just barely, and not much else. A sip confirmed the vanilla, but it brought along with it a passing bit of fruit flesh that was just at the edge of discernible. I'd say it was a dish of ripened plums and well bruised apples.

The finish was medium in length—which is a generous description on my part. Incredibly airy, the only thing about the Proper No. Twelve that lingered past the short marker was the sense of alcohol and the sugary juice collecting at the bottom of the dish (which I'm guessing is copper) of fruits from the palate. It wasn't necessarily unpleasant, however it just wasn't emitting the proper proof one might need to verify this is indeed a whiskey at all.

I'm going to do a little searching into the history of the man behind this particular edition—Connor McGregor—the UFC fighter from Dublin. I'll nose around the internet a little and see if I can discern if he's one of the ninety-nine billion.

If not, then we'll know for sure why this whiskey is a little outside the boundaries of proper order.

WEST CORK, ORIGINAL IRISH WHISKEY, 40%

The moment was beautifully awkward.

Crossing the clothing store parking lot, my twelve-year-old daughter, Madeline, stepped into stride beside me and slid her hand into mine. Only slightly arched, her thin fingers barely gripped my palm. Her grasp was awkward. But it was beautifully awkward in that the gesture was unprompted.

We strolled along, and as we did, had I not kept hold, her hand would've fallen away. She was letting me lead. She was letting me do the holding—as if she were little again.

Once we arrived at the store's entrance, the sliding glass doors parted to reveal a busy row of clerks serving lengthy lines of back-to-school parents shepherding their own lambs—some of whom were teenage boys. Madeline gave a gentle tug. I knew why, but I didn't want to let her go. And yet, I did. The defectless moment, as easily as it had come, dissipated into the fluorescent noise of the crowded store.

Still, it was a moment I'll never forget.

It's not that I don't hold either of my daughters' hands, making this an otherwise odd occurrence. In fact, my youngest daughter,

Evelyn, is still found hurrying into such times with her father. Madeline, however, is becoming less inclined to offer herself this way, and so when it happens, it's most certainly intentional, and thereby affecting. It's in these moments with my children that I feel the weight of Marcus Aurelius' words when he meditated: "Some things are hurrying into existence, and others are hurrying out of it; and of that which is coming into existence part is extinguished."

A most unfortunate verity.

A few evenings later, I was stirred to recall the occurrence while reviewing a dram of the West Cork Original Irish Whiskey. I'm thinking it came to mind because, like that memorable instance in the parking lot with Madeline, the West Cork nestled in beside me and offered a most unexpected pleasantness.

With a gentle, almost dainty hand, the whisky is more than inviting. It's engaging. It reaches up and out of the Glencairn, brushing scents of malt, creamy vanilla, and citrus into the nose. With those same digits, its touch is soft to the palate, rendering the very same delights already teased.

The finish is short, leaving behind a fast-fleeting dash of peppered caramel and the sense of having enjoyed something that you wish was a little less temporary.

Like the short-lived days of a father who loves to hold his little girl's hand.

CANADA AND FRANCE

CROWN ROYAL, BLENDERS' SERIES, BOURBON MASH, 40%

I was an Australian trying to sound like a Jamaican.

As a clergyman, I probably shouldn't do some of the things I do in public. And why? Because there's always the chance that the passing observer to any of my odder interactions will one day visit my church, and when they discover me in the pulpit, who knows what their reaction will be.

It's not like I do anything offensive. I don't swear or throw up rude hand gestures or anything like that. My concern is that I am more than ready and willing to use my innate weirdness to lob a curve ball at pretty much anyone when they invade my space. I don't do it to be a jerk. Most often I do it because the moment is a teachable one, and the people are boldly crass enough to initiate the interaction. Other times, I do it just to keep things interesting. Consider the following example, and decide for yourself which of these you think was in play.

I have a t-shirt that I like to wear when I'm doing work around the house. It's one that Jennifer bought for me at Walmart a few years back. It says "England" across the breast and has the Union Jack prominently displayed. I like the shirt. In fact, I like it a lot, and I happened to be wearing it one day while visiting the local Home Depot in search of wood screws and wall plates for some electrical outlets I installed in my basement.

I found the wood screws first, and then I made my way to the main aisle that would lead me to the section where I'd find the remainder of my required items. To get there, it was necessary to pass the appliance department. On approach, there was a rather rugged looking fellow who appeared to be guarding multiple flatbeds, each bearing some larger appliances—things like dishwashers and microwave ovens. It was an impressive stash of items he was preparing to purchase. But even with his remarkable train of products, the man himself stood out as most notable in the collection. He was decked in red, white, and blue from top to bottom. Everything on him bore an American flag, from his bandana to his pants. Even his shoes participated in the pageantry. Admittedly, being the patriot that I am, I was impressed, and I felt almost as if I should remove my hat and put my hand over my heart as I passed him.

But I didn't, and that's because as I made my way toward him, I could more than tell that he'd locked onto me with a stare. Having forgotten what was on the t-shirt I was wearing, I didn't know why.

And then he spoke.

"Nice shirt," he intoned sarcastically. I smiled and kept my passing pace. But then he added, "Ashamed of your own flag, friend?"

Now, I suppose most folks would probably just have allowed the man his space and kept walking, relegating his rudeness to the obvious fact that he's an overly-zealous nutjob. I mean, I don't need to tell him that I'm not ashamed of my country's flag. I love America. I also love the freedom I have to wear my England t-shirt while working on my home. Still, it was the urge I acted upon next that I posited at the beginning of this little jaunt as something I should probably stop doing because it could get me into trouble.

As immediately as he spoke, I turned and offered in my best British accent something like, "Oy, mate! It's 'ard enough I've to drive my motorcar on the wrong side o' the road, but must I also be coerced into 'splaining me bloody shirt?!"

Although I didn't remain long, I stayed put long enough to note that the surprise on his face was worth at least a couple quid.

Returning to my previous pace, I continued my quest. I certainly didn't want to continue the engagement, anyway, and mainly because if I found myself drawn into an actual conversation, one in which I'd have to keep the charade alive, he would've eventually noticed that I can't keep the accent going for too long before it devolves into something more attuned to an Australian trying to sound like a Jamaican.

I can't say for sure, but I do think he tried to apologize as I walked away. I think he said something about respecting America's allies. Well, whatever. I turned the corner of the aisle I needed, grabbed my wall plates, and then took the long way back to the checkout lanes, traveling first among the ceiling fans and then through the outdoor garden department, all in an effort to evade my star spangled antagonist and the possibility of betraying my covert tactics.

In a way, the sample before me of the Crown Royal Blenders' Series Bourbon Mash that I received from my friend George reminds me of the scene I just described. It's a Canadian whisky, but it's pretending to be from Kentucky. And while it does a pretty good job at first, the longer you spend with it, the more you realize it's just another syrupy edition from Crown Royal.

The nose of this whisky is splendid. It carries some pretty typical Bourbon sensations, at least enough for an initial convincing if this were a blind taste test. In addition to these particulars, there is a more notable scent of simmering butter and glazed peaches.

A taste reveals the Bourbon influence but betrays its non-native birth. Firstly, there's a wash of creamy vanilla and a shake of the fruit from the nosing, but no sooner had this commentary begun than did it turn with an aftertaste of sour artificial flavoring eased only slightly by a drop of honey.

The finish is where its attempts at being a Bourbon cease and it wholly becomes what I most recall about Crown Royal. With a short to medium fade, the whisky suddenly feels thicker than you remember, coating the tongue with an overly-sugared stratum.

For Crown Royal fans, this whisky may put forth a Bourbon flag, but in all, it will be the candy-like and velvety experience you'd expect from your homeland. For all others, I suspect that this dram will serve only to confirm a thankfulness for genuine Bourbon while reaffirming any alternate choices you may have made with regard to the Canadian whiskies you prefer. Either way, just know that it probably doesn't matter what shirt you're wearing while you drink it.

CROWN ROYAL, XO, CANADIAN BLENDED WHISKY, 40%

You know what doesn't come to mind when I say "gumbo"?

There are certain words that carry an innate potency. When you hear them spoken, the mind immediately begins to stir, and in due course, the particulars associated with the words are brought to remembrance.

For example, if I were to say "double-decker bus," right away you might imagine a giant, candy-colored transport filled with tourists and navigating the narrow streets of an ancient and gray city, stopping along the way at places like Westminster Abbey, Trafalgar Square, and the Tower of London.

If I were to mention the R.M.S. Titanic, perhaps your mood would change as you contemplate the icy waters of the northern Atlantic consuming more than 1,500 people aboard the infamous ocean liner heralded as the ship that not even God could sink. Or maybe your mood soured because you thought of Leonardo DiCaprio, Kate Winslett, and a certain song by Céline Dion. If this is more the case, then I'm truly sorry for bringing it up. Allow me to make haste toward a different image.

What comes to mind when you hear the word "gumbo"? For me, I see a product born in Africa but raised in Louisiana. I see images of the coastal American south beginning to coalesce like spirits conjured by a voodoo priestess. I see snakes winding through patches of swamp grass, Spanish moss hanging from primordial trees, well-used and rusting fishing boats tied in harbor, and open fires cradling kettles filled with simmering stews of shrimp, chicken, or beef and the holy trinity of southern vegetables—onions, bell peppers, and celery.

You know what *doesn't* come to mind when I say "gumbo"? Canada.

Now don't get me wrong. Canada is a wonderful place. It's just that eating gumbo made in Canada is sort of like flying an American flag made in China. For purists, it's tantamount to sacrilege. I'm led to assume that the folks at Campbell's know this, but they found themselves in a bind. Like any business-savvy company, they intended to market their product as "authentic," but when the labels rolled out, the lawyers stepped in. Pointing to the fine print of the trade agreement, the lawyers reminded Campbell's of the requirement to prominently display the product's Canadian origin.

And so they did.

Along the same lines, I used to feel the same with regard to Canadian whisky as I do now regarding Old Glory being produced and sold by a communist state. In other words, I used to think that Canadian whisky could never be considered as authentic as other whiskies—at least not as legitimate as Scotch or Bourbon. But that's because my only interaction with the country's booze was with the likes of Canadian Club. But over time, I tried others, and in so doing, I became aware of my incredible wrongness. Canada does indeed have some really great distilleries producing some really great whiskies.

Then there's Crown Royal. I've tried several different renditions from this well-beloved distiller, but I've not found love for any of them. And yet, today has delivered something altogether different— the XO edition—and it is changing what comes to mind when I hear the words "Crown Royal."

The nose of this delightfully creamy dram is one of toffee edged with dark chocolate and sprinkled with toasted oats. This much concentrated sweetness would typically cause me concern, because it suggests a syrupy character that I do not prefer and yet have found to be characteristic of most Crown Royal editions. But here, the nose is not heavy, but lighthearted, and such lightheartedness communicates something crisp will follow. And it does.

The palate is oak spice, baked apples, oats, and vanilla. There's a tad bit of nip near the end of the savoring, but it comes along at just the right time with a measure of dryness that helps to keep the syrupy character at bay.

The finish is quick, almost hurriedly so, leaving behind a trace of the oak, apples, and oats.

I know this stuff has been around for a while, but with every invocation of the Crown Royal name, I've shrunk from any desire to give it a whirl. I thought I knew what to expect. Good or bad, I've arrived to the party—or better yet, a sample of the XO was brought to me from the party. Obligated, but still giving it an honest go, I realize now that Crown Royal deserves its status as an authentic favorite for many. And since this is true, then maybe, just maybe, we should try a spoonful of Canadian gumbo, because you just never know.

DILLON'S RYE WHISKY, THREE OAKS, BATCH 01, 3 YEARS OLD, 43%

Mr. Miyagi would have been proud.

You know you've raised your kids right when you're in the middle of a thumb war with one and the other in the room breaks right into the montage song from the 80s film *The Karate Kid*. Suddenly, the significance of the bout becomes altogether different when you hear, *"You're the best around! Nothing's ever gonna keep you down!"*

Mr. Miyagi would be proud.

That song alone—as bad as it was then and still is today—put magic into that moment and turned what could have been simply passing-the-time-at-the-doctor's-office into twenty minutes of full-fledged stretches, thumb warm-up routines, and a final sweat-drenched, digit-flicking moment of father and son combat stupendous. The only things missing were the karategi uniforms, cheering spectators (although, we did have one), and the Oriental-themed motivational posters made especially for adorning the walls of a dojo.

It doesn't matter where you are or what you are doing, kids have a way of making certain moments much more enjoyable. But this means you have to give in, at least a little, to their expectations. It means dropping yourself into their imaginary worlds as soon as they appear, filling any of the particular roles they've designed. This doesn't mean you go along with the storyline completely. I rarely do that. In fact, I do what I can to twist the story's expected outcomes and make it a little more fantastical. That never ends with sour faces.

Take for example the thumb war I shared above. When Evelyn began to sing, right away Joshua assumed the role of the movie's protagonist, Danny LaRusso. At one point, he even did the infamous crane stance. I became Johnny Lawrence, the leader of the Cobra Kai gang and Danny's arch rival. Of course Evelyn was rooting for Danny, the underdog, the one who is supposed to win. I was talking smack and pretending to be tough and unforgiving.

And then I actually was. I beat him down badly—seriously— and in the end, I told him to leave my girl Ali alone, get his loser self out of the valley, and go back to Jersey.

Yeah, sort of harsh. I guess he wasn't the best around. I was. Still, the moment was unforgettably gratifying even as it was unexpected. We all laughed. At least I think I remember that Joshua laughed.

The Dillon's "Three Oaks" Rye was a bit of a surprise, I must say. It's not that I expected it to be either good or bad, but rather I've only ever experienced such a multihued involvement with Scotch. Sometimes with Japanese whiskies, but never with Canadian whiskies. Almost certainly never with Bourbons.

And yet, kind of like when we were thumb-warring at the doctor's office, this whisky has a chorus singing in the background that makes it a bigger deal. The nose alone has lemon, ginger, and maybe even a toasted and well-buttered bagel.

In the mouth, there's a coconut sprinkled doughnut dipped in cinnamon applesauce. The spice gives it some bite.

The finish is the whisky's only hang-up. With a medium to long draw, it wanders away from everything I just described and lands in a vat of sour chews that never actually received the sugar required by the recipe. Everything was looking good for Danny, until Johnny dodged that crane kick and knocked the Italian kid's nose a little bit left of center.

Still, in all, it's a complex whisky. And maybe even fun. It won't get "Best Picture," but it will be remembered for a long while as having used up a moment on the timeline in a most enjoyable way.

FORTY CREEK, CONFEDERATION OAK RESERVE (2015), LOT 1867, 40%

Remind me never to vote for you in an election.

"It's time to convene the gummy bear council," the younger of the two girls announced, having just finished making several miniature Play-Doh bears from a mold.

"Yes, it is," the older one replied. "We have much to discuss."

Rarely do I intervene in such fanciful moments, but I had a pressing matter that involved me sharing the content of an article with the boys who were upstairs worshipping at the PlayStation altar. Apparently, the World Health Organization announced recently that video game addiction is now an official diagnosis among mental disorders.

Anyway, as I rose from my chair preparing to employ my best, most annoying dad voice for my sons, I asked Madeline, "What exactly does a gummy bear council discuss?"

"Plenty," she answered. "We talk about waging war on other groups, accepting their peace treaty offers pretty much after we've conquered them, and building a bridge over the river of tears. We need more bridges from Gumdropolis into the wastelands. It's depressing over there."

"Anything else?"

"We talk about our alliance with the frog people and the ginger bread people. They were fighting, so we conquered them both and then forced them to be friends."

"Why were they fighting?"

"Because the ginger bread queen got mad at her husband about something, and then she did something that made the frog people really mad."

"What did she do?"

"I don't remember," Madeline said, tapping a slender finger to the side of her head and bringing her story to a pause. "But I remember that all of her servants died in the war."

"How many servants died?"

"About a thousand."

"Wow. Sounds like a brutal place," I said. "So, what's the council going to talk about today?"

"We're going to talk about who else we should conquer," she replied with pep. "Maybe plan out some stuff. Or figure out what color to make our new gummy bear clone army. There are a few more places around us we want to make really happy."

"Remind me never to vote for you, Madeline, if you ever run for office," I said very plainly. "Although, if at some point you do manage to seize power in America, I'd like to be your Minister of Whisky."

"Why would I give you one of the most important roles in my kingdom if you didn't vote for me?"

"I'll wait and watch the polls," I said. "If it looks like you're gonna win, I'll go ahead and pull the lever for you."

"Good," she said with a smile and finished arranging the gummy bears at the plastic plate serving as the council's table.

"Just promise me the position," I said, begging confirmation of my soul's sale. "And that you'll outlaw video games."

"Yes to the position," she said. "But I'll think about the video game idea."

"That's good enough for me."

"You'll like that I'm already planning to move the White House to Florida."

"Girlfriend, you sure know how to sell your candidacy to the undecided voter," I called from halfway up the stairs. "I'm definitely voting for you, now, honey."

I took a moment to share with my sons that their mental disorders had now been officially recognized, and then I made my way back to my unopened whisky stash to choose what would be forever remembered as the celebratory dram for the day I was pledged a place in my daughter's cabinet. Today's choice: The Forty Creek Confederation Oak Reserve.

Tragically, my memory will be forever seared by a lack of enjoyment with this one.

Initially, the nose gave a vinegary trail, one that just couldn't get far enough out of the way to let shine what I suspected were caramel and fruity undertones. They're there, but I'm guessing they're in chains in the gummy bear dungeon below Gumdropolis.

For the most part, the palate was fine enough, offering some peace-keeping morsels at the foot of the gummy bear queen's throne—nibbles of chocolate, lemons, and whatever that stuff is inside of a Cadbury egg. The problem, however, is that everything is overly peppered with cloves and wood spice, causing the overall balance to be off.

The finish was short and dry, offering only a fingerprint of the alcohol and a pinch of barrel spices.

As prophetic as the selection was, I suppose I should have chosen differently. I'm guessing that if the time ever comes for my daughter to impose her happiness upon the rest of us, many among us may be thinking the same thing.

P.S.   Let the reader know that after my review, I let this whisky sit for about an hour before coming back to it to finish it off. Apparently, this was just enough time for the dram to rid itself of the sour that seemed to be hiding its better qualities. The problem, however, is that no one opens a bottle, pours a dram, and lets it sit for an hour. That's dumb. The positive side to this as a prophetic dram is that perhaps after some time ruling over all of us, my daughter will get better rather than worse.

FORTY CREEK, COPPER POT RESERVE, 43%

Mele Kalikimaka

"I don't think she can do it," I said.

"Yes, she can," Harrison argued.

"No, she can't," I replied.

"Yes, she can," Jen said, taking his side. "She's pretty intuitive."

"But not that intuitive," I answered. "She'll never figure it out."

"I'll bet she can do it," Evelyn chimed.

"You stay out of this," I said, pointing.

"Me, too," Joshua interrupted. "I think she can do it."

"And me," Madeline added, giving a glance from behind the protection of her older brother.

"Whatever," I said, in mid-turn toward the device. "Hey, Google," I continued, using exceptional enunciation, *"it looks like you are going to have a chance to prove your worth."*

"I'm sorry," came the device's friendly female voice, "but I can't help you with that just yet."

"See," I said, waving my hand in the diminutive machine's direction. "She can't even have a reasonable conversation when I'm making sense. How's she gonna figure out what you're trying to get out of her?"

"She can do it," each offered with certainty.

And so a wager was set. If she accomplished the task, I'd say I was wrong, and that, dear reader, is as big a deal as anything else to these squatters—especially the miniature ones.

"Well," I prodded, "give it a shot. Let's see what this baby can do."

"Hey, Google," Jen called, "play that mackalacka shamacka lalacka dacka fracka song."

"Okay," the virtual assistant replied almost immediately. "Playing 'Mele Kalikimaka' by Bing Crosby. Here it is playing on YouTube."

The song's notes teemed through the kitchen and living room like a Hawaiian stream. The whole family cheered, some demonstrating their prideful joy with arms outstretch and swaying like palm tree branches nudged by an ocean breeze. Others celebrated with some pretty uncoordinated hula moves.

Indeed, she did it.

I admitted my wrongness, turned to my whisky cabinet, and poured myself a dram of the Forty Creek Copper Pot Reserve, which I must confess, I approached with the same level of expectation as our Google Home device. Because of the bottom shelf price, I just didn't think it would succeed.

But once again, I was humbled.

The nose of the Copper Pot Reserve delivers a carefully enunciated phrase of caramel and sour citrus. That's it. Nothing else.

The palate repeats word for word what it received from the nose, and then it adds a bit of clarifying commentary—roasted pecans and a cup of Tim Horton's coffee, which in my opinion, is more tart than other coffees but still quite enjoyable.

At first, the medium finish leaves behind something metallic, but only for a moment. It dissipates quickly in an agreeable conversation of caramel and rye spice.

A smile, a gulp, and the Canadian gem is gone. Yes, I'm wrong. Again.

"Hey, Google. Do me a favor and pour me another dram of the Forty Creek Copper Pot Reserve."

"I'm sorry, but I can't help with that just yet."

"Hey, Google, you're useless."

"Got it. Wikipedia.org says that Ulysses S. Grant, born Hiram Ulysses Grant, was an American politician, soldier, international statesman, and author, who served as the 18th president of the United States from 1869 to 1877. During the American Civil War Grant led the Union Army as its commanding general to victory over the Confederacy..."

FORTY CREEK, DOUBLE BARREL RESERVE (2012), LOT 25, 40%

Take two whiskies and call me in the morning.

It's Saturday during my Christmas break, the one bit of down time I've been eagerly anticipating since September, and I've been dreadfully ill since Tuesday. The whole break is spent. Go figure.

It started with some pretty incredible chest pain. It was so bad, in fact, that I thought I might've been having a heart attack. Nevertheless, I took some Tylenol and went to bed. I know my eternal fate, and so with that, I figured that if Jennifer discovered the next morning that I was dead, she'd be sad, but she knows it, too, and in the meantime she'd be able to collect on a life insurance policy that would make life a little bit easier.

I'm definitely worth more dead than alive.

But I didn't die. I woke up Wednesday morning, and apparently at some point during the night, I'd traded my chest pain for full body aches, an irritating cough, a massive headache, skin and muscle sensitivity, and chills. I must have been swindled in that midnight exchange because I'd gladly take the chest pain over the way I'm feeling right now.

Needless to say, the only real positive thing I have to share with you about this long-anticipated but swiftly shattered time of rest is that while I've lost my taste for all things edible, I haven't lost my taste for whisky, which is why I'm actually willing to steam forward and write a review for you even in my current state of abysmal anguish.

It's all for you, friends. And me, too, I guess.

Whisky is medicinal, you know. Seriously. Whisky has ellagic acid, which is an antioxidant that absorbs rogue cells in the blood stream. Among the many gatherings of data, a Harvard University study and "The European Journal of Clinical Nutrition" both settled on what they would call "beneficial drinking," which is defined as seven drams a week, or at least one dram a day. Doing this, they say, reduces the risk of heart disease and heart failure. It's a good thing I'm pretty much on track with what they discovered, which is probably why I didn't die on Tuesday night. And there's an additional perk here. The National Institute of Health discovered that folks who keep to such a regimen are half as likely to get dementia, which means I'm not likely to forget to thank the Lord above for not calling me home just yet on Tuesday night.

Also, and finally, whisky fights common cold and flu infections. Funny thing is, this is nothing new to anyone who spends time enjoying whisky. We've known it for years. Like five hundred years to be a bit more precise. Truly. Take a look at the following paragraph from page eight in *Volume VI* of Raphael Holinshed's *Chronicles of England, Scotland, and Ireland* published in 1586. He gives a pretty explicit listing of everything whisky (or "aqua vitae" as they called it during his day) is good for curing.

THE soile is low and waterish, including diuerse little Ilands, inuironed with lakes & marrish. Highest hils haue standing pooles in their tops. Inhabitants especiallie new come, are subiect to distillations, rheumes and fluxes. For remedie whereof, they vse an ordinarie drinke of *Aqua vitæ*, being so qualified in the making, that it drieth more, and also inflameth lesse than other hot confections doo. One Theoricus wrote a proper treatise of *Aqua vitæ*, wherein he praiseth it vnto the ninth degrée. He distinguisheth thrée sorts thereof, *Simplex, Composita*. and *Perfectissima*. He declareth the simples and ingrediences thereto belonging. He wisheth it to be taken as well before meat as after. It drieth vp the breaking out of hands, and killeth the flesh wormes, if you wash your hands therewith. It scowreth all scurfe & scalds from the head, being therewith dailie washt before meales. Being moderatlie taken (saith he) it sloweth age, it strengthneth youth, it helpeth digestion, it cutteth flegme, it abandoneth melancholie, it relisheth the heart, it lighteneth the mind, it quickeneth the spirits, it cureth the hydropsie, it healeth the stranguric, it pounceth the stone, it expelleth grauell, it puffeth awaie all ventositie, it kéepeth and preserueth the head from whirling, the eies from dazeling, the toong from lisping, the mouth from maffling, the teeth from chattering, and the throte from ratling: it kéepeth the weasan from stifling, the stomach from wambling, and the heart from swelling, the bellie from wirtching, the guts from rumbling, the hands from shiuering, & the sinewes from shrinking, the veines from crumpling, the bones from aking, & the marrow from soaking. Vlstadius also ascribeth thereto a singular praise, and would haue it to burne being kindled, which he taketh to be a token to know the goodnesse thereof. And trulie it is a souereigne liquor, if it be orderlie taken.

There's a lot of stuff in that list, eh? As I said before, no surprise here. Of course, today we know a little bit more about why whisky is a formidable foe for such pesky human ailments, namely the common cold and the frightful flu. Whisky dilates blood vessels, which means that more ellagic-toting plasma can make its way through the system shackling the bad guys, more widely opening up the mucus membrane, allowing for the body to deal a little more conclusively with the residual gunk. I'm living proof of the science. I rarely get sick. So when I do—like right now—you can pretty much guarantee it's not the flu, but rather I've been infected by an otherworldly microbe that fell from space and is trying to gestate in my abdomen. But even as it does, my daily regimen of whisky is making it far too difficult for the xenomorph to actually grow into a mature chest-burster. Although, it sure felt like the little bugger was close to hatching the other night, which is why I fought the good fight with a dram before tucking myself into bed.

Today's medicine is a little sampling of the 2012 edition of the Forty Creek Double Barrel Reserve which I received from my pal, George, in Canada. But before I share my thoughts, you need to know that Forty Creek and I haven't gotten along too well in the past. In my opinion, it pretty much always has a caustic exit from the bottle, and it's one that lingers through each of the stages of review.

Unfortunately, this time it was no different. The first gale across the nose is a briny mixture of alcohol and vinegar from a jar of mild peppers. This doesn't mix well with what seems to be a secondary gust of wood spice and caramel. It leaves the impression that the wood is rotting and the caramel is spoiled.

The palate is considerably better, offering up some rye, a scrap of cornbread, some buttered popcorn, and a remnant of the wood spice from the nose. All of this carries over into a medium finish that matches its beginning. Its end is sour, but it's a stale sour, as if whatever is making it sour sat out all night on the kitchen counter when it should have been placed into the refrigerator. That kind of sour.

In the end, I'd say the whisky serves well alongside the white blood cells at the battlefront, but it's not necessarily one that I'd recommend to anyone in search of something that will help to turn an illness-influenced frown upside down. For that, you need to look somewhere else.

GOODERHAM & WORTS, LITTLE TRINITY, 17 YEARS OLD, 45%

Did you die, Bob?

So, how do you respond to someone who walks out of the Christmas Eve worship service and says to you in the greeting line, "Thanks for calling me out for never coming to church except at Christmas and Easter"?

I hope that responding with "You're welcome" suffices, because that's exactly what I did.

Of course, there were a few other things I managed to say, softer words like "We miss you here at the church," and "Let's get together for coffee sometime—I'll buy—and we'll figure out what's keeping you away." Funny thing is, the gentleman returned the next day to the Christmas Day service which, for the most part, isn't well attended.

Nevertheless, the particular portion of the Christmas Eve sermon that I'm guessing stung the most was when I discouraged the listeners from resting too comfortably in the privilege of calling themselves Christians if their only motivation for attending the night's service was due to their family dragging them along by a leash of guilt, or because they were sensing the first of the only two seasonal obligations to their church community that they feel all year, the other arriving at Easter. From there I pressed that calling oneself a Christian means having an innate and steady awareness that not only knows that there's no other place on earth for a Christian to be on Christmas Eve than in worship, but that regularly attending worship is crucial for healthy faith.

I don't know how that meets with your senses, but I would surmise that almost anyone who knows me also knows how I feel about tiptoeing around issues. It never works. Most often, in fact, it only makes things worse. It's better to steer into the painful discussion and deal with it. It's rarely easy. Sometimes it takes a good long while before results are seen. Sometimes results are never seen at all. Other times it's all that was needed and things turn around right away. I'm convinced it's best to pull back the curtain and shine the light on both the truth and the excuses.

Besides the paragraph above, I'll give you another example. Here's a pretty typical conversation that takes place in a church on Christmas Eve:

> "It's great to see you, Bob!" the pastor says with a pleasant smile.
>
> "Yeah, well," Bob replies sheepishly, "things have been pretty busy. Life just gets so busy."
>
> "Oh, I know," the pastor offers, missing his chance. "Life keeps us running. Be sure to say 'hi' to the kids."

I'd rather see the conversation go this way:

> "It's great to see you, Bob!" the pastor says with a pleasant smile.

"Yeah, well," Bob replies sheepishly, "things have been busy. Life just gets so busy."

"Did you die and then come back to life?" the pastor asks, seizing his chance. "Or have you been in a hospital quarantine since last Easter? You know, being dead or infirm are some of the only allowable excuses in the Scriptures for missing worship. And even with a quarantine, when you can't go to church, the church is supposed to go to you. I'm sure they would've let me speak to you through your plastic bubble."

Another example might be:

"It's great to see you, Bob!"

"Yeah, this evening worship service works out pretty well. With everything going on in my week, it's really hard for me to get here for the worship service on Sunday morning."

"How's that new TV working out for you?"

"Wha—?"

"Yeah, that 70 inch flat screen I saw you carrying out of the electronics store at 4:30 in the morning on Black Friday. How's the picture on that bad boy?"

The point is, be ready for the typical defenses, and then be ready to steer into them in a way that shows the person you aren't so easily fooled. I guarantee that a conversation—easy or hard—will be stirred by the effort. If it's an easy one, roll with it, and then be glad that a door has opened for an honest and contrite conversation between two people. If it's a hard one—one in which you find yourself in the crosshairs of a venomous person doing everything he or she can to project the guilt upon you—roll with that one, too. When they point to your failures and inconsistencies as a person— shining the light on all of your warts—take it in stride as best you can, maybe even agreeing to some, and then steer back into the topic at hand. The humility and diligence will eventually accomplish something.

Unfortunately, I fear that in our post-modern, radically individualistic society filled with "who-the-hell-do-you-think-you-are-to-tell-me-I'm-wrong" kind of people, the chances are better that they will leave the church. This, too, you must take in stride. Consider that the seed has been planted, and if they transfer to another congregation's roster, maybe what you've given to them in honesty will be to their good, maybe even helping to encourage them to keep connected in the new place. Or maybe they'll just stay put because they've realized the friend they have in their pastor, and they know that with such an association, they have a friend with whom they can exchange their warts for something better—namely, a churchly dram from Gooderham & Worts. And I must say the 17-year-old "Little Trinity" edition is an exceptional reward for heartfelt repentance and faith.

Inspired by the namesake church that Gooderham built for his employees in Toronto, the nose of this whisky is one of vanilla soaked pears and coriander with a touch of cinnamon. This complexity carries over to the palate, revealing in the first sip a wash of raspberries atop a rye bread slice and gladdened ever so slightly by the already familiar vanilla.

The finish is shorter than I expected, although even in its hasty passing, there's enough time to gather wood spice and a pale sense of the pears from the nosing.

In all, when it comes to the opportunities for giving the best dosage of lawful reality to certain folks, Christmas and Easter are some of the only chances I get. And so, in these instants, I try never to shy away from seizing the sermonic moment before a relatively captive audience. That being said, if you're the listener in the pew, let the whisky description above be an enticement to venture beyond the horizon of insufficient excuses to your clergyman. We're not all as dumb as we look, and we've probably heard—so many times before—everything you're about to invent. It's really not new. And like I said, with the possible endpoint iterated above—at least in my church—you might be really glad you came clean.

J.P. WISER'S, 35 YEARS OLD, 50%

35 has its own Wikipedia page.

Thirty-five.

Just in case you needed to know, thirty-five has its own Wikipedia page. Yep. It says pretty dryly, "35 (thirty-five) is the natural number following 34 and preceding 36."

Looks like someone had some time on his hands.

I'm not interested in following this person's trail of boredom, although I'm guessing it has been happening for some time because a lot of other numbers have pages, too. I can tell you with certainty that there's no page for 2,005,017. I looked. Although, typing that number into Google will bring up IRS Notice cc-2005-017, which speaks to the topic of "Interim Procedures for 'Ballard' Type Issues." Now there's a reverse-the-earth-on-its-axis effort on the part of the federal government, wouldn't you say? What is a ballard, anyway? I suppose I could read the document and find out.

Nah. For the moment, I'd rather stay focused on the number thirty-five.

Did you know that thirty-five is the atomic number of bromine? Of course you did. Everyone knows that. But I'll bet you didn't know that 35 mm film is actually 34.98 mm wide, and it was first introduced by Thomas Edison and William Dickson back in 1892, although apparently it was noted at the time as 1.375 inches.

I was thirty-five years old when I was ordained. It's also the last time I remember being relatively pain free in my body. Now I have back and knee pain like crazy, and I also get pretty severe migraines.

The BBC offered an article in 2017 suggesting from data collected from a few various surveys that one is officially considered boring and old sometime in the mid-thirties. Thirty-five, to be precise, was marked as the critical age for no longer being considered young. I was glad to read that, because I was under the impression that the pastoral office was killing me physically. Turns out it's the number thirty-five.

The results from a University of Kent study suggested that at age thirty-five, men reach "peak loneliness" and women reach "peak boring." It's also noted as the age when folks are more likely to begin hating their jobs.

None of these aforementioned particulars much matter in the case of the J.P. Wiser's edition before me. Having "35-years-old" on the label communicates anything but lackluster or deleterious. Instead, the number thirty-five heralds a numerological vantage of depth and experience that many whiskies might covet but few claim. And when it comes to this whisky, the envy is merited.

The nose is a sweet and creamy custard of vanilla and tangerines stirred into a cup of light-roast coffee. In the mouth, the cream continues, but adds to the regimen a spryness of cinnamon and oak.

The finish is a medium draw of overly ripened pineapple, cocoa powder, and cinnamon.

J.P. Wiser's has done a splendid thing here, and if anything, they've given a trophy dram to those of us noticing the wheels beginning to come loose. With this 35, we can celebrate the accomplishments that come along in the years following thirty-five—careers, a little more money for better booze, lasting love, a few kids, a little less money for better booze, a few more kids, a lot less money for booze, wisdom, and so many other things that the club-hopping twenty-something millennials are flittering away to a much more distant future under the fleeting guise of "youth." Personally, I look back on my twenties and remember them as friend-filled and interesting, but from my current perspective, I now recall them as lonely and, in most circumstances, less than inspiring. It's only in the current time that life is about as interesting as it gets. With four kids running around, I'm never alone. And with everything else involved with marriage and parenting, I'm rarely bored.

So, call me old if you'd like. Just know that in the grand scheme, a good many things get better with age. The J.P. Wiser's 35-years-old Canadian Whisky is an icon of this truth.

J.P. WISER'S, COMMEMORATIVE SERIES, CANADA 2018, 43.4%

Dihydroergotamine. Say that five times fast.

It's migraine season—and I just emerged from one.

It's hard to be funny when you have a migraine. It's hard to be, do, or say just about anything when you have a migraine.

Light hurts. Noise hurts. Moving hurts. Life in general hurts.

And then the nausea.

I started getting migraines about five years ago. The first one landed on me right in the middle of Holy Week, which is a time in the Church Year when I have multiple worship services on multiple days from Palm Sunday to Easter Sunday—about eleven services in all. Each requires a different sermon, and so I do a lot of writing. It's a killer time for a pastor. A migraine multiplies the struggle.

The first migraine I ever experienced hit me on Maundy Thursday. And when I say it hit me, I mean hard. It started before the service, and by the time I got to the sermon, everything on the inside of the left side of my head felt like it was being scrambled and prepared as an omelet. My sinus cavity was throbbing, from head to toe my skin was extremely sensitive to touch, and I was ready to puke. Eventually I did.

Not in the middle of the service, of course. But it was close. Thankfully the former pastor of my congregation was there in the pews. Though retired, he robed up and finished the service. I went to my office to empty the contents of my stomach, and then Jennifer took me to the Emergency Room.

I spent the next eight horrible days in the hospital with a gathering of specialists hovering above me attempting to sort out the mess. They drew blood, performed tests, ordered up CT scans, X-rays, and MRIs. After a while, they discovered the problem.

"You have a severe migraine," the chief neurologist said that final day. "At first we thought your brain had shifted by three millimeters, which would have suggested a particular disea—"

"—You thought I had a disease that shifts my brain?" I interrupted.

"Yeah," he said. "But you don't. Good thing, huh?"

"Yes. Good thing."

"Essentially, it's a severe migraine you're dealing with," he continued.

"A migraine?"

"Yeah, it's probably seasonal, coming on because of changes in the weather—maybe barometric drops and such. You'll probably get them every year from now on. This was the first."

"So, what do I do?"

"Well," a negligible doctor beside the chief doctor began, "if it isn't necessarily the weather, then you'll need to discover and watch for the triggers."

"Triggers?"

"Usually migraines are triggered by something—stress, chocolate, something. Your wife said you're under a lot of stress.

That could be part of the problem. You need to figure out how to get rid of the stressors."

"I'm a pastor," I said, my eyes locked shut from the pain. "My stressors are people. You're counseling me to commit murder."

They laughed among themselves.

"We've ordered up something called Dihydroergotamine—DHE for short," the chief said. "It's one of the most powerful medications out there for slowing these things down and getting a handle on them."

"Got it," I replied, dryly. "DHE. How about we get it into me and get me the hell out of here?"

The next few hours were spent feeding the DHE into my body. Within a half hour of the first dose, the migraine began to subside and I was feeling better. In fact, for the first time in over a week, I was finally able to open my eyes to look around the room.

"How're you feeling?" the nurse charged with my care asked from the doorway.

"A lot better," I replied. "The headache is still there, but it seems to be dissipating."

"That means it's working."

"Can I ask you a question?" I pried as she moved among the various devices that shackled my body's diagnostics to the nurses' station in the hallway. "When this whole thing started, it felt like it began on the left side of my nasal cavity. Could there be something going on in there?"

"It sounds like the doctors checked everything," she said. "If something was out of sorts in there, they'd have found it."

"Well," I said, looking to the window timidly, "what if I did this to myself?"

"What do you mean?"

Do you know what a neti pot is?" I asked.

"Yes," she answered. "It's a little teapot-like thing that you fill with warm salt water. You tip yourself upside down and you pour the water into your sinuses to clean them out. A lot of people swear by them."

"Yeah, well, I'd never used one until about three weeks ago," I said, continuing the diffidence.

"Yeah, so?"

"Well," I started, "I felt what I thought was a head cold coming on, and since Holy Week was approaching, I got sort of nervous. I didn't want to be out of commission during the busiest time of the year with a sinus issue. My parish administrator suggested I try a neti pot, and so I did."

"And?"

"And instead of using warm salt water, I figured I'd go full guns and destroy the bugger."

"What did you use instead of salt water?"

"Scotch."

A few seconds of uncomfortable silence passed between us.

"You…poured Scotch…into your sinuses?" she asked, a look of disbelief now adorning her kindly face.

"Yes," I replied. "But don't worry. It wasn't good Scotch. It was Scoresby, which is really bad Scotch."

"Seriously?"

"Yes," I answered.

"Didn't…didn't that hurt?"

"It was a little warm," I said. "But trust me, I'm a guy who can handle whisky no matter how or where it gets into my body."

"Really?"

"That didn't sound right, did it?"

"Not at all."

"So, anyway," I said, attempting to shift conversational gears. "Did I permanently damage my sinuses with Scoresby?"

She drew another breath, betraying a tenacious surprise as well as her attempt to get her bearings in the discussion. "While that's probably not something you should be using," she said, "I'm sure it has nothing to do with your current situation."

"Are you sure?" I pressed. "Maybe I should've used a good single malt instead of a crappy blend—maybe something from The Macallan, or maybe The Balvenie?"

"If I were you," she said, maintaining a straighter face, "I'd just use the warmed salt water...like you're supposed to. Don't put whisky into your sinuses."

"Gotcha," I said. "No more whisky up my nose."

As I said, several years have passed since that conversation, and now instead of cleansing my sinuses with Scotch, I shoot up with DHE every few days during migraine season. It seems to keep the demons at bay. More importantly, I haven't had to murder anyone in my congregation.

Also, I suppose there's a greater success to attribute to the DHE. In the midst of a cranial storm, my thirst for whisky goes away. The DHE helps it to return. I'm glad for this, because it means that the sample of the J.P. Wiser's Commemorative Series Canada 2018 edition sent to me by my friend George could be thoroughly enjoyed here in the aftermath of the most recent bout.

And indeed, it was enjoyed.

A nose of tangerines, spiced marmalade, and rye, the whisky's scent speaks to the bright beaming sunshine of an uneventful summer day, one well beyond the reaches of the relentlessly unstable migraine purgatory that is springtime.

The palate is a tongue gloss of treacly caramel and the darkest of red cherries, both sensations warmed and then served together on nearly burnt rye toast. The juice from the cherries seeps into the toast to soften it. The caramel holds the whole snack together.

The finish is shorter than expected, although not thin or unenjoyable. The corn finally comes out to embrace the sweeter rudiments mentioned in both the nose and palate.

Overall, this is a well-balanced bit of joyful relief to a recent migraine—relief that was had with neither murder nor neti pots. And yet, since the nurse assured me that putting whisky up my nose wouldn't kill me (even though I gave her my word that I wouldn't), this particular dram is far better than Scoresby, and with that, I'd certainly consider using it the next time a head cold chooses my already sensitive sinuses for a dwelling place.

The only problem is figuring out how to swallow it through my nose while upside down. But then again, it's me we're talking about. If anyone can do it...

J.P. WISER'S, RARE CASK SERIES, SEASONED OAK, 19 YEARS OLD, 48%

If you love Jesus, you'll repost this.

If you have to end your super-serious, tragically misspelled, cookie-cutter Facebook post with the words, "I'll bet only my true friends will repost this," then you are a person of great emptiness. Only the neediest among us would post something on social media and try to guilt people into sharing it.

And yet, memes such as this continue to plague the internet. One doesn't have to scroll for too long before discovering the loneliest among us. In fact, here's one I just read about the American flag.

> This flag was bought and paid for with American lives. Let's make this go viral! Only 2% of you will show you have a heart by reposting. The other 98% will continue to take freedom for granted.

Seriously? By not reposting I'm taking my American freedoms for granted?

Yes, the freedoms we enjoy in America weren't cheap. They cost lives. But the complete measure of my national devotion is by no means reflected in whether or not I share your carelessly constructed image of a bald eagle and a flag. Instead, I'd like to think that the 98% aren't withholding their sharing because of their frivolous patriotism, but because they know you're a dope and they don't want to feed the tiger that is your emotional barrenness.

Here's another one:

> Aaron is 8 and has cancer. All he wants before he dies is 1,000,000 shares. Let's help him get there! I'll bet I already know which of my friends will actually share this to help Aaron.

While you're betting on which of your friends will share this, a few of us are betting you didn't realize your list of friends just got a lot shorter.

Again, these are easy to find. Here's one more:

> Repost if you ♥ Jesus. If not, just keep scrolling to show your true colors.

The problem I had with this one was that it had been recycled and reposted so many times that the heart in the image was blurry and looked more like a smudge. With that, I kept scrolling…because I'm not Jesus. Although, once I did figure out what the meme was communicating, I took the liberty of signing the particular friend up to receive email updates from some of the better known pharmaceutical companies dealing in antidepressants.

> Repost this if you love Jesus' gift of antidepressants. If not, just keep scrolling…all alone…in your pajamas…in the dark…with your only friend, a pizza.

As you can see, I have neither tolerance nor empathy for such childish things. Leave it to the Kindergarten teachers to sit through this gobbledygook. The rest of us sitting at the adult table will exercise and enjoy our freedoms by raising a glass to our nation, praying for the suffering ones, and thanking the good Lord for His gifts—one of which is the J.P. Wiser's Rare Cask Series Seasoned Oak 19-year-old. It's the perfect sipper for soothing an irritated soul under assault from guiltmongers making a racket over at the kids' table.

This particular edition—a kindly gift from my Canadian friend, George—has the sweetly scent of raisins, vanilla cream, and cinnamon. The tiniest drop of water enhances the raisins and cream.

The palate takes concentration. At first it suggests the cool of something peppermint. But if you're paying close attention, it turns back to the sweeter tendencies it shared by way of the nose, adding to the gathering an unmistakable orange zest and oak.

The finish is incredibly charming. Having reached a splendid peak in the palate, it takes to a medium soar on the well-balanced wings of caramel and wood spice.

This is a good one. If you happen to find it, buy it. And if you have a heart, share it. Although, I'll bet only one percent of you actually will—and we all know who you are.

LEGACY, CANADIAN BLENDED WHISKY, SMALL BATCH, 40%

So, let's sound it out. Buh, buh, buh, car.

"Maddy, honey," I heard Jen say from the kitchen. "You need to help him sound it out."

I remember that Madeline was very young at the time, maybe only five or six. I was sitting at the dining room table listening as she attempted to teach her younger brother, Harrison, how to read. Bright eyed and interested, he was sitting beside his kindly sister watching and listening.

"How do I do that?" she called back to her mother with an innocence of intent. True to the blossoming character she possesses today, she desperately wanted to see Harrison succeed in the effort, and so she was determined to learn the best method for securing her goal.

"You could show him the sound that each individual letter makes," Jen suggested.

"How do I do that?" she asked again.

"Which word are you working on?"

"Baby."

"Well, maybe you could do it like this," Jen said, walking to where the two were sitting where the dining and living rooms met. Crouching and finding the word, she pointed to its first letter. "This is the letter B," she said. "It makes the *buh* sound." Maddy's eyes were on her, registering every detail of her mother's impromptu lesson with precision. Jen pointed again, and Harrison followed her finger to the first letter of the word. "*Buh, buh,* baby," she said. "What sound does the letter B make, Harry?"

"Buh," he said proudly.

Maddy's eyes widened. "Thanks, Momma," she said. She knew what to do. "Let's move to a different word, Harrison."

"Otay," he said agreeably.

Jen made her way back to the kitchen while Maddy scanned the opposite page, eventually settling on a new word.

"Okay, Harry," she said, pointing confidently. "Let's learn this word." Her little finger pressed to the page. "This is the word 'car,'" she said. "Do you know what letter it starts with?"

"I doan know," he said, putting his little hands into the air beside his shoulders. "Wassit?"

"It's the letter C," Maddy answered. "We need the letter C to make the word 'car.'"

"We do?" Harry said, playing his part so that his sister could play hers.

"Yes, we do," she answered. "So, let's sound it out. *Buh, buh, buh,* car."

Jen looked at me. I looked at Jen. It took immeasurable strength to keep the laughter contained.

Okay, so maybe she missed the mark on that one. It doesn't change her history as one who rarely complains about anything, is kind-hearted to everyone she meets, is always ready to help, and is an all-around sweet human being. I'm even willing to admit that if it weren't for Saint Paul's truthful words in Romans 3 reminding that all have sinned and fallen short of the glory of God, I'd be in danger of heresy as I consider this little girl to be one of the few treading ever-so-closely to sinlessness.

Not so for the Legacy Blended Canadian Whisky Small Batch edition.

While the nose of this youngling seems cheerful as it promises singed oak and spiced apples, the palate attempts to sound these sensations out, but in the process, reveals a lack of depth. There's a little bit of the fruit—in syrup form and with a little bit of pepper sprinkled in—and some rather obvious cloves. But they're soft and sour as opposed to edged and sweet as one might expect.

The finish is medium in length, and thankfully, its contours make the dram worthwhile. The spiced apples are there, but, in a short moment, chocolated cherries begin to mingle. These were a nice surprise to an otherwise unexciting dram.

At this point in history, I wonder if the future of the Legacy, an effort from Buffalo Trace and Drew Mayville, will one day prove similar to that of my daughter, Madeline, whose name, when uttered, prompts smiles as well as thoughts of genuine glee from nearly all who know her. I hope so. But admittedly, at this point, I'm concerned that it's *buh, buh, buh,* uncertain.

Lot 40, Cask Strength, Canadian Whiskey, 12 Years Old, 55%

God fought for me today.

"You'll be so happy, Daddy!" the little girl delivered with a brightly beaming smile as she hurried through the door.

"Why's that, honey?" I inquired, attempting to match her exuberance.

"God fought for me today," she said confidently and dropped her jacket to the floor.

My interest piqued, I opened my arms to what I thought was an approaching hug. "What did He do?" I asked, as she ran past me.

"On the way home," she called, slamming the door of the bathroom near the kitchen, "I had to go potty so badly."

"You did?!" I called back, changing my excitement to a tone of faux concern.

"I didn't think I'd make it."

"So," I said assumingly, "God helped you hold it until you got home?"

"Oh, no," she said resolutely. I could hear her spinning the toilet paper roll. "I totally would've peed in the car, but God didn't let us get stuck at Satan's stoplight!"

My daughter was right. The event she described clearly involved the hand of the Divine.

There are two traffic lights in our little town. One of those lights I've come to believe is controlled by Lucifer. Even my kids have learned to call the stupid thing by a variety of names—Lucifer's light, Satan's stop light, the thorn of the Devil in Daddy's side.

This particular device designed to foster traffic safety has garnered these titles for a good reason. Over the past four years we've called this place home, I've rolled up to this singular traffic light at least a thousand times, and I can tell you with all certainty that it's only been green maybe three or four times. All other times, no matter the traffic volumes or the time of day, I always get the red light. The fact that the light turned green—most especially when my daughter was about to let loose in the minivan that I, earlier that day, had spent an hour cleaning—and the fact that my wife was allowed to roll right through like the people of Israel crossing the Red Sea is nothing short of the Holy One boxing back the Devil. It has to be. I always get stopped at that stupid light. It's possessed by Satan.

Maybe Jen got through because she called out "The power of Christ compels you" on approach. Or maybe the hidden factor in this scenario is that I wasn't in the car. It wasn't me in a dreadful hurry. If it would've been me needing to pee, the car would be at the detail shop right now. Or at the auto auction in Flint. There's no way I'd be keeping it.

Or maybe my wife and child are actually in cahoots with Satan and he gave them a pass. I sometimes wonder.

Anyway...

The more likely scenario is that God just favors them more than me. He knows the best way to chastise me, and, apparently, the traffic light at the corner of Silver Lake Road and Hyatt Lane is one of His preferred means.

It's my lot in this mortal sphere.

But I do have other, more enjoyable lots in this life, too. I mean that literally. At this very moment, one of them is the Lot 40 Cask Strength edition.

A sample I received from my friend George, this 12-year-old Canadian Rye is proof that even as the Lord chooses to chastise me, He often deigns to shine the bright beams of His love upon me, too.

With a nose of walnuts, cinnamon, and salt, this whiskey is reminiscent of the sweeter scents wafting in the little bakery downtown at Christmas time.

A sip reveals the bite you might expect from a cask strength edition, although it is in no way unpleasant. The elixir maintains its nuttiness—namely walnuts sautéed in a butter-soaked mixture of cloves and cinders.

The finish is the only downside to the dram. I figured I'd get a minute or two out of this one, but alas, its butter-cream goodbye was less than half a minute.

Oh well. I suppose not everything can last as long as the eternal two or three minutes I sit alone at Satan's stoplight.

Ninety, Decades of Richness, Canadian Rye Whisky, 20 Years Old, 45%

Use what you have learned.

I'm sitting on a bench in the waiting area of the dojo where my son, Harrison, only recently began learning Tae Kwon Do. A moment ago, there was a young girl a few paces from me talking to a friend's parent and telling him the tale of her brother who was bullied at school today.

As the story goes, the young boy tried to walk away, but the bully kept pushing him, ultimately landing a thrust to his chest that caused him to fall backward and hit his head on the floor. Apparently, all of it was caught in a pretty lengthy video and has since been shared with school administrators who are promising to do something about it. According to the young girl's mother, who was standing beside the young girl as she told the story, when she and her husband saw the recording, they were furious, and rightfully so. But in light of the situation, the expression of their fury was curious.

I know the boy. I've seen him here at the dojo. He's not a big kid, but I'm pretty sure he's one of the students preparing to test for a black belt. In other words, he has some skills that could easily dispatch a bully on the playground. And yet in their anger, the advice mom and dad gave to their son was to take a stand against the bully by matching action for action. She fervently reported that she'd told her son that if the bully pushes him, he is to push back. If the bully calls him a name, he is to call him one back. If the bully takes something of his, he is to take something from the bully.

I'll admit that I don't know the fuller history to the situation, but from what I do know, I was stunned by the advice because it seemed as though they were pressing for their son to deliberately escalate the problem. The only thing I could think was, *Have you forgotten where you are right now and what your son has been learning for the past few years? He hasn't been coming here every Tuesday and Thursday for who knows how long to train for a black belt in Tae-Learn-How-To-Make-Things-Worse-Do. And he certainly isn't preparing to demonstrate the proper technique for falling and hitting his head against the floor.*

My advice: Forget returning malice for malice. Be humble and controlled, but put your skills to work. With the first shove, warn him. With another shove, warn him again. After that, landing one of those round-house kicks you've been perfecting against his teeth should just about do it. Certainly we don't want anyone to get hurt, but if pain infliction is going to be a part of the unfortunate equation, let it be used for bringing the situation to a speedy conclusion, and let it be leveled against the bully and not the victim. And besides, your kid will probably end up being a YouTube sensation and maybe even land a spot on "The Ellen Degeneres Show."

In summary, what's the point of taking the time to gather the necessary tools for success if when the time comes to employ them, you don't? Such context is reminiscent of the Century Distillers' 20-year-old Ninety edition. At such an age, and with such experience, this whisky should be taking out schoolyard bullies left and right, but instead, it's more of a confused amalgam that wants to be caught off balance.

The nose of the Ninety is a syrupy sauce of alcohol-soaked caramel apples. A follow-up sniff reveals salt and stale caramel corn.

The palate is the nose's identical twin, although the two are easily discernible by the fusty animal cracker mole on the palate's chin.

The finish is a medium stroll of sullenness through the schoolyard, one in which the tongue is oppressed by bitter rye and wood spices. There's a sense of depth waiting to be discovered, and a couple of drops of water offer aid toward its revelation, but in the end, the whisky just won't dig any deeper to become what it could be. Instead, it falls back and hits the floor.

As I already mentioned, my son Harrison is currently a student of Tae Kwon Do, and as far as I know, he isn't being bullied at school. But I assure you that if he were, I have a small stack of monthly invoices from a dojo down the street that both assumes my permission to dig deep while foreshadowing a swift end to the situation.

PIKE CREEK, 21 YEARS OLD, 45%

Chance favors the prepared, especially when it comes to flies.

A s the saying goes, chance favors the prepared.
But not this time.

There are two things you need to know. First, when I'm ill in a way that affects my voice, before a worship service begins, I'll put a glass of water inside the pulpit so that if I need to relieve vocal irritation during a sermon with a sip, I can.

Second, there's one particular problem that I would imagine many churches struggle with: Flies. With the constant opening and closing of doors at various ends of the building, vaulted architecture adorned with massive lighting fixtures, and less-than-insulating stained glass in the windows, during the colder months of the year, you can almost guarantee that flies will find their way in. Once inside, they'll buzz skyward to keep warm—and to multiply—in or near the sconces of the light fixtures. It is also expected that most will, at some point, go out to explore the boundaries of their new resort, and as they do, they'll meet with the colder temperatures near the windows and they'll spin into a frozen coma, ultimately coming in for an upside down landing on a sill, the altar, or some lady's hat.

Because no one wants to share his or her space with what can only be described as a breakdancing fly buzzing around on his back and doing all that he can to get back to his feet even in the throes of death, before every worship service it's quite necessary for our elders or ushers to traverse the worship space with a little handheld bug vacuum equipped with an inner electrocution wire and designed to suck up the dizzy little buggers and introduce them to the afterlife.

But just because you clear the scene of flies before the service doesn't mean the overall process has ceased, and with that, I think you know where I'm going with this. Chance favors the prepared, that is, unless you reach for your glass during the sermon only to observe a sputtering fly being overcome by the waves within. In that case, chance has laughed at both the fly doing what he can to survive his arctic locale and the preacher who sought to prepare accordingly for a sermon's delivery.

"Sorry, guys," chance giggles, "but this time you both lose."

Thankfully, I saw the fly in there, because I'm guessing that jetting a spray of fly-infested creek water from my mouth across the finely dressed people in the front row isn't very churchly and could be interpreted as offensive. Although, now that it comes to mind, and depending upon who's in the front row, I might catalogue the excuse for future use.

"Oh, yeah, Sam," I'd say. "Sorry about spitting that mouthful all over you during the sermon this morning. I took a sip and discovered a fly in my glass. What? Oh, no, I didn't do it on purpose. And besides, thankfully it was only water, and it will dry up and disappear quickly, unlike those nasty, but untrue, things you said about me to Mark."

At this point, I must shift gears and admit that some creek water is worth savoring, and that neither troublemaking flies nor seditious humans would cause me to eject a sip of the 21-year-old Pike Creek edition. Seriously, if a fly landed in a dram of this Canadian prize, while it isn't necessarily the best I've ever consumed, it is worth the effort to scoop him out. And yet, if I were unsuccessful, I stand on the conviction that you don't want to waste what's been poured, and so down the hatch he'd go.

Let me tell you why.

A swirl and a sniff of the Pike Creek opens the front doors to barely a hint of smoke that immediately carries upward into a holy space of spiced and simmering honey and ripened strawberries. A sip brings what I've described to a more graspable plane where you not only experience the honeyed fruit, but are also given the opportunity to lie back and consider the spices mixed into the honey—cinnamon and cloves and maybe even some thyme.

The whisky exits in medium fashion, leaving cinnamon applesauce behind.

You won't find yourself desiring to spit this stuff out. In fact, you preachers out there may be tempted in your preparations to forsake the transparent glass of water for a suspiciously opaque coffee mug of this stuff.

WARENGHEM, ARMORIK, SINGLE MALT CLASSIC, 46%

My remote control has a "WHY BOTHER?" button.

I watch very little TV, so when I do, you can be pretty sure that whatever I'm watching is something I made plans to view. Usually it's a presidential debate, or something like that, which should tell you just how often I schedule my preferred TV time.

There is something that I don't have to schedule as it relates to the TV, and it is iconic of a true if/then conditional statement. What I mean is this.

If there is smoke, then there is fire. Where there are rain clouds, rain will follow. *If* I sit down to watch something important to me, *then* all four of my children will have sudden, personal problems that must be met by the help of a parent lest the world come completely undone.

Seriously. I sometimes feel like there's a button on the remote control that I've pressed by mistake, and it signals some part of my children's brains. I do all that I can to press only the button which reads "POWER" followed by the buttons clearly marked for controlling the channels and volume, but somehow in my non-texting and technologically unskilled manner, I manage to hit the "INTERRUPTING CHILDREN" button. And of course, there are mere seconds between the moment I'm situated and the moment the first child comes running in to tell me the toilet is backing up. And even as I'm still gathering enough energy to rise from my chair to seek out the plunger, I can hear the next in line charging down the stairs to announce that the hamster has escaped. The other two children are out in the garage, so, while I don't know it yet, it will only be a moment before one will need to tell me that the other's shirt got caught on the garage door and he was pulled up into the rafters when it opened.

I think I'm going to scratch off the word "PAUSE" on the DVR portion of the remote and write "WHY BOTHER?" in its place. That certainly seems more appropriate.

Well, at least when it comes to if/then conditional statements, I'm learning that *if* I have a dram of Warenghem's French whisky in hand during these tumultuous events, *then* they are sure to be much less traumatic to my own inner stability.

Tonight's edition: the Armorik Single Malt Classic.

A quick sniff of the delightful vanillas, blood oranges, and warmed barley and I'm ready to meet with a stubborn toilet bowl's contents swirling at its uppermost edge. A sip from the Armorik—one which reveals creamed barley stirred with a sauce of honey and lemon—and I'm prepared to reach into the ductwork to find Fernando, the hamster who considers his benevolent keepers as no better than Alcatraz prison guards.

The finish—fine, indeed. Its medium cling of lemon zest and cinnamon gives me just enough time to set the folding ladder in place in the garage that I might ascend and work to dislodge my son from a ceiling truss.

And then back to my chair where I press the "WHY BOTHER?" button in order to continue in peace.

"Daddy," the little girl says, tapping on my shoulder, "I accidentally put all of the Crayons into the microwave and cooked them for nine minutes on high. A fire started right around the eight minute mark and now the kitchen is burning. Can you help me?"

"Honey," I say, sipping my whisky and maintaining my lock on the TV. "The fire extinguisher is in the pantry."

WAYNE GRETZKY CANADIAN WHISKY, ICE CASK, 43%

Taco Bell at the DMV

I arrived at the DMV around 9:30 AM. It wasn't until 12:21 PM that my number—95—was finally called.

171 minutes later.

I made my way forward to the kiosk, but before taking that final step to begin conducting my business, I turned back to the ever-increasing swarm of people, many of whom had been there just as long, and I said with my preacher's voice, "Assuming any of you actually go to church, remember this day the next time you get the urge to drop one of those little comment cards into the suggestion box near to your congregation's front door. Remember this day when you feel the need to complain that the worship service is too long or that your pastor should work to shorten his sermons."

I allowed a moment for the announcement to sink in. There were a few chuckles, and maybe a few uncomfortable coughs. An older woman in the front row, bearing a slight smirk, leaned forward and said in a partial hush, "Pray for us, Father."

"I have been, my child," I answered. "For three hours, I've prayed."

Most of the folks just stared, but I didn't care, and so I added one last time, "Remember this day." With that, I turned to the clerk who'd only moments before called my number. She was frowning. Again, I didn't care. The place has twelve stations, but only two people on duty. And of those two, she was the one who managed only one customer every twenty minutes while the other accomplished two in that same amount of time.

I know. I timed them both. But what else was I supposed to do? I used up all the juice in my smartphone by 10:45. Sure, there were TVs in the place, but the only thing showing on them were PowerPoint type slideshows about traffic safety. Did you know the average time it takes to glance at a cellphone while driving and cause an accident is three seconds? There also were a few cycling news clips from well before last year's national election which only served to enhance the rage of the people in there who were beginning to feel as though they'd already been there for a year. I should mention that I counted all the ceiling tiles—727 in all, if you're counting the tiny triangular ones as individual tiles.

Meanwhile, I was surrounded by all that serves to remind me how devolved our society has become.

Two rows ahead of me was a man holding a one-year-old girl and talking on his phone to who I'm guessing was his boss, trying to explain to him that he was at the DMV trying to get the license he needed but hadn't yet acquired. From what I gauged, he was dealing with a couple of DUIs and an arrest and conviction in Detroit sometime last year. To make the scene even more disheartening, he took a moment to swear at his little girl each time she squirmed in uncomfortable boredom.

To my right was a woman. Having noticed that her number was 96, which was just after mine, I attempted to make friendly small talk.

"I'll bet right before they call my number, the clerks are going to go to lunch," I said, leaning slightly toward her. "That would be just perfect for us, wouldn't it?" She acknowledged my words with a glance and an awkward grin, but then put her face even more closely to the "People" magazine in her hands in order to let me know she wanted nothing to do with me.

To this woman's right was another woman—a mother—who tapped at her smartphone while her three-year-old son sat popping open an empty Pez dispenser and staring into oblivion. No talking. No attempt at engaging the lad. She was too busy talking to her virtual friends.

Behind me, leaning against the wall, was a heavier set man who I'm guessing before he arrived ate an entire bag of chupacabras or chalupas or whatever the heck those things are called from Taco Bell. Every now and then he'd let a little fart go, and with each release, he'd shift his stance and glance around the room as if observing something important. I got the sense that he truly believed none of the people around him could hear what he was doing. Calm and cool, he stood. There were a few moments when I found it necessary to put my face into my sleeve.

The whole experience was truly hell on earth. In fact, I'm pretty sure I read about this place in Dante's *Inferno*. The only thing that could have made the experience worse would have been for me to hear my number called and then to arrive at the kiosk to discover I didn't have all of the items required for my transaction—and then to be startled awake by one of the gaseous breezes from the man behind me, revealing that I'd only dreamt that my number had been called and I was still sitting in the plastic chair near the back of the room.

By the way, I shouldn't forget to mention that in the midst of my transaction with the slowest clerk in the place, a man emerged from a back office and told her to take her lunch after she was done with me.

Take that, you cold-hearted-anti-social-People-Magazine-reading lady in the back of the room!

Oh my. Did I just write that? Do you see what a morning at the DMV has done to me? Oh, these poor people.

The next time I need to purchase transportation, I'm buying a horse instead. Or a goat. Or even some ice skates. I'd rather strap ice skates to my feet and struggle against the pothole infested pavement we call roads here in Michigan—anything to stay the hell out of the DMV. And besides, as a means of transportation, ice skates would probably work here in Michigan since we experience winter's frigid darkness for at least eight months of the year. We certainly have a lot more of winter than we do summer.

Speaking of ice skates and "more than less" circumstances, I wish I had a lot more of this Wayne Gretzky Canadian Whisky Ice Cask edition than what's in this kindly sample I received from my friend, George. This served as a fine calming agent following the experience I described above.

A swirl and a sniff reveals the whisky's impending sweetness. Essentially, it's honeyed cognac and some concord jam.

It's easy on the palate, too, carrying along the sweetness already described. But then in that moment between the savor and the swallow, a heftier dough-like batter arrives, bringing along with it a dash of nutmeg and rye.

The finish—a pleasant sweet cream married to the concord jam from the nosing—totters in length between short and medium.

Unlike my purgatorial time at the DMV. By the way, forget about the ice skates and instead, think on a name for my goat.

WAYNE GRETZKY CANADIAN WHISKY, NINETY NINE PROOF, SMALL BATCH, 49.5%

Facebook never fails to display the worst of us.

My relationship with Facebook is a tenuous one. Some days we get along pretty well. Other days I can't think of anything I despise more. Today is one of those days.

Today's reason is because Facebook has once again proven itself to be a platform for catwalking the worst about us—which in this case is the inability to admit when one is wrong.

Let me explain.

You may or may not care to know, but the topic was "closed" versus "open" communion. I happen to be a pastor in a particular branch of Christianity that subscribes to closed communion, which means that unless you confess the real presence of Christ in, with, and under the bread and the wine for the forgiveness of sins, you shouldn't participate in the sacrament. This practice gets a bad rap from most mainstream protestants as being cold and unfriendly, but while I don't have time to go into all of the reasons as to why it's exactly the opposite, just know that I tend to agree with Saint Paul and his instruction in 1 Corinthians 11:27-30 and am therefore a closed communion subscriber.

Still, even as I take the administration of the Lord's Supper very seriously, I won't go out of my way to hassle you if you practice open communion. I'll answer to God for my practice. You'll answer for yours. Done. Let's go get a whisky.

Anyway, open communion is as it sounds. Anyone who believes anything about anything regarding the sacrament is welcome to participate. And why? Not because its chief significance is Christ's presence and the giving of forgiveness, but rather because it is a memorial meal of remembrance for all who, at a minimum, acknowledge Christ.

So here's why I hate Facebook…

A gentleman in favor of open communion chimed in and said that since Judas participated in the very first Lord's Supper that must mean that Jesus was in favor of open communion.

That's a huge leap. Still, for some, I'm sure the argument sounds convincing. At the time of the Lord's Supper, Judas was an unbeliever, a man set on betraying Jesus to the ruling council. If Jesus allowed someone to receive His holy supper even as an unbeliever, then He must be suggesting that Paul's words in 1 Corinthians 11 with regard to discerning the real presence aren't as paramount in the practice as Paul teaches.

But there's a problem. Judas wasn't even there during the Lord's Supper. He'd already left to go and get the guards and doesn't get mentioned again until the arrest in Gethsemane. How do I know this? Because each of the four Gospels provides various pieces to the timeline. As it relates to Judas, John 13:18-30, the place where the betrayer ducks out to do his deed, occurs right between verses 21 and 22 of chapter 14 in Mark's Gospel account. It's the same for verses 25 and 26 of chapter 26 in Matthew's account. It's a very simple logging of the evening's events. And by the way, don't forget that logistics apply in these circumstances, too. Judas didn't own a teleportation device, so if he stayed through until the end of the meal, and then went with Jesus and the disciples to Gethsemane, to accomplish his task he must have been a track star, because he covered a lot of ground in a very short period of time. I mean, how would he have managed to get all the way back into the city, gather the guards, and get right back out to the garden without a single one of the disciples noticing or the Gospel writers mentioning it?

That's why we have John 13:18-30. That's when Judas left. John tells us—rather explicitly—so that we know.

With that, Judas wasn't there. Facebook Guy's point is nullified as a proof text for Jesus supporting open communion. Now, maybe the point could be made somewhere else in the Bible that the Lord promotes open communion. But if so, I don't know where that is. I know it isn't here in this argument regarding Judas.

I hate Facebook, because it is a safe place for potshot stupidity in conversations that you can simply delete or abandon what you've said rather than apologize and admit to error. Or, you can do what the one making the argument did in response. You can type something like, "Well, at least we can admit that Judas was there that night and probably ate with Jesus."

Man, I hate that. Sure, we can admit Judas was there. But we can assume that there were bugs in the room, too, since I doubt they had regular visits from the Orkin man in first century Jerusalem. Does that mean that bugs are invited to participate in the sacrament? The point is that the sacrament was instituted for human beings—at a minimum, human beings of faith—and when it was instituted, Judas wasn't there. With that, just apologize for being wrong about this particular proofing effort, and let's move along to a discussion point that actually has something in its middle—something that we can discuss. How hard is it?

I think it's really hard. I've shared with all of you before that one of the most courageous things a person can do is admit fault and seek forgiveness. It doesn't take much courage to defend error. Fear defends error. But it takes an unearthly measure to set oneself below another and admit fault. Those kinds of people are the ones I respect the most.

So, I don't care which camp you're in. I really don't. But if you are going to argue one position or the other, you should at least be somewhat familiar with the basics of the biblical narrative—you know, the place where we get the stuff used in a debate about open or closed communion. What if the folks making whisky just started throwing useless assumptions together thinking that would result in the perfect recipe for a fine dram? My guess is that's how the world ended up with Scoresby Scotch. Thankfully, Wayne Gretzky's group isn't doing that. They seem to be carrying truth into the process, and with that, the results are worth your while.

Take, for example, the Ninety Nine Proof edition. The nose of this little gem is a wash of dark cherries, wood spice, cinnamon, and a little bit of something to singe the nostrils—not in a bad way but in an enlivening way.

In the mouth, the Ninety Nine is creamy cerate of fruit and caramel. The Cabernet Sauvignon cask is more than influential, and it binds to the caramel, which you also notice has been enhanced with a dash of the wood spice from the nose.

The medium finish is one of the better conclusions I've experienced lately, being a consolidation of both the nose and palate. In fact, I'd say it unapologetically held the nose and palate together very well—unlike the argument from the guy who tried to support open communion by insinuating that Jesus communed Judas.

But Jesus didn't commune Judas. You're wrong. Judas wasn't there. And catwalked unapologetic stupidity makes me hate Facebook.

WAYNE GRETZKY CANADIAN WHISKY, RED CASK, 40%

I bought a hotdog with her money.

"Oh, you're selling books," the woman said scanning my table at the craft show.

"Yes, ma'am," I replied with a smile.

"And you're signing them, too," she chimed with surprise.

"Indeed, I am."

"Did you write them?"

"Um…"

Now this could have gone one of several ways. The one that happened in my mind but never made it past my lips sounded something like:

Oh my, no, I didn't write these books. I stopped by a bookstore and grabbed a bunch of random volumes written by other people. I figured I'd set up shop here at the craft show and sign my name to their works. So, wanna buy one? I've got a pen. It's not my pen. I stole it from the bookstore where I got the books.

Fortunately for both of us, I managed to keep from such a response. I steered clear of it by restraining the effects of the hormone oozing from my sarcasm gland. But I'll admit, it was a struggle—even more so when she walked away without purchasing a single volume.

By the way, after her comment, she offered some casual conversation as to how her pastor just wrote a book, as well—a collection of ten of his best sermons.

Oh, did he write the sermons?

To at least participate in the conversation, I mentioned to her that if I collected all my sermons into a single volume, at about five pages of text per sermon, I'd have about five thousand pages in my book.

"You mean you never reuse the old ones?" she asked. "My pastor does that all the time."

Oh, so he's not doing his job, huh? That's cool. Well, at least now you'll not only be able to hear the same sermons over and over again, but you'll be able to read them, too. Maybe after a while you won't even need to listen to your pastor anymore. Heck, you might not even need to step foot in the church ever again.

As you can see, my gland's beta-cells were working overtime. Unfortunately, other versions of the same conversation happened at least three or four more times throughout the morning. On the bright side, I used some of my profits from the books I sold to buy a hotdog and a bar of scented soap.

I ate both—one to quell my hunger, and the other to punish myself for my sarcastic thoughts. Sort of like that bar of soap mom would grate into my braces when I said something I shouldn't say.

Believe it or not, I feel bad when these thoughts pop into my head. I guess I felt I needed to go a little further with this one.

Okay, so maybe I didn't eat the soap. But I thought about it. I also thought about how having a flask in my pocket during such conversations would be just as salving to the soul as a punitive soap munching. I own three flasks, and with that, I won't be making the same mistake the next time I do a book signing at a craft show. I might even bring along the Wayne Gretzky Canadian Whisky Red Cask edition.

In the midst of an elementary school hallway filled with essential oils, overly fragranced lotions, and homemade pumpkin spice holiday candles, a nosing of the Red Cask offers a distinctness of character that cuts through the hovering cumulus with rye spices and a dry sauvignon. A little more concentration added to a second and third sniff reveals the smoked, but damp, finishing barrel.

The palate—a milky and well-balanced amalgam of raisins, vanilla, and allspice—teases interest in what other wonderful concoctions might be hiding just over the border at Gretzky's distillery. The medium finish of biting berries and nougat affirms the desire to find out.

As I noted before, it's a pacifying dram, and I suppose that had I been fiddling with a flaskful in my back pocket while entertaining conversations that require me to coldly explain why it would be ridiculous for me as an author to be signing books that weren't my own, knowing that a sip was only moments away, all would be much easier to swallow. And I dare say that the hotdog probably would have paired well with it, too.

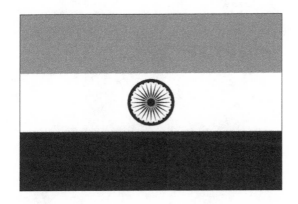

GUAM, INDIA, AND WALES

GUAM'S OWN WHISKEY, 40%

Kiss me, I'm Irish.

It's Saint Patrick's Day, and you know what that means in America, right?

It means celebrating a sainted missionary while dining on corned beef and cabbage and drinking green beer chased by Irish whiskey.

Sounds good. Sounds holy.

Unfortunately, it means a number of other things, too.

It means donning green apparel and four-leafed clover stick-on tattoos. It means some among us skipping all that and going full throttle toward sanctity with a leprechaun costume.

It means rehashing stereotypical castings of Irishmen as irate drunkards with red hair and freckles.

It means stroppy pecks for a woman wearing a Walmart t-shirt that reads "Kiss me, I'm Irish" even though her maiden name is Sienkiewicz.

It means performing dances that apparently can only be properly executed while completely intoxicated. It means raising a glass and shouting, "They may take our lives, but they will never take our freedom!" even though the line is from a movie about a Scotsman.

It means drinking Shamrock shakes from McDonald's until the middle of May—because that's about the time McDonald's finally runs out of the green syrup.

It means sitting at the bar and learning from a friend that the only kind of furniture you can't purchase anywhere else but Ireland is Paddy O'Furniture.

It means a whole lot that has very little to do with Saint Patrick.

Having all of this in square focus, I've decided that this year I'm celebrating the blessed saint with a whiskey from Guam. Yes, Guam. And why not? Guam has as much to do with Ireland and its patron saint as any of the other doings mentioned.

For example, the nose of Guam's Own is most certainly a wafting of Ireland in every way. With a twist of the cap, the first available scent is that of canned green beans, and because said beans are deeply green, they're perfectly associated.

The palate confirms the appropriateness of the whiskey's observance. The soggy green beans are back, except now they're warmed in a briny sauce of salty seaweed and cloves, both of which are clearly appropriate for the celebration. The seaweed mixture is obviously Irish, and not only because it's green, but because it matches the salty attitude of every red-haired fighter on the Emerald Isle. Of course the word *clove* fits because it is but one letter from being *clover*. That was easy.

The finish is short like the Irish temper, and it's syrupy in ways that even McDonald's would consider giving a glad eye.

Praise be. It was nothing less than the luck of the Irish that I had this on hand.

For the record, I don't believe in luck. I'm with Emily Dickinson on this one. She's the one who said, "Luck is not chance—It's toil—Fortune's expensive smile is earned." But then again, Miss

Dickinson was clearly an American poet, so, what would she know about something so Irish?

JOHN DISTILLERIES, PAUL JOHN INDIAN SINGLE MALT WHISKY, "BRILLIANCE" EDITION, 46%

I'm not trying to exit. I'm trying to escape.

In a sense, I suppose that brilliance is synonymous with genius. Both terms communicate a certain level of exceptionalism that isn't common to all. And by exceptionalism, I don't mean skill alone. An athlete making fifty million dollars a year is doing so because he has talent, but that doesn't necessarily assume he's brilliant. German philosopher, Arthur Schopenhauer, is the one who said, "Talent hits a target no one else can hit; Genius hits a target no one else can see."

As artless as these words were, Schopenhauer's brilliance beamed through them. They show that true brilliance requires a pairing of both intellect and skill, and his words hint to the fact that brilliance is often more a spark than a bonfire, more something of simplicity than a complicated matrix of overthought confusion. Einstein and his theory of relativity being prime examples—a man and a tiny equation giving birth and contour to so much. Mozart, another example, heard simple tunes in his head that became extravagant orchestrations on paper and in performance.

I only wish more of the brilliant minds among us were at work building things like parking garages rather than helping to design neutron bombs and writing musical compositions. I say this because earlier today I spent thirty-five minutes—yes, five minutes past half an hour—in a long line of cars circling heavenward in a hospital parking structure only to discover not a single available space at the top. Once up there, I waited another fifteen minutes until someone left before I was actually able to park. Perhaps worse, had any among us in the joyless line changed our minds along the way, having become uncommitted to being where we were, there were no avenues for exiting the lemming-like death march to nothingness. We were trapped. I don't know about any of the others, but I certainly couldn't call for help—you know, maybe at one point around the third level trying to get a call out for an evacuation chopper to meet me on the roof. The concrete and steel monolith in which I was being digested was more than confusing my mobile phone signal.

Hey geniuses—get to work figuring this out, okay? I guarantee that no small number among the populace would appreciate it. And while you're at it, you know what would make us smile while we traverse the corridors of your state-of-the-art parking garage? If you changed all of the shepherding departure signs with arrows that say "Exit" to something a little more intellectually honest. I already have a suggestion. Change the word "Exit" to "Escape," because in the end, that's what we're really trying to do.

Interestingly, when I finally did escape and return to my office, I discovered a box on my desk that contained a bottle of the Paul John Indian Single Malt Whisky "Brilliance" edition sent to me by John Distilleries in Goa, India. I have to admit that when I receive whiskies for review directly from the distilleries, I get a little nervous. I know it's not the same, but I have to imagine that when the procedure is done, if the news is bad, it's a splinter of what it's like to be a surgeon tasked with telling the family in the waiting room that their loved one didn't pull through. I don't enjoy being the one to do this because I know how much time and effort goes into any particular edition. With that, it's an unpleasant thing to see it fail.

But I assure you in this case, the name of the whisky—*Brilliance*—is fitting. This is one that meets with Schopenhauer's words. It proves John Distillery's skill for hitting the target while at the same time imagining and reaching new ones unseen by others.

The nose is a splendid structure, one of overly buttered caramel poured into a mix of spicy malt. A slight draft comes at its end, the kind of tickling breeze you get while simultaneously smelling and sipping a glassful of Coca-Cola. I almost expected some carbonation with the first sip.

The palate matches the nose's equation but, at its end, adds a little something more to its intriguing character. The first sip beams the spicy malt. A second realizes the buttered caramel. Both form a mixture rightly measured. A third sip adds to the recipe a nip of citrus jam and well-browned sourdough toast, bringing the whole experience to a balanced level of exceptional loveliness that's certainly present in other whiskies—but not necessarily attainable by most.

The finish is a medium casting of what has been shared coupled with a bite that reminds you you're drinking whisky and not something for the faint of heart.

Overall, the Paul John "Brilliance" edition is a demonstration of what guys like me would like to see accomplished by other whisky makers, especially here in the United States. In fact, maybe the Paul John folks could visit us here in the states and share some of their insight. And I suppose while they're here, if it isn't too much trouble, perhaps they could stop by and weigh in with whichever think tank in Washington D.C. has concerned itself with infrastructure. It's obvious we need a little more brilliance when formulating architecture meant for accommodating the public masses.

John Distilleries, Paul John Indian Single Malt Whisky, "Edited" Edition, 46%

I'm rooting for the sun.

I started a Ketogenic diet a few days ago, and I have to say it's going pretty well.

For starters, I'm hungry all the time. My wife and four children say I've become incredibly irritable. I can barely gather enough strength to lift my toothbrush to my mouth let alone walk up a flight of stairs without feeling like I need a nap. I have more headaches than usual. I have a hard time concentrating, although I was able to gather enough focus for planning my funeral...which I'm expecting will be sometime next week. Probably Tuesday.

And I think the sun stopped shining. I'm serious. Since I've been on this diet, I'm almost certain that the joy-filled brightness allotted to any particular day has been snuffed out. Or maybe the scientists have been wrong about the sun all along. Maybe it doesn't burn hydrogen and helium but rather carbs, and it has decided to go Keto, too.

Great. Give it all you've got, Sun. I'm not sure you actually exist anymore, but just in case you do, know that I'm rooting for you.

I suppose I could be mistaken. Maybe the sunshine seems distant because it's being blocked out by the sizeable list of "no" foods to which I am now subscribed. The "yes" food list, the low carb list, I've learned is comprised primarily of savory construction material—wood, replacement windows, cement, beef jerky, door knobs, paint, coaxial cable, caulk, nails, pork rinds, and pretty much anything else you can purchase at your local hardware store. But the "no" list is far more grand. It contains all things either simple or extravagant that might stir one to smile at a life lived fully—doughnuts, pizza, joy, spaghetti, happiness, Frosted Flakes, waffles doused in maple syrup, enjoyment, and other flavorful things.

Thankfully, there's a wide assortment of thirst-quenching fluids on the "yes" list. I can choose anything from among the seemingly endless spectrum of water and water. Apparently any water is good—tap water, pool water, downspout water, sewage water—as long as it doesn't taste very good, you should be fine.

I don't know for sure if whisky is on the "yes" list. I'm kind of afraid to check. I suppose if I had to guess, it's probably on the "no" list. Why? Because it's an enjoyable thing, and if you recall, joy is a no-no in this life-editing exercise.

But there you have it. Since bending all reason in submission to my current life-editing routine is a part of what I'm doing to torture myself right now, then I'm sure it'll be fine to stretch my reasoning a little more to find a place for enjoying a dram of the Paul John "Edited" edition while I chew on a low carb, butter-dipped corner of vinyl siding.

And so, with high hopes for even a moment of rescue, the cork is popped and I'm giving it a try.

Refreshingly, the nose of this whisky is the first real sunbeam to pierce my dreadful gloom in days. Alongside a somewhat vegetal scent, a touch of forbidden chocolate and fleshy fruits—plums, perhaps—is carried along by a lazy and shapeless draft of peat.

The palate offers another few rays of liveliness—glimmering beams of warmed vanilla and overly ripened gala apples—both pleasant enough to penetrate the shell of anyone's misery.

The finish is a medium stream of faintly strolling smoke and a more prominent barrel spice that spends its time nipping at the tongue with a lovely reminder that this is only the first sip and the bottle is still very full.

Another sip brings a satisfyingly consistent sameness. A little water, however, lessens the palatable joy, and that's probably because water is on the "yes" list. The "yes" list things are meant to murder enjoyable things.

Overall, this is another edition from Paul John that, if you can find it, is worth your attention. It may stir disappointment from your dietitian, but I can pretty much guarantee that your therapist will offer a commending grin.

I think the diet is on track for accomplishing its goals. I'm fairly confident that I can keep at it for another seventy-two hours or so before altogether forfeiting in order to choose happiness again. But if I do decide to press on, if I do decide that suffering is the preferable road to better health, even as I go to bed hungry, at least I'll sleep peacefully knowing that the Paul John "Edited" edition is within reach and I have five other people in my home who can pour it for me when I've grown too weak to lift the bottle.

PENDERYN, WELSH GOLD, MADEIRA FINISH, 40%

The Flimsy Barrier of Personal Interest

D o you want to know how I know that alien lifeforms aren't being kept alive in captivity or stored in glass jars filled with formaldehyde in a government vault somewhere?

Because it's hard to keep secrets from a pastor.

Most folks take us for innocent dolts. But they forget that we interact fairly regularly with the underbelly of mankind's visceral grotesqueries. Infidelity, drug abuse, you name it. I've seen and heard just about every veiling lie for covering a human's tracks. I'm more than accustomed to the facial expressions, and I'm overly familiar with the accompanying body language.

If you're hiding something from me, ninety-nine percent of the time I'll know just by listening and watching. It's almost eerie how accurate I can be in this regard, too. And again, it's also why you can trust me when I say we've never experienced first contact.

Here's why.

The President of the United States holds absolute executive authority. Absolute executive authority assumes full access to all government facilities, programs, and documentation. This means that no sitting U.S. president is subject to security clearance requirements. It follows then that the only thing keeping a U.S. president from knowing every single one of the highest tier secrets of our nation, past or present, is the level of his own personal interest.

You'll never convince me that any of the men who've ever achieved the highest office in the land did so without feeding the beast of self-interest. And so once again, the reason I know the U.S. government isn't keeping any otherworldly secrets hidden away in steely bunkers six miles below the earth is because if it was, the presidents would have been asked this on camera, lied about it, and ultimately been discovered by guys like me who know what to listen and look for.

I mean, just think about it simply. They're human, like the rest of us, right? Not that we're all chronic liars, but just imagine if either of us were newly elected as president. You and I both know that one of the first things we'd want to know is what's going on in Area 51. Upon learning that we've been visited by beings from another planet, and after we've held their technology in our hands, do you really think either one of us would be able to hide this knowledge so easily behind a stale-faced persona? I don't think so. Certainly, we'd hold to the oath of office and wouldn't betray the secret verbally. But my guess is that most regular human beings would betray it visibly before the cameras as they struggle to find any bit of interest in the major geopolitical situations going on around them. My guess is that at the first run-of-the-mill press conference with another world leader, it would be easy to tell they'd learned something fantastical.

"Thank you for taking my question, Mr. President," a reporter would say, his recorder outstretched toward the two dignitaries. "You've only been in office a few days, so, what points of discussion took place between you and the French Prime Minister regarding the war in Syria?"

"Yeah, well," the President would reply, a distant stare revealing his struggle to care much about the here and now. "I told him some stuff. He told me some stuff. Then we ate lunch."

"What did you eat for lunch, Mr. President?" another reporter would call with a chuckle from the back of the room.

"Well, the Prime Minister had soup. I had an alien spaceship—I mean, um, an Episco*palian* sandwich."

"Sir," the same reporter would ask, "what makes a sandwich Episcopalian, exactly?"

"Um, because, everything on it is out of order. The meat's on the outside and the bread's on the inside. Very weird. Thanks, everyone. No more questions."

It's true that the government lies to us about a lot of things, but alien contact probably isn't one of them.

Do you want to know how I know that the folks at Penderyn must be lying about using Buffalo Trace and Evan Williams barrels for the aging of their whiskies? Because Penderyn whisky is good. It's well balanced and crisply sweet—especially this particular edition of the Welsh Gold finished in Madeira casks.

Okay, so maybe Penderyn isn't lying and I'm merely betraying my dislike for Buffalo Trace and Evan Williams. With that, the truth to Penderyn's story remains sturdy, just as Oliver Wendell Holmes said truth would be:

"It will not break, like a bubble, at a touch; nay, you may kick it about all day like a football, and it will be round and full at evening."

No matter the barrels, Penderyn has a fine dram here. It's round and full all day long.

The nose of the whisky is one of malt and dark fruits—black raspberries, perhaps. There's a flow of warmed vanilla that tapers into a stream of honey.

The palate is generous with the malt. At first, it feels like the whisky might be hiding something metallic behind this particular flavor, but it comes clean on the copper still used in distillation, and rounds the corner toward balance with a well-timed dash of wood spice.

The whisky's medium finish is as it began in the nose—malty, fruity, and warm. It's the perfect dram for a summer evening on the deck beneath the stars. It's even better to have in hand if that star-filled night is suddenly disturbed by an alien spaceship landing in the back yard. Your best bet for establishing peace between two worlds is to make the strange beings an Episcopalian sandwich and then let them wash it down with this particular edition from Penderyn.

NOT WHISKY

Bottega, Limoncino, 30%

Genuine French furniture! We ship directly from Italy!

I've been encouraged on more than one occasion to run for public office.

It's true that I'm fairly engaged in the public square. And I suppose that if I did seek to run, I'd probably have enough folks in my community who know me that they'd at least be willing to send me up the chain to occupy some irrelevant position.

The biggest problem with the idea is that I'm perfectly happy not being an elected official. No matter the station, every official is beholden to someone. That's the way our system of government works. It's held together by strings. I suppose the first time I fail to cast a vote as my biggest donors would expect, I'd find my re-election campaign in jeopardy.

The second biggest problem is that I'm a teacher at heart. Too often I'm looking through the lens of teaching others a lesson.

Yes, that is exactly as it sounds, which means if you're up to anything criminal, you wouldn't want me serving as the judge in your court case.

Abusing your children? I'm a creative guy. I have some ideas on how to rehabilitate you, one of which involves a wiffle ball bat. Did someone die as a result of your driving drunk? I've sometimes wondered what it looks like to be waterboarded with Scoresby. Are you a child sex trafficker? I'd be okay with letting you soak for a few hours each day in a tub full of Drano. Are you behind Daylight Savings Time? Well, I've already decreed your fate in my review of The Balvenie Single Barrel First Fill Cask in *The Angels' Portion, Volume III.*

Are you a charlatan dealing in counterfeit goods? Do you own and operate a store in an Orlando shopping mall entitled "French Furniture," which is a seemingly high class establishment brimming with gaudily designed and extravagantly priced furnishings, a place that makes every visitor feel as though he or she has just stepped into the world of "Beauty and the Beast"? Do you sell these items and the experience they suggest knowing that everything in the store is actually made in and imported from Italy?

Liars.

My best, most imaginative notions for punishment were born from the prospect of penalizing liars.

Stephen King said it best: "The trust of the innocent is the liar's most useful tool." When innocence is lassoed by lies, people end up spending $4,000 on a curvy nook table and chairs reminiscent of Audrey Hepburn in Paris.

Okay, so maybe it's no big deal. Products are made in various countries and sold as authentic to others all the time. Still, I remain a purist, and false impressions fall beyond purism's borderlands. I say if you want something that's truly French, get it from France. If you want something that's truly Italian, try the Bottega Limoncino.

Limoncino—also referred to by many Americans as Limoncello—is a sipping liqueur original to Italy. It's typically made from lemon zest and grappa, and most often is served cold. And for the record, you'll know the authenticity of the one serving the drink if they deliver it to you in an equally chilled ceramic cup.

I received this bottle as a gift from a friend who visited Italy. I'll admit it was a kindly gesture; however, in order to maintain the integrity of my efforts here—and to stay in Stephen King's good graces—I won't pretend to like it.

"But you just told all of us to try it!"

Yes, I did. I said if you want something that's truly Italian, try this particular edition of Limoncino. I said that because it's actually from Italy. There are plenty of booze hagglers out there making stuff they call Limoncino, but Bottega Liqueurs does their work in Veneto, which is a town situated in northern Italy. A winery dealing in grappa, they've been making and selling this stuff for almost half a century—long before anyone anywhere else decided to set aside a vat in order to try their hand at emulating this regional spirit.

Still, I maintain I'm not one to enjoy the drink. It's too sweet for me. Also, I should note that while I consumed the dram chilled, I nosed it at room temperature. I did this because the scents from chilled drinks have a tendency to fall rather than rise, and when that happens, you miss the wider array of the gifts they bring.

That being said, the nose of this specialty drink is butter, and as one would suspect, lemons. There's a fraction of allspice and a hint of plums that come along to the palate. I'm guessing the plums are due to the grappa. I don't know what would stir the spice. I imagined the lemon pomace.

The finish is long and oily. It coats the mouth with a stratum of lemony sugar that goes far beyond what most whisky drinkers would consider polite or enjoyable. And don't think you can sip some water to cleanse the palate after drinking this stuff. It doesn't work. My only success was found in eating a ham sandwich stacked with tomatoes, cheese, mayonnaise, and mustard. And then I washed it down with The Balvenie I mentioned before.

And then I brushed my teeth and took a shower.

But again, if you're seeking an authentic Italian experience, I recommend this as opposed to what they're selling in that little room just off of the kitchen of your favorite Italian restaurant.

You know the one.

PALINKA, HOMEMADE ROMANIAN PLUM BRANDY

It's been 9:20 AM for over an hour.

It's the same every year while on holiday, and its timing is predictable. At some point during the time away I have a terrible dream, and it usually happens sometime around the half-way point.

I'm not sure what this means, but I would imagine somebody out there knows the answer. My only guess is that when I reach the vacation's midpoint, my body and mind both know that I'm not so much moving further into a much needed time of rest as I am passing through and out of it.

The days are numbered, and very soon everything will begin again.

Last night I dreamt that an unrecognizable couple showed up at the church on a Sunday morning right before worship expecting me to perform their marriage ceremony. I was vested and ready to begin the regular service when I came down the hallway from my office to the church's entryway and discovered them with a large party of family and friends. They approached me and thanked me for scheduling the event, but also revealed a concern that so many people were already in the church but were not on their overly scrutinized guest list.

I was at a loss. Of course the church was full. It was Sunday. And I didn't know who these people were. I didn't remember anything about the event—which means I couldn't recall the typical pre-marital counseling sessions, the service planning, or any of the other detailed conversations that go into scheduling a wedding.

Our Sunday morning service begins at 9:30 AM. I looked at my watch. It was 9:20.

I apologized to them, promising to do what I could. Since I apparently scheduled the event, I would perform the wedding, but it would have to happen after the regular service and Bible study, which means they'd need to wait until about noon.

The situation grew heated. The bride began to cry. The groom tried to console her. The bride's mother—who I didn't recognize, but for some reason was the only one I sensed as familiar—stormed away. Her husband remained behind and worked to convince me that it was only right to tell the rest of the congregation that the church had been reserved and they needed to leave.

I apologized again and again for the mix up, but assured him that I was not going to tell the members of the congregation they had to leave their own church to accommodate a wedding ceremony for a couple that none of us knew, even if I had mistakenly scheduled it.

I looked at my watch again. It was still 9:20.

The bride's father was furious, and in his rage, he belittled me, creative with his disgust that a man like me could ever be a Christian pastor.

Then there was a moment when, even though I knew my opponents had somehow made a serious error or were simply at the wrong church, I felt like I was in the wrong and should do what I could to accommodate. Working over the shouts of the bride's father, I even tried to suggest that it wouldn't be entirely inappropriate for the ceremony to serve as the beginning of the service.

But he wouldn't have it, and he assured me that if I didn't ask the people of my congregation to leave in order for the wedding ceremony to take place, I would be hearing from his lawyer.

I looked back down to my watch. It was still 9:20.

I told him I couldn't do it, that I was sorry, and that if he wanted to speak more at a later date, I'd be more than willing. The mother of the bride returned. I told her the same, even as she motioned and shouted to the whole group, "Let's go folks. This ungodly reverend is kicking us out."

With taunting scowls, the whole group filed through the church's doors and into the parking lot. I looked at my watch. It was 9:20.

Feeling like I wanted to throw up, I gathered myself and then made my way into the narthex where I was greeted by the ushers and the Elders on duty.

"Hey, pastor!" they all said exuberantly. "How ya doing this morning?!"

Apparently, none knew what had just happened.

"Pretty good," I replied. "Everything ready in here?"

"Oh, yeah," they said. "The candles are lit and we have two youth assistants. We're all set."

"Great," I said, proceeding to gather the group for pre-service prayer.

Just before we bowed our heads, I heard the prelude begin. I looked at my watch. It was 9:29.

I'm not sure what any of this means, but to break free from the trepidation this kind of thing stirs, a kind word or a warm embrace from someone who doesn't hate you—like a spouse, a child, or a good friend—will do the trick. Even better, life has a softer hammer when one of those folks reaches to you with a bottle of something they fought hell and high water to get to you, like the bottle of homemade Romanian whisky my good friend Paul delivered to me this past spring in a plastic bottle (which I hastily transferred to a glass one). In such moments, you know that you're never truly trapped at 9:20, but rather are but a few seconds from 9:30.

Palinka, the dram at hand, is the traditional spirit from the land of Dracula. It's made from plums and usually runs at an octane of about 25% to 65% ABV. Again, the stuff I'm trying was crafted by someone in a village in the Carpathian Mountains. And from its initial nosing, I'm guessing this stuff is most certainly at the upper end of the ABV scale.

It's rough to take it in at first—very chemical, very medicinal, with only a minor hinting to dark fruits—and almost certainly something its distiller sells as an all-purpose tonic in the village medicine shop. In fact, the elixir's fumes were so potent, I had to tape the cork to the bottle lest it keep popping off. I get the sense that this stuff would be a standard potion for dealing with pneumonia-like symptoms in the midst of a frigid Carpathian night.

The palate of this beast was as bitter pine, scalding raisins, and acidic solvent. The plums were there, but in vampiric fashion, more dead than alive.

All of these things together made for a long and sour finish, one that tells me that while I'm incredibly grateful for this gift, it's going to take me a long while to consume it. I'll most likely only turn to it for the same reason the villagers from its birthplace do—to fight back the invading hordes of sickness-inducing germs that could ultimately snatch away life. That is, if the bloodstream is not preemptively teaming with tiny Romanian soldiers that can hold them back.

Or I'll keep this incredibly potent cocktail at the ready in a hip flask so that when I'm confronted by crazy and compassionless people in the church's entryway demanding things of me that I cannot provide, in a stealthy effort toward peace, I can offer them an almost instantaneously immobilizing gulp, put them on a cart, and roll them down the street to the neighboring church that I know will pretty much give them whatever they want. That's probably the place they meant to visit anyway, and so when they wake up, they'll be pleased.

Yeah, I think that sounds like a good idea.

TOMMYROTTER DISTILLERIES, CASK STRENGTH BOURBON-BARREL GIN, 61%

I've been seduced by another.

So many things have clumsy beginnings—driving a car, doing your taxes, love, changing a diaper, mudding and sanding drywall. The list is relatively inexhaustible.

This could be a clumsy first for me—reviewing gin, that is.

I just don't drink gin all that often. But I suppose you knew that already, didn't you?

It's not that I don't appreciate it. There was a time when a careful measure of gin in chilled tonic water and adorned with a fresh lime would be a near-flawless potation at the edge of any summer sunset. But even as tranquil as such scenes were, I never found myself committed to gin in the same ways I'm committed to whisky. Gin just never had a depth or vibrancy about it, at least not enough that I felt drawn to investigate it. The better known gins—Bombay Sapphire, Tanqueray, or Hendrick's—I employed them all. But even so, until today, I remained relatively certain of gin's charmless and settled form.

It was Albert Camus who suggested that charm is what's needed for getting a yes without asking a question. It was Ambrose Bierce who mused that being certain means being mistaken at the top of one's voice. It was John Stuart Mill who offered that all good things in existence are fruits of originality.

The rudimentary bells of these three statements tolled my foolishness with the first take of the Cask Strength Bourbon Barrel Gin from Tommyrotter Distilleries.

The nose of this spirit affirms Camus' perspective. Indeed, charm has her way of getting through and stealing an affirming nod. This particular edition gives charming tracks of spicy licorice root, burnt sugar, and barely a hint of oak. Of course there's the typical pine-like aroma because of the juniper berries—or more properly, the berry-like seed cones—which are standard to gin production. But the familiarity of the scent is anything but typical. The nose of this gin is crisp, almost cold. In my wandering mind, it betrays a vast and untouched pine forest, one with snow-covered hills just beginning the transition to spring.

Charming, indeed. I could live in a place like that. I could even sit and sniff this gin on the front porch of a little cabin in a place like that. I wouldn't even need to drink it.

Ah, but I would experience the desire to consume it, because the palate is now carrying me into Bierce's words. I say this because just as this gin began to come to life with a more distinctive barrel spice, wintry juniper, and maybe even a little bit of lemon pepper, I was immediately reminded of the fact that at one point in my distilled spirits journey, I was all but shouting that I would never discover a Bourbon worthy of cleaning my toilet let alone drinking for enjoyment, and yet over the course of the years I've happened upon so many that I truly adore. A sip from this gin is an invitation to remember that there are plenty of enchanting doors in life that are yet to be opened. This gin is one of those doors.

The finish, just shy of being medium in length, insists that we agree with Mill's observation. This is a good gin, one born of originality. It carries along at its end in a way that rejoins its beginning, giving over the root spice and hint of barrel oakiness. It commends itself to you as thoughtful and unique, and it reminds you that it isn't as you've known before. It isn't Bombay Sapphire. It's not Tanqueray or Hendrick's. It's Tommyrotter. And it's definitely better.

Having now been seduced into another arena of spirits discovery, I suppose at some point I'll give Tommyrotter's American Gin a try. I have to. All the other gins I've known are now distant and clumsy beginnings, and something tells me that the Tommyrotter Distillery and its offerings could be a field where any one of us might actually begin a more seasoned stride.

DILIGENCE AND LEISURE

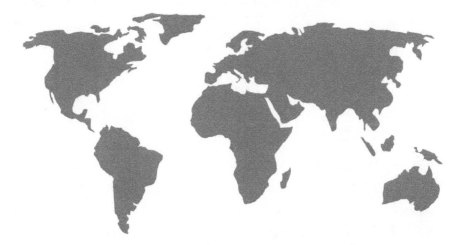

KEEP YOUR HUMOR AND WITS ABOUT YOU

I have puke in my mouth and it's not mine.

My wife, Jennifer, posted to Facebook, saying, "If my kids really do know so much, then why is my life so difficult?"

At first glance, her statement seemed a bit bizarre. But it only takes a moment for her words to make complete sense to those of us who exist in the strange trans-dimensional world where the supposed wisest among us—the children—require us to tell them not to do stupid things they apparently already know are stupid and shouldn't do.

And how do we know that they know? Because they tell us.

"What are you doing?! Don't stand on the tank of the toilet!"
"I know."

"Why are you eating the Play-Doh?! Don't do that!"
"I know."

"How many times do I have to tell you to stop taping your sister's dolls to the ceiling fan?! You're going to break one of the blades!"

"I know."

"Are you out of your mind?! Don't test the flammability of your inhaler! It could explode!"

"I know."

"And at least go outside if you're going to try to blow your hand off!"

"Yeah, I know!"

It's been said a million times, still, it never loses its gravity: *Parenting isn't easy.*

It really is one of the hardest jobs on the planet. This is true not only because of the level of physical exertion it so often requires of the adults. Sleepless nights. Back-breaking contortions with car seats. Birthday party cleanups. The list of sweat-drenched labor is endless. But these things aside, it's equally difficult because of the mental taxes it continually levies. Concern for a fever that won't break. Compounded worries as the 8th grader becomes a freshman. And who could've known that, well before this, you secured the responsibility for having destroyed any chance he might've had for a happy life just because you told him to eat his dinner? His animated response in the moment confirmed his future was lost.

This is our guilt.

Or is it?

I don't know about you, but after four children, I had a portion of my guilt gland removed. It was an elective surgery. But I did it in order to embrace a very important verity. I've learned that to accomplish what needs accomplishing among the smaller versions of myself, a stale face and a plain tone sprinkled with a little bit of "horrible" is necessary. I can assure you that since the surgery, life has become considerably less maniacal.

"Eat your food."

"I don't like mashed potatoes."

"I don't care."

"Can I have a bowl of cereal instead?"

"Nope."

"But I don't want this!"

"I don't care. Eat it."

"But I don't like it!"

"Okay, how about this? I'm going to count to five. When I reach the number five, I'm going to put that food into you through one of the various holes on your body. Right now, you can choose to do it through your mouth. But sweetie, if I get to five, I'll choose the hole. I don't know which one it'll be, just yet, but you need to know that'll be the next stage of the meal and the end of this conversation."

By the way, after a scene such as the one I've just described, you should know that the adults in the Thoma house now live five seconds at a time during meals. But in all honesty, it's a small price to pay. And it really only took a few moments involving a spoonful of mashed potatoes and a child's flared and angry nostril as a reasonable entry point to set the pace. The cereal-munching beasties are now convinced that my words, while non-aggressive, are by no means hollow.

"How do those mashed potatoes taste?" I ask with a kindly tone.

"I don't know," she replies in a huff, doing all she can to hold back tears of defeat. "They're in my nose."

"Well then, honey, how do they smell?"

You have to keep a sense of humor when it comes to children. Humor is the one lens that allows the crispest view of the things that are truly memorable. Humor will grab hold of any scene and make it wholly unforgettable—even the most horrific scene of a laughing father joyfully lifting his giggling toddler into the sky, over and over again, only to have him throw up in his father's mouth.

I wouldn't know anything about such things. But if I did, I'd assure you that even as it was a sour moment, the memory is laughably sweet.

Without humor, I dare say you risk aging much more quickly than the clock requires.

You also need to keep your wits about you. But that's for an altogether different reason, which, in a way, has to do with what the English novelist, Graham Greene, referred to as those moments in childhood "when the door opens and lets the future in."

What I mean is that, in general, while children are not very good at listening or sitting still or eating the food we put before them or remaining on the floor instead of perching on the tank of the toilet like a bathroom gargoyle, for all the things they do poorly, there is something they do magnificently.

They imitate adults.

I suppose if I have anything of value to share by way of this leisurely stroll meant to accompany your "the kids are finally in bed" evening whisky, it's the encouragement not only toward maintaining one's humor (and maybe getting the elective surgery I mentioned previously), but also to remember who you are as a parent, and as I said, to keep your wits about you. Be mindful of the many and various ways to shepherd your children, and be cognizant that you serve as the door for letting in the best future possible.

Attentive to this, as parents, we work hard. We choose the best words in a tough situation. We deal honestly with others. We admit when we're wrong. We say thank you. We go to church. We show love to family and friends—and yes, even our enemies. We engage with other human beings in ways that teach our little ones that integrity matters. They behold this in us, they emulate it, and the kindly beams of a bright future are welcomed in.

On the other hand, I suppose if you want to disregard all of this, there's always adoption. But don't ask me to take in any of your children. I'm still suffering from nightmares about puke in my mouth.

CALL, DON'T TEXT

My family mocks me.

For those who know me personally, I'm not one for texting. I do my best to accommodate the circus, but in the end, it's not a way of communication that I appreciate.

Don't get me wrong. I'm not completely annoyed by it. Well, maybe I am. I just don't appreciate it as so many others do.

One reason I don't like it is because it takes me far too long to craft a text message. I'm a rigid perfectionist when it comes to writing stuff. With this, texting is difficult and impractical. Even worse, it has placed a target on my back in my own family. From youngest to oldest, they all tease me. They mock as I tap out complete sentences, sure to take the time to punctuate everything fully and correctly. They poke fun at my frustrated exhaustion, laughing as my struggle among lowercase letters, capital letters, symbols, and numbers comes to a tired end.

Another reason I'm not much of a texter is that it's inconveniently convenient, giving a vast majority of people the false sense that they'll receive an instant response to any question they ask, even if that question could've waited until another time. I suppose I should add to this that sometimes I don't even understand what people are so hurriedly communicating to me. I know it sounds ridiculous, but for as savvy as I may be in social media circles, I literally just learned ten days ago what "smh" and "lmk" meant. I had no idea. I would see these in a text or online post and just move along as an admitted outsider in the SMS language community. I never cared to learn these lazy phrases. As a result, I suppose that many appropriate replies went unsent over the years because I didn't realize someone was telling me to let him or her know. I'm pretty sure that when people typed that to me, I responded with something like, "Are you okay?" because as far as I knew, it meant "Landed on My Keys!" And all of us, most especially the pastors, should show concern for someone who suffers such an accident, right?

Well, whatever. We have bigger problems than your clumsy handling of keys. The world is facing the prospect of an entire generation bent on jettisoning punctuation, and it has me sweating.

You doubt me? Then think on the ramifications from a misplaced comma or two. Consider the following cover of "Tails" magazine from October of 2010. Even as it was proven to be fake, the forgery proves the point rather well.

Without commas, we might assume Rachel Ray realizes her innermost creativity while sautéing both her family and pets.

Again, care in these things matters. Texting sacrifices clarity for efficiency, and I'm not so sure that's the best trade-off. I'd much rather have a phone conversation than a text or instant messenger conversation, anyway. I find that a phone conversation—or even better, a face to face conversation—has a much better chance of ending well, especially when it comes to the contentious situations in which we find ourselves in the virtual world.

Perhaps the drollest aspect to all of this is that folks will send me a text message saying they didn't want to call because they know just how busy I am, not realizing that by contacting me in this way, they were slowing my pace even more than if they had called. I had to stop, thumb out a reply, do a thorough proofreading, send it to the editors in my mind, make their recommended changes, and then hit *send*.

A phone call would've been better.

And for the record, I'm never too busy for a phone call from anyone. Never. Except maybe a phone call from a politician. Or someone trying to sell me the latest video series from Joel Osteen. I suppose I can let those particular reach-outs land in voicemail.

In the end, I guess you could say that I'm a guy who believes that words matter, that the language structure they rest in matters, that the time spent in contemplative care of the words matters. There's already enough acknowledged communicative confusion in this world, texting seems counterintuitive to the solution. It has me asking myself, "Would a little more time and precision in our efforts to communicate really be all that bad?"

I suppose you can answer that question for yourself. When you do, be sure to *lmk, k*?

CONCLUSION

Of what use is a philosopher who doesn't hurt anyone's feelings?
—Diogenes

I sure hope you're not one of those folks who, before reading a book, jumps straight to its conclusion to see how it ends. If so, then you need to know three things.

First, even if you only read four sentences, the author is still getting paid.

Second, the concluding pages of *The Angels' Portion* volumes are always very different than the content that precedes them. I usually try to wind down through the "Diligence and Leisure" section before finally coming to an end with something that not only leaves you with a sense of having been entertained, but also that you've been nudged beyond the safety of your own intellectual borders by something a bit more substantial.

Third, you may not know me as well as you think you do, and because I write about whisky, you might be under the assumption that I'm one of those edgy, carefree clergymen who has tattoos, wears flannel while preaching, and prepares all of his sermons mindfully considerate of which images and music will serve best for a PowerPoint presentation.

If that's what you think is happening, then you should stop right here and go back to the beginning, because that's definitely not me.

I'm as historically liturgical as they come. I'm the kind of guy who believes that if you jumped into a time machine, zipped back to the third century, kidnapped a reverent worshipper, and brought him back and dropped him into one of the worship services in my church, he'd know exactly what was going on in the place. He may not speak the same language, but he'd certainly know what we were doing and why we were doing it.

I'm also the kind of guy who thinks that the words "Christian" and "pastor" are descriptors proving themselves rather empty these days—which explains why I appreciate booze more so than the average clergyman, and it's probably why I sometimes find myself tempted to punch other pastors in the face.

Seriously. Some pastors need what Saint Nick offered to the heretic Arius—a swift right cross to the jaw.

I say all of this because I believe that weak-kneed, inane pastors are the reason for increasingly typical scenarios like the one that follows:

"I don't have to go to church to be considered a Christian," the man said defiantly to the other in the clerical collar.

"Yes, you do," the clergyman replied.

"No, I don't," he insisted. "I just need my Bible."

"Yes, you do need to go to church," the clergyman answered again.

"That's just your opinion," the man said, his resoluteness building.

"No, actually, it isn't," the man in black rejoined, maintaining his calm.

"Well, anyone who thinks sitting in church can make you a Christian must also think that sitting in a garage can make you a car."

"Garrison Keillor said that," the clergyman replied. "That's well worn, and also quite wrong."

"You better watch out, Reverend," his opponent fired back, "because he's a Lutheran just like you."

"No, he's not a Lutheran," the clergyman said. "The man who taught Jack Daniel how to make whiskey, Reverend Dan Call, he was a Lutheran. Garrison Keillor's barely an Episcopalian."

"Well, whatever. He's a Bible believer, just like me."

"Do you know what else Garrison Keillor believes?" the clergyman asked.

"What?"

"He said that if an expecting mother discovers her child is disabled, the child should be killed, no matter the stage of pregnancy. He also said that the folks in America concerned with pornography are a bunch of 'shrieking ninnies' and 'pompous blowhards,' making clear he doesn't take much issue with it."

"I didn't know that."

"I figured," the clergyman said. "But you do realize these beliefs are counter-biblical, yes?"

"Well, whatever," the man said, waving a carefree gesture. "I still don't have to go to church to be a Christian."

"Dear friend," the minister began to recite, "let us hold unswervingly to the hope we profess, for He who promised is faithful. And let us consider how we may spur one another on toward love and good deeds, not giving up meeting together, as some are in the habit of doing, but encouraging one another— and all the more as you see the Day approaching."

"That's just your opinion," the man shrugged.

"Would it change your mind if I told you Garrison Keillor said it?"

"Did he?"

"No. That was from the Epistle to the Hebrews. It's in the New Testament."

"Well," the man shrugged again, "I guess I don't need the New Testament to be a Christian, either."

Truth be told, I'm using this true-to-life conversation to conclude this book because I fear that such depthless scenarios are the American pastors' reward. They're nothing less than recompense for engaging in similar thought processes.

Now before I go any further, I humbly ask that you give me a second with this, because whether you might call yourself devout, quasi-spiritual, or even a hard and fast atheist, there's no harm in continuing in order to see if you agree.

I think you will. In fact, I'm confident you will.

Divinely inspired or merely good literature, it can't be argued against that the Bible refers to the Christian Church—all believers from all times and places—as "holy." Quite literally, the term means to be set apart. That's easy enough to understand. In this world, the Christian Church is to consider herself set apart, distinct, different in her existence.

In addition to this, just as unarguably true as the descriptor "holy," there are moments in the Bible when the Christian Church is instructed to be "godly." For example, the Apostle Paul speaks this way in 1 Timothy 2:2. In the original *Greek*, the word he uses is εὐσεβείᾳ, which may be equally translated as "reverent." Pedantically, reverence is the emittance of a piety born from adherence to the tenets of the Christian faith located in the Word of God—the Bible. This piety has an innate integrity that becomes visible through its practices, which that one particular guy in the Bible we know as Jesus often refers to as being in place to communicate the faith to others.

Now, take a quick moment to refill your whisky glass before continuing. If you're a pietist, go get another Coke.

Got it? Okay, good.

My concern is that, for the most part, the Christian Church in America has lost almost entirely what it means to be *reverent*. And so my question for all of the flaming Evangelicals fighting the culture war among us becomes: You're trying to make yourselves more palatable to the culture, but do you realize the incredible sticking point that emerges from your anything-goes practices? Do you understand how this actually aligns with the culture, which at this point in human history has as its main goal the imposing of palatability and inclusivity upon you?

Now I'm not arbitrating what a church should or should not do in relation to its doctrine or evangelism efforts. I'm just pointing out the inconsistency among the churches that claim to be counter-cultural in their theology. It seems awfully uneven for such a church to demand that the world refrain from instructing God as to how He should operate when that same church also gives the impression, by her practices, that the God of the Bible is flexible with His boundaries, His distinctions in comparison to the world around her.

So, here's where my words get rough, and while those of you who skipped to this conclusion probably don't know me very well just yet, I'll go ahead and share some things I've shared before with those of you who do.

Thinking on this whole topic, I encourage you to give honest consideration to the data being produced by reliable sources such as George Barna and the Pew Research Center, as well as a good number of other prominent observers of the culture so many claim to admire. These sources are reporting that far too many of the practices we see in full bloom across the landscape of American Christianity are hurting the Church and not helping as she attempts to engage the world around her.

The data speaks of trends sixty years in the making, beginning when, collectively, all of the denominations began seeing a decline in attendance and income. In response, churches began jettisoning anything the culture might not consider palatable. Like him or not, it was Matt Walsh who wrote: "You can easily track the church's stunning decline over the past several decades and see that it corresponds to the church's shredding of Christian orthodoxy…"

Certainly churches held onto their message of salvation, but they reached to the culture for answers to their problems. The culture responded by telling them they needed to do a better job of selling their message, that they needed to be less conspicuous in who they were as churches. And so they hired consultants who told them to take "Lutheran" or "Methodist" or "Presbyterian" off of their church signs. Some hired more aggressive consultants who told them to change their names altogether, ultimately disfiguring their own histories as Saint Luke Lutheran Church or Saint John Episcopal Church for names that sound more like nightclubs—"Benchmark" or "Epic" or "Elevate" or even names that are so hip they're only numbers.

And by the way, there will always be consultants out there willing to take a church's money in exchange for a transformative program.

G. Shane Morris, a senior writer for the Colson Center for Christian Worldview, wrote that the longstanding data speaks against making such moves. He said that longstanding data actually reveals the unchurched are less than half as likely to view churches without denominational identifiers as "honest," and are almost five times more likely to perceive such churches as "disingenuous" and "trying to hide what they believe."

Again, like him or hate him, Ben Shapiro wrote an honest piece for "National Review" entitled "Goat Yoga is a Poor Substitute for

Religious Observance." By it, he cited examples of synagogues so desperate to entice newcomers that they replaced the traditional rites and ceremonies during the most reverential days of the year with conga lines, goat yoga, and mosh pit benedictions in beer gardens.

Many branches of Christianity are doing this, too.

We've seen entire denominations departing from historic Christianity and the Bible it claims to adore—which is the same Bible that actually describes the nature of the Church and her worship as something that exists in contrast to the ways of the culture. Books of the Bible like Leviticus, Ecclesiastes, Matthew, Luke, Romans, First and Second Corinthians, and the Book of Hebrews all reveal boundaries established by God. All of these are written with the assumption that when it comes to the Church's identity, she doesn't need to make herself relevant. She's already the most relevant entity on the planet.

Forfeiting this essential truth, the culture warriors betray a shame in their truest identity. Even worse, they've given license to anyone claiming Christianity to re-write the Church's creeds and sometimes even Christ's own words.

For example, I served a congregation in Pennsylvania that believed most folks could no longer grasp the words of the Lord's Prayer, and so there was talk of rewriting it. I resigned and left less than a month later.

Another example: I attended a funeral in a conservative church, one that claims to take the Bible seriously. The whole place was designed like a movie theater. But there wasn't a single crucifix on the premises. A week later I visited an extremely liberal church in Detroit, one that would just as soon employ readings from the New York Times as opposed to the Bible. I experienced the exact same thing there. Neither the conservative nor the liberal church communicated an entering into a completely different sphere—into an existence comprised of completely different expectations. Both churches had altogether traded away their distinctive altar and worship spaces. Their narthexes are now coffee bars. They've exchanged vestments for skinny jeans. They've forfeited traditional adornments for projector screens and industrial beams clad with stage lighting. Their holy spaces are venues, and their pastors are considered entertainers.

And why not? Remember where this rant began. The pews must be filled to meet the bottom line, and so why wouldn't there be a shift toward selling the Church as opposed to *being* the Church? And as a result, why shouldn't we expect there to be a larger evolution of entire denominations massaging the Bible's contents to make it less offensive?

The unfortunate result to all of this as it meets the post-modern church in America today is that now the culture looks upon the Church with very little wonder or intrigue. The Church has more than become a mirror image of the culture, making the efforts of the warriors impotent. The culture doesn't see the Church as a formidable foe guarding sacred truths. It hasn't the slightest concern that she might rise up if she were to be pushed to betray that which she holds dear. In July of 2012, noted atheist and popular social critic Christopher Hitchens mentioned during his opening remarks in a debate with Dinesh D'Souza that the Church is finding herself in scrapes because her preaching lacks the confidence of former days. In many cases, the Church has already surrendered so much of who and what she is, and with that, the culture has been more than happy to consume and digest and ultimately produce piles of fecal Christianity—a religion that can effortlessly disregard the New Testament, choosing instead to exist on little more than smart-sounding tidbits from folks like Garrison Keillor.

Again, and I suppose in conclusion, all of this comes together to form at least one of the reasons why I drink and write about whisky. It's an outlet—cathartic therapy of sorts—something very necessary during those times when I'm overly frustrated by the splashing of my friends here in the Christian swimming pool. In those moments, whisky and its subsequent world become gifts of God capable of calming the soul and keeping guys like me from beating stage-pastors wearing Garth Brooks styled microphones to death with their acoustic guitars.

And trust me, it works. It's nearly impossible to swing a guitar at someone while holding and sipping a dram. The spillage is far too great to make it worth anyone's while.

INDEX

Also by
Reverend Christopher I. Thoma

There's a Bug on the Floor
Ten Ways to Kill a Pastor
Type One Confessional: God, a Pastor, and a Girl with Type 1 Diabetes
Kids in the Divine Service
Feeding the Lambs: A Worship Primer for Teachers of Children
The Homiletical Canvas: Poetry in Service to Preaching
Where Dreams Ponder People
The Angels' Portion: A Clergyman's Whisk(e)y Narrative, Volumes I, II, & III

Visit Reverend Thoma at
AngelsPortion.com.

CPSIA information can be obtained
at www.ICGtesting.com
Printed in the USA
LVHW020521170920
666268LV00002B/16/J

9 781734 186154